OBLIGATIONS

For my mother and father

OBLIGATIONS

Martin Hogg LLB, LLM

Solicitor; Lecturer in Law, University of Edinburgh

Avizandum Publishing Ltd
Edinburgh
2003

Published by
Avizandum Publishing Ltd
58 Candlemaker Row
Edinburgh EH1 2QE

First published 2003

ISBN 0-9543423-4-8

British Library Cataloguing in Publication Data
A catalogue record for this book is available from the British Library.

Typeset by Hewer Text Ltd, Edinburgh
Printed and bound by Bell & Bain Ltd, Glasgow

Preface

My purpose in writing this book is to explore how the obligations recognised by Scots law relate to and interact with each other. In researching and teaching on the law of obligations, I have found such relational and interactive issues to be of the greatest interest, yet because of their nature, they cross obligational boundaries and are issues which have tended to be addressed only tangentially in the standard works dealing with discrete obligations. As such, there seemed to be an obvious need for a work such as this, which takes the relationship between obligations as its primary subject matter.

This is not a book about the whole of the law of obligations. There are many topics within the law of contract, unilateral promise, delict, unjustified enrichment, and *negotiorum gestio*, which are not addressed in the book, and for which a treatment may be found in the standard texts on these obligations.

The subjects addressed in this text cover diverse matters, among them concurrent liability between obligations, the utility of unilateral promise (a much neglected obligation in our law), the availability of unjustified enrichment remedies in situations of void, voidable, frustrated and broken contracts, liability for pre-contractual expenditure, and the concept of unjustified sacrifice. The importance of topics such as these stretches far beyond the concern of the academic, as the large number of commercial cases discussed demonstrates.

The bulk of this text was written at the Law Faculty of the University of Stellenbosch, South Africa, in July 2002. I am extremely grateful for the hospitality of the Dean and Faculty, and in particular I should like to thank Professor Gerhard Lubbe for his many kindnesses. He ensured that I had a roof over my head and a desk at which to work—baie dankie. I am also grateful to my two research assistants, Andrew Jessop and Peter Webster, who rooted out more obscure authorities and questioned any doubtful propositions which I might make. My colleague and mentor, Professor Hector MacQueen, was kind enough to take time off from his many duties as Head of the Edinburgh Law School to offer suggestions on a draft of the text, for which I am most grateful. Above all, I should like to express my thanks to Avizandum Publishing, and to Margaret Cherry especially, who had sufficient faith in my idea to see it through from tentative suggestion to finished publication. As ever, any faults which the reader may perceive in the substance of what follows must be laid at my door alone.

Martin Hogg
Edinburgh
September 2003

Contents

Contents

Table of Cases

Table of Cases

Tables of Legislation

TABLE OF STATUTES

TABLE OF STATUTORY INSTRUMENTS

Chapter 1

Introduction

THE NATURE OF AN OBLIGATION

1.01 Scots law derives its concept of obligation from Roman law.[1] An obligation is a legal tie (*juris vinculum*) by which one or more parties is bound to perform or refrain from performing specified conduct.[2] An obligation thus imposes upon a party the duty to perform (or refrain from performing), and simultaneously creates a corresponding right to receive performance on the part of the party to whom such performance is to be tendered. Strictly therefore the term obligation encompasses both the duty and the corresponding right.

1.02 The term 'obligation' is thus used in its classical sense to denote the whole relationship binding a party or parties at law. The term is also used in at least two further senses. It may also describe:

(1)   a subject heading within the law, for instance 'the obligation of contract', or, at its broadest, simply 'obligations', when it describes the whole of the law concerned with obligations. In this sense it is being used to describe not a specific legal tie between parties, but a taxonomic division of the law; or

(2)   a specific duty imposed upon a party, for instance 'the obligation to make payment under a hire-purchase contract'. In this sense 'obligation' is being used as a synonym for 'duty'. This sense of the word is frequently adopted by the layperson, who may only conceive of 'obligation' as referring to the duty side of the equation. This use is also adopted by practitioners and academics, however, and so long as it is not productive of confusion it is perfectly acceptable.

1.03 Scotland has for long recognised the law of obligations as a distinct division within private law[3]. The subject headings of this division are as indicated in this map of the law:

---

1 The Roman jurist Gaius distinguished rights deriving from obligations (personal rights) from rights deriving from property (real rights), while recognising that both kinds of right formed part of a person's assets. This taxonomy was adopted in Justinian's *Institutes*.

2 In Justinian's *Institutes* an obligation is defined thus: 'An obligation is a legal tie [*iuris vinculum*] which binds us to the necessity of making some performance in accordance with the laws of our state' (Inst 3.13).

3 See for instance the treatment of obligations as a distinct category of private law by Stair.

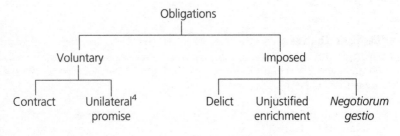

Figure 1.1

1.04 Each obligation shown in the above map may be defined briefly:

(1) A contract is an agreement, enforceable at law, between two or more parties to do or refrain from doing specified acts.
(2) A unilateral promise is an undertaking, binding on one party alone, to do or refrain from doing specified acts.
(3) A delict is a harm occasioned to a person or property as the result of wrongful behaviour.
(4) An unjustified enrichment arises where a gain is made by one party at the expense of another in circumstances where the retention of such gain cannot be justified.
(5) *Negotiorum gestio* is the administration of another's affairs where the other is unaware of, or precluded from consenting to, such administration.

The definition of each of these obligations is explored in depth in the succeeding chapters of this work.

1.05 It is conceivable that one might describe a contract not as an obligation but as a collection of obligations, meaning either a collection of legal ties (both the rights and the corresponding duties) or a collection of duties to be performed. The doctrine of the mutuality of contract in Scots law might be said to encourage this, recognising as it does that certain specific duties of a party within a contract may be viewed as the counterpart of specific duties of the other party's. One could thus see each duty pair as a separate obligation. This use of the term obligation is an additional meaning of the term to those already listed above. Such a conception of contract would be perfectly correct, but it does not detract from the fact that the whole contractual relationship is also properly described as an obligation. A contract may thus equally be seen as a legal tie or a collection of legal ties. Whichever description is chosen will depend upon the context of the debate.

---

4 The obligation may be referred to simply as 'promise', as there is no other type of promise recognised by Scots law as a complete obligation. As David Sellar has commented, in 'Promise' in *A History of Private Law in Scotland*, vol II, at p 253, the prefix 'unilateral' seems unnecessary. We do not, for instance, call the obligation of contract 'bilateral contract'. However, it is common among commentators to include the prefix.

Types of obligation: voluntary and imposed

1.06 The distinction between those obligations which are assumed voluntarily by the parties—contract and unilateral promise—and those which are imposed by the law regardless of the will of the parties—delict, unjustified enrichment, *negotiorum gestio*—was first drawn clearly by Stair in the late seventeenth century, who distinguished obligations undertaken 'by engagement' (that is, those voluntarily assumed) from those which were 'obediential' (that is, imposed by the law). For Stair, this distinction was crucial in explaining certain fundamental differences between contract and promise on the one hand, and delict, unjustified enrichment and *negotiorum gestio* on the other hand[5].

1.07 The distinction between voluntary and imposed obligations remains important today in explaining in part certain features of the law of obligations. The following list indicates how certain features of contract and promise stem from their conception as self-imposed obligations, while in delict (for instance) other features flow from its conception as an imposed obligation:

In contract: the understanding that implied terms in contract depend upon the presumed intention of the parties; that no contractual terms may be implied which contradict express contract terms; that proposed terms amount to a contractual offer only where there is a clear intention to be bound to such terms; that parties may in a contract provide for any matter affecting the parties' relationship, including the consequences of breach or external frustration; that only terms of which sufficient notice was given prior to the formation of the contract will be incorporated into the contract; the primary interest protected by the measure of damages;[6] the availability of specific implement.

In promise: that a unilateral promise is to be distinguished from an offer by the former requiring a clear intention immediately to be bound to an obligation.

In delict: that so long as the type of injury can be foreseen, it is irrelevant that the extent of liability could not; that in personal injuries claims one takes one's victim as one finds him; the primary interest protected by the measure of damages.[7]

1.08 Whilst in order to properly understand the law of obligations it is important to distinguish voluntary and imposed obligations, one should not overlook certain commonalities between the two groups:

(1) It should be borne in mind that both types of obligation will arise only as a result of voluntary conduct undertaken by the relevant party or parties. Thus, it may be stated that a contract is formed only where the parties have voluntarily accepted liability; likewise a delict is only committed where the

---

5 Stair's terminology is not always that of the modern law. The term 'delinquence' is used to describe delict, and the duty to compensate another in delict is styled the duty to make 'reparation' (I.9.1,5); the term unjustified enrichment is not used by Stair, but rather the actions of 'recompense' (I.8) and 'restitution' (I.7).

6 Discussed further at **1.37**.

7 Discussed further at **1.37**.

conduct which is described as wrongful was undertaken voluntarily.[8] A note of caution must be sounded, however, about the growing use of the notion of an 'assumption of responsibility' as a basis for imposing liability in delict.[9] Despite the use of the phrase by the courts, it is unhelpful. Whilst a party who commits a delict must have *acted* voluntarily, the idea that delictual *liability* is voluntarily assumed runs counter to the understanding of delict in Scots law as an obligation imposed by the law rather than assumed by the wrongdoer. 'Assumption of responsibility', suggesting as it does a voluntary action, is a phrase which is particularly inept to describe the compulsory imposition of delictual liability on a wrongdoer.

(2) Many contractual duties are now implied in law (or, one might say, imposed) without reference to the intention or agreement of the parties. Such terms have proliferated as a result of statutory provisions[10] as well as judicial creation.[11] In this respect, many contracts now therefore contain duties which have not been voluntarily accepted by the relevant party.

Types of obligation: unilateral and bilateral/multilateral

1.09 A further distinction may be made between types of obligation, namely between obligations which are unilateral and those which are bilateral or multilateral. One common understanding of these terms (the **'first** definition') holds that the difference lies between those obligations to which only one party is bound (unilateral obligations) and, on the other hand, obligations to which two or more parties are bound (bilateral and multilateral obligations respectively). On this view, contract is always considered bilateral, even where the contract is gratuitous, for even where one party alone comes under a duty, there are in strict terms two parties who are bound to the obligation. Promise, per contra, is always unilateral, for even if the promisee requires to fulfil a condition before the promised benefit may be claimed, there is only ever one party (the promissor) bound to the obligation. The term 'unilateral contract' is encountered in English law, and, as will be seen[12], appears to have been created to remedy the lacuna in English law of enforceable unilateral obligations. Scots law, which recognises the obligation of unilateral promise, has no need for a concept of unilateral contract and (at least under this definition of unilateral and bilateral) in consequence does not recognise it.

---

8 A party who is physically compelled to act or who is not in control of its actions at the time the harm was committed is unlikely to incur delictual liability. See for instance *Waugh v James K Allan Ltd* 1964 SC (HL) 102, 1964 SLT 269.

9 See for criticism of the notion of assumption of responsibility, K Barker, 'Unreliable Assumptions in the Modern Law of Negligence' (1993) 109 LQR 461, and S Whittaker, 'The application of the "broad principle of Hedley Byrne" as between parties to a contract' (1997) 17 LS 169.

10 For instance, the terms implied under the Sale of Goods Act 1979 and the Supply of Goods and Services Act 1982.

11 See for instance *Malik v BCCI* [1998] AC 20, [1997] 3 WLR 95, [1997] 3 All ER 1, HL.

12 See **2.34–2.44.**

1.10 A variation of this first definition, although essentially encapsulating the same idea, is to say that a unilateral obligation involves the participation of only one person in its constitution; a bilateral (or multilateral) obligation per contra requires the participation of two (or more) parties before it can be constituted. Hence, promise is always unilateral because only one party constitutes the obligation, whereas contract requires a second party to participate by consenting to the obligation before it can be constituted. This variation may perhaps help to explain in a more convincing fashion the nature of some obligations. For instance, it may make more sense to talk of two parties being required to constitute the obligation of *negotiorum gestio*, one to administer the affairs of another (the *gestor*) and one to have his affairs administered (the *dominus*), than to talk of two parties being 'bound to the obligation', when the 'binding' of the *gestor* appears to be nominal.

1.11 A very different view from that of these two variations on a theme is arrived at if one defines unilateral and bilateral as follows (the '**second definition**'). On this view unilateral means that, at the time of the constitution of the obligation, only one party is obliged to perform any duties under it; a bilateral obligation per contra is one where two parties are bound to perform duties. Under this view, unilateral is in essence synonymous with gratuitous, and bilateral is synonymous with onerous (or mutual). On this view, a contract might be unilateral if only one party were obliged to perform under it, that is, if it were a gratuitous contract.[13]

1.12 It is not really possible to say that one or other definition is objectively correct. Any legal system may define its terminology as it wishes. So long as the definitions chosen are then used coherently and consistently there is no problem whichever option is adopted, although there may be difficulties in undertaking a comparative dialogue. Unfortunately the Scottish legal system has not authoritatively defined these terms, not even, it is suggested, in the current statute on the requirements of writing.[14] It may be said, however, that a weakness of the second definition outlined above is that it unnecessarily duplicates terminology. If unilateral is synonymous with gratuitous, then why not simply use one of the terms and dispense with the other? The first definition has the merit that, in distinguishing the meaning of unilateral from that of gratuitous, it permits a more precise analysis of obligations, and for that reason it is suggested as preferable.

1.13 The following chart uses the two definitions of unilateral and bilateral outlined above to indicate the nature of the different obligations recognised by Scots law:

---

13 R Black, 'Unilateral Promises', in the *Stair Memorial Encyclopaedia*, vol 15, at p 280, appears to adopt this viewpoint.
14 See the discussion of the Requirements of Writing (Scotland) Act 1995 at **2.10** below.

Type of obligation	Unilateral or bilateral – applying definition 1	Unilateral or bilateral – applying definition 2
Contract	Bilateral	Bilateral or unilateral – dependent on specific contract
Promise	Unilateral	Unilateral
Delict	Bilateral	Unilateral
Unjustified enrichment	Bilateral.	Unilateral
Negotiorum gestio	Bilateral	Bilateral

Figure 1.2

1.14 On either variation of the first definition of unilateral/bilateral, promise is the only unilateral obligation in Scots law: only one party is bound to the obligation, or, to put it another way, it requires only one party to participate in order to constitute the obligation.[15] On the first definition, all the other obligations are bilateral, because two parties are bound into the obligation (even if only in a nominal sense for one of the parties), or, to express it using the second variation, because two parties require to be involved in the constitution of the obligation. It is proposed to explore this more fully in relation to each obligation in the relevant chapters of this book, to which reference is made.

1.15 Using definition two, however, the picture is slightly different. Contract may be bilateral, if both parties have duties imposed upon them, or it may be unilateral if only one has duties. *Negotiorum gestio* is bilateral, as both *dominus* and *gestor* have duties imposed upon them.[16] Delict and unjustified enrichment are more tricky. Taking a definition of unilateral/bilateral based upon the concept of the number of parties who have duties, it is suggested that delict would be unilateral for the injured party has no duties placed upon him.[17] In relation to enrichment, it would seem that only the enriched has any duty imposed upon him. Once the enrichment has occurred, the impoverished party merely has a right to its return, but no duties.

15 Whilst a promisee must be contemplated, the promisee is in no sense required to participate in order to constitute the obligation. Indeed the promisee need not even be in existence when the obligation is constituted.

16 This is discussed further at **5.07**.

17 Mitigation of loss by the injured party is generally not conceived of as a duty, as it cannot be compelled by the wrongdoer as a matter of right: see **3.13**, fn 19. On the other hand, as everyone has a duty to take care for his own safety, an injured party whose own negligence aggravated the loss caused by the wrongdoer might be said to have breached a duty to take care for his own safety. This is best conceived of as a free-standing duty, however, rather than as the reciprocal side of the wrongdoer's duty to make reparation for the wrong.

Types of obligation: gratuitous and onerous

1.16   There is some academic disagreement as to the definition to be accorded to the term 'gratuitous obligation'. This is discussed more fully, with particular reference to the nature of promise, in chapter 2.[18] The Scottish Law Commission suggested that:

> 'Whether an obligation is gratuitous or onerous is determined at the time when the obligation is constituted and while matters are still entire; if at that stage there is no counter-stipulation prestable against the creditor the obligation is gratuitous.'[19]

This correctly states the position. A gratuitous obligation is one where the obliged is, at the constitution of the obligation, unable to compel performance from any other party. A gratuitous obligation is thus the opposite of an 'onerous' obligation, the term onerous denoting that, at the time of constitution of the obligation, a performance is offered in exchange for a counter-performance. The term 'mutual' can also be used as a synonym for onerous. A contract between parties *A* and *B* is properly described as onerous so long as there is some element of counter-performance on the part of *B* for the performance of *A*, even if there is not reciprocation by *B* of every single duty to be performed by *A* under the contract.

1.17   In a multilateral contract, it is conceivable that not every party will have duties imposed on it in terms of the contract. For example, a four-party contract might be constructed along the following model:

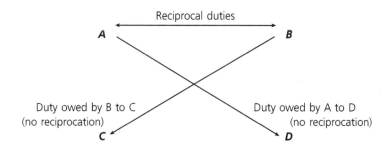

One might analyse each obligation to see whether it was gratuitous or onerous, but as a contract will be concluded as an overall package and thus, as has been suggested already, is correctly described as an obligation itself, the contract may appropriately be described as onerous, as there is counter-performance for at least some of the duties owed.

---

18 See **2.06–2.11**.

19 Scottish Law Commission Memorandum No 39 on Constitution and Proof of Voluntary Obligations, 1977, p 41.

Analysing obligations: one-stage or two-stage

1.18   In respect of the voluntary obligations of contract and unilateral promise, it is possible to talk of two stages in the existence of the relationship:

Stage 1—occurs when the contract or promise is created.

Stage 2—occurs when the obligation, whether contract or promise, is either broken or performed. Where the obligation is broken, the law intervenes to require that liability for the breach be imposed upon the offending party. Where performance occurs, the law deems the obligation to have been exhausted and therefore to be, in some sense, 'completed'.[20]

For the obediential obligations, however, only a single stage is relevant, corresponding to the second stage of voluntary obligations. The very nature of an obediential obligation presupposes that there has been no voluntary assumption of the obligation at a first stage. Instead, certain conduct has occurred which the law deems to give rise to correctional liability. The very essence of a delict, for instance, is that offending conduct has occurred. One moves immediately to reparation of the delict. There is thus a sole stage for obediential obligations:

Stage 1 (sole stage)—the delict is committed. The law intervenes to impose the duty to make reparation for the harm committed.

BASIS OF LIABILITY IN OBLIGATIONS

1.19   The traditional analysis of the basis of liability in the law of obligations is, as discussed above, that obligations are to be divided into those voluntarily assumed and those imposed by law. In the former category (comprising contract and promise) liability is held to be the result of a party having voluntarily agreed to accept such in the event of a breach of the obligation occurring. In the latter category (comprising delict, unjustified enrichment, and *negotiorum gestio*) liability is imposed regardless of whether a party would have wished to accept it, but rather because certain conduct performed by that party attracts liability. The type of conduct varies with the obligation in question: in delict, it is the commission of a wrongful act or omission; in unjustified enrichment, it is the retention of a benefit in circumstances where such retention is deemed to be without justification; in *negotiorum gestio*, it is having benefited from the administration by another of one's affairs.

1.20   In recent times, some commentators have suggested, however, that liability in the whole of the law of obligations may be explained by reference to a single principle or theory. It has been suggested by Atiyah, for instance, that wherever a benefit has been received by *B*, or wherever *B* has relied to its detriment upon the

---

20   Although some contracts, for instance, may impose ongoing obligations after the stage of performance.

behaviour of *A*, this will give rise to liability in the law of obligations.[21] Such a theory may be objected to on several grounds. First, the single principle theory does not properly reflect the state of the law as it is. For instance, the law recognises the validity of executory contracts where no benefit has been conferred or where no reliance has occurred, although such contracts should not be recognised if Atiyah's view were correct. Second, it is suggested that Atiyah's view is too simplistic to explain the diversity of liability in the law of obligations. For instance, delictual liability is not wholly about detrimental reliance—many delicts are committed in circumstances where reliance is wholly irrelevant or impossible. Third, Atiyah's benefit-reliance scheme has no room to accommodate the obligation of unilateral promise recognised in Scots law. It is clear that whilst it is perfectly possible to map out the bases of liability in the law of obligations, it is not possible to do so using a single principle such as the benefit/reliance principle.

1.21 The division between voluntary and imposed obligations provides the best starting point to explain the nature of liability in obligations in Scots law, a division which has served the law well for over three hundred years. It is, however, possible further to classify the obligations according to the nature of the event which gives rise to liability in each case, a classification which is dealt with shortly. It will soon become evident that the nature of the events is so varied that the search for a single unifying principle of obligational liability is the quest for a non-existent grail.

Identifying further aspects of each obligation

1.22 It is suggested that it possible further to analyse the nature of liability under each obligation, beyond dividing them into voluntary and imposed obligations, and beyond analysing them as one or two stage obligations, by reference to the following features:

(1) whether the obligation may be formed as a result of positive conduct (action), or as a result of negative conduct, ie a failure to act (inaction);
(2) the specific nature of the conduct which triggers liability under each obligation;
(3) the effect(s) that the events giving rise to the obligation may have upon the party who is entitled to performance under the obligation.[22] The effect of the events giving rise to an obligation may improve that party's position (either physically or economically) in comparison with the position before the obligation came into existence, may preserve its position as it was, or may worsen its position;
(4) what expectations, or 'interests', in the obligation the party entitled to enforce the obligation may have protected by virtue of the legal remedies available to it; and
(5) the principal remedies which the party entitled to enforce the obligation is permitted at law.

21 P S Atiyah, 'Contracts, Promises and the Law of Obligations', in *Essays on Contracts*, (Clarendon Press, 1986).
22 There will be two such parties under contract, but for the sake of simplicity *B* alone is considered in the following table.

These features may, together with the appropriate definition, be plotted on the following graph:

Obligation	Created by action or inaction?	Effect upon the party entitled to performance under the obligation	Conduct/ event triggering liability	Primary expectation/ interest protected by principal remedy/-ies	Nature of principal remedy/ -ies
Contract	*Stage 1 (formation):* Action of A and B *Stage 2 (breach):* Action or inaction of A[23]	May improve B's position, preserve it as it is, or worsen it[24]	Breach of contract	In receiving **performance** of the right(s) under the contract	Specific implement and/or payment of damages
Unilateral promise	*Stage 1 (formation):* Action of A *Stage 2 (breach):* Action or inaction of A[25]	May improve B's position, preserve it as it is, or, exceptionally, worsen it	Breach of promise	In receiving **performance** of the right(s) under the promise	Specific implement and/or payment of damages
Delict	Action, or exceptionally inaction, of A[26]	Worsens B's position (which may include failing to preserve it)	Wrongful conduct	In being **restored** to position prior to harm (**status quo ante**)	Payment of damages
Unjustified enrichment	Action of A and also, in some cases, of B[27]	Worsens B's position	Retention of gain by A without justification	In **disgorging gain** made by A (restitution)	Disgorgement of benefit retained
Negotiorum gestio	Action of B[28]	Worsens B's position	Expenditure by B to safeguard A's interests	In being **restored** to position prior to expenditure (**status quo ante**)	Compensation for expenditure undertaken

Figure 1.3

This is a complex table and its component features require to be explained in turn.

23 Where A is the contract breaker.
24 It may be questioned, however, whether this may be an *intended* effect. Certainly one cannot contract to have physical harm inflicted upon oneself. Such a contract would be illegal. However, one could contract to have one's property or interests worsened, eg a contract to demolish one's house. In any event, regardless of intention, any of the three effects noted may be obtained.
25 Where A is the party who breaks a promise.
26 Where A is the party who commits the delict.
27 Where A is the party making the gain and B the party suffering the loss. A's action may be relatively passive in some cases, eg simply receiving a mistaken payment. In some cases of enrichment involving interference with B's rights, B may be an inactive victim of loss.
28 Where B is the gestor.

Action or inaction

Contract/Promise

1.23 A contract requires positive action to be constituted (stage 1)—silence or inaction cannot conclude a contract. Thereafter, a contract may be broken by action or inaction (stage 2). Thus, a party who is obliged to deliver a specific car under a contract of sale, may breach its obligations by selling the car to someone else (*action*).[29] On the other hand, a photographer required to take photographs of a wedding may breach his obligations by failure to appear on the due day (*inaction*). The same principles apply to promise: stage 1 requires action; thereafter, stage 2, the breach of promise, may be the result of action or inaction.

Delict

1.24 The law's basic policy is to require action before a delict can be said to have been committed. Inaction, or an 'omission' or failure to do something, is not usually sufficient. Confusion can arise, however, as a result of differences in expression. A failure to properly exercise a duty of care can be described as an 'omission', on the basis that one has omitted to perform properly one's duty. It is suggested that this is misleading however. The term omission should not in this context be understood to refer to an omission to perform a duty. 'Omission' or 'inaction' describes rather a failure to undertake any conduct, whereas 'action' refers to the taking of such conduct. So much for the general policy of the law. However, there are some exceptions to this principle. First, where parties have had some prior contact through which one has come reasonably to expect that the other will confer a benefit upon it, then an omission to do so (or failure competently to do so) may constitute a delict. Thus, a professional who has been asked by a client to perform a task and has failed competently to perform it may be liable in delict for this omission. This is discussed more fully under the heading 'Effect upon the party entitled to performance under the obligation'. Second, the existence of a 'special relationship' between parties may impose a duty to take positive steps upon one to safeguard the position of the other, if necessary through the performance of positive conduct. Thus, a parent or a person *in loco parentis*[30] and an employer are two categories of person who may be required by the law to take positive steps to safeguard the child or employee respectively. An omission to take such steps may constitute a delict in Scots law.

Unjustified enrichment

1.25 For the obligation to be constituted, the impoverished party, *B*, must have undertaken action by which he has been impoverished, save in those cases where

---

29 Such behaviour would be classified as anticipatory breach of contract.
30 See for instance: *Carmarthenshire County Council v Lewis* [1955] AC 549, [1955] 2 WLR 517, [1955] 1 All ER 565, HL; *Dorset Yacht Club v The Home Office* [1970] AC 1004, [1970] 2 WLR 1140, [1970] 2 All ER 294, HL.

B's rights have been interfered with by *A* without *B*'s knowledge or consent. The enriched party, *A*, must have taken some action, even if it is relatively passive, eg the receipt of a mistaken payment. Mere inaction on *A*'s part will in general be abortive of the constitution of the obligation. Thus if *B* paints *A*'s house while *A* is on holiday, *B* cannot raise an enrichment claim against *A*. *A* has taken no active part in the process.

Negotiorum gestio

1.26 For the obligation to be constituted, some action by *B*, the *gestor*, is required. On the other hand, *A* must not have taken any active part in the constitution of the arrangements, the point of *negotiorum gestio* being that *A*'s affairs have been administered in circumstances where *A* could not consent to the administration.

Effect upon party entitled to performance under the obligation

1.27 When a party interacts with another in terms of any of the recognised obligations, then its position may be improved, it may be preserved, or it may worsen. Its 'position' may be taken to include both its physical integrity and its patrimony (including its financial resources):

Contract/Promise

1.28 A contract is most often undertaken by a party with the expectation that its position will be improved. However, a contract may also be undertaken to safeguard a party's position, to prevent it from being diminished. The net effect here will be zero. Thus a contract of insurance is undertaken with the intention that, should any of the insured risks materialise, the contract of insurance will ensure that the insured party is no worse off.

1.29 Occasionally a contract may be undertaken to worsen a party's position. Thus, I may contract to have property of mine destroyed if I wish. Thus, contracts may be undertaken with the intention of any of the three effects outlined being obtained. However, the *intention* of the party undertaking the obligation does not universally correlate with the *effect* that may be obtained: I may enter a contract with the expectation of gaining under it but, through making a bad bargain, the effect may be that my position is worsened. Similar comments reply in respect of promise.

Delict

1.30 A delict will always worsen the victim's position. That is of the very essence of the concept of a delict as a harmful act which causes loss. 'Worsen' should be understood to include, in certain circumstances, a failure to preserve an individual's position. Thus, where a professional party has been requested to undertake services to preserve a party's position, a failure to effect such preservation will entail that the victim is worse off. This failure to preserve a party's position will only be applicable where there is a positive duty to act. As has been seen, such a positive duty to act will only apply in limited circumstances.

1.31 The recognition that a failure to preserve a person's position, that is, a failure to confer the benefit of preservation upon him, may give a right to delictual damages does not in any sense infringe upon the preserve of contract. As shall be seen below, the voluntary obligations alone confer a right to enforce performance (including improvement or preservation) upon the party having the right. This important feature is not comprised by a delictual right to damages in some cases where the injured party's position has not been preserved.

Unjustified enrichment

1.32 The existence of the obligation of unjustified enrichment requires that the impoverished party's position has been worsened. Without a loss there can be no action.

Negotiorum gestio

1.33 The existence of the obligation of *negotiorum gestio* likewise requires that the *gestor's* position has been made worse by the administration undertaken on behalf of the *dominus*.

Expectations (or interests) protected by law

1.34 When one considers the principal remedy or remedies to which an aggrieved party is entitled for breach of each obligation, it is possible to say that in respect of each the remedies available protect a specific primary 'expectation' or 'interest'[31] which is embodied in the obligation. The 'interests' protected by the law of obligations are as follows:

(1) **Performance interest**. [32] The remedies of specific implement and damages for breach of contract are designed to protect the interest a contracting party has in expecting performance to occur. If *A* does not perform, then *B* is entitled to protect this so-called 'performance interest' by seeking enforcement of the contract via the remedy of specific implement or, where this is not granted, by seeking damages in an amount representing the position in which *B* would have been had the contract been performed. The same may

---

31 The terminology of specific interests was first proposed by Fuller and Purdue in their seminal article 'The reliance interest in contract damages' (1936) 46 Yale LJ 52 (part 1) and 373 (part 2). See further for Scots law: L Macgregor 'The expectation, reliance and restitution interests in contract damages' 1996 JR 227, and W Stewart 'The theory of the Scots law of contract' 1996 JR 403.
32 See D Friedmann, 'The Performance Interest in Contract Damages' (1995) 111 LQR 628.

be said for promise. The performance interest is sometimes referred to as the 'expectation interest'.[33] This is an unhelpful and misleading term. Under a contract, one may well 'expect' to receive performance. However, the language of expectancy may also be used of the other obligations. If a delict is committed against me, I 'expect' to be restored to the position I was in before the delict occurred; if another is unjustifiedly enriched at my expense, I 'expect' to be able to have the gain made by that other transferred to me. For this reason, in *Figure 1.3* above the term expectation has been used as a synonym for the term interest. If I have an 'interest' in certain states of affairs being the case, I 'expect' them to happen.[34]

(2) **Restoration interest** (also sometimes referred to as the **'status quo ante** interest' or the **'reliance interest'**[35]). Where *A* commits a delict against *B*, *B* has a legitimate interest in being restored to the position he was in before the delict occurred, that is, to be restored to the *status quo ante*. Delictual damages are assessed on that basis. There is no question, however, of improving upon *B*'s *status quo ante* position, as is possible with the performance interest, as it runs contrary to the nature of delict as a non-voluntary obligation that a party upon whom a delictual duty is imposed should be compelled to improve another's position, as may happen under the performance interest.[36] That is the proper province of voluntary obligations. The *status quo ante* interest also applies in respect of *negotiorum gestio*—where *B* has expended time and resources in managing the affairs of *A* in circumstances where consent to such management could not be obtained, *B* has an interest in seeing that the reasonable expenses incurred in such administration are recoverable by him. He thus wishes to be restored to the position he was in before the management occurred.

(3) **Restitutionary interest** (or **'disgorgement interest'**). Where *B* has been unjustifiably enriched at the expense of *A*, *A* is entitled to seek restitution of the enrichment or recompense for the gain *B* has made. Such restitution/ recompense does not fulfil any expectation of *A*, nor will it necessarily restore *A* to a prior position (as the enrichment made by *B* may in fact be

---

33 The term coined by Fuller and Purdue: see fn 31.

34 Jane Stapleton, though adopting a slightly different terminology to that suggested here, also prefers to use the term 'expectation' in a different manner from that in which it has traditionally been used. She styles the contractual interest the 'entitled result' measure, and the tort interest the 'normal expectancies' measure: see Stapleton, 'The Normal Expectancies Measure in Tort Damages' (1997) 113 LQR 257.

35 On the basis that we are entitled to rely upon not being injured by culpable conduct. However, as some delictual situations require a more specific instance of reliance to occur (eg misrepresentation) not required in other situations (eg a road traffic injury), it is suggested that the term 'reliance interest' is apt to confuse, and 'restoration' or 'status quo ante interest' should be preferred. Moreover, use of 'reliance' may confuse with the primary contractual interest, as it may be said that one 'relies' upon a contract being performed.

36 However, where a delict prevents the pursuer from having improved his own position, for instance by earning employment income, such loss can properly be considered as an aspect of the restoration or status quo ante interest. See further J Stapleton, 'The Normal Expectancies Measure in Tort Damages' (1997) 113 LQR 257 at pp 266–67. Note, however, that Stapleton uses the term 'entitled result' measure to refer to what in the present text is styled the 'performance' measure, and the term 'normal expectancies' measure to refer to what in the present text is styled the 'restoration' or 'status quo ante' measure.

greater or less than the loss suffered by *A*). In essence the interest *A* has is in disgorging *B* of the benefit acquired at *A*'s expense.

1.35 Thus far, one might imagine from a reading of *Figure 1.3* above that there is only one interest to be associated with each obligation. In fact, as the heading in the table disclosed, what was listed was the 'primary' interest in respect of each obligation. That is not the full picture, however, for, as shall be seen below, a party may on occasion be entitled to have an interest other than the primary interest protected. This may be an important option, as the value which can be claimed by a party may differ depending upon which interest or interests are protected.

1.36 Consider the following scenarios. They explain how calculation of damages may differ depending upon which interest is used (though as shall be seen, a free choice is not available to the injured party in most of the scenarios):

Scenario 1: *A* contracts to sell goods to *B*. The contract price is £500. *B* intends to sell the goods on to *C* who has offered to pay £600 for them. *B* pays for the goods but they are not delivered, as *A* has meanwhile sold them to *D* from whom it has received the higher price of £700. If *B* is entitled to damages correlating to its performance interest it will receive £500 (the price paid for the goods which were not received) + £100 (the profit expected from the resale) = £600. On the other hand if *B* is entitled to recover in the amount of its restitutionary interest, it will be entitled to claim £500 (the price paid for the goods which were not received) + £200 (the amount of the gain made by *A* over and above the price *B* would have paid it) = £700.

Scenario 2: *A* commits a delict against *B*. *B*'s losses are £500. *A* makes a profit of £1,000 out of this delict. If *B* is entitled to damages representing its restoration interest it will receive an amount to put it into the position it was in prior to commission of the delict, namely £500. On the other hand, if *B* is entitled to seek protection of its restitutionary interest, it will be entitled to disgorge the profit made by *A* and will thus be entitled to £1,000.

Scenario 3: *A* agrees to buy goods from *B* for £300. *A* pays the price but *B* fails to deliver the goods on the appointed day. However, by the delivery day, the value of the goods has fallen to £100. If *A* is entitled to damages representing its performance interest then it will receive £100, being the amount that will place it in the same position as if the contract had been performed. However, if *A* is entitled to protection of its restitutionary interest it will be entitled to the amount of £300, being the amount of the benefit unjustifiably retained by *B* at *A*'s expense.

Scenario 4: *A* owns a small cinema. It contracts for the installation of a new high technology cinema projection system in the cinema, to be purchased from *B* for £10,000. *A* incurs £5,000 in costs in converting the cinema in preparation for the installation of the new system. It expects to make £30,000 profit from the installation of the new system. Before the new projection system is installed, it becomes superseded by an even newer system. *A*'s expected profits from installation of the new system now fall to only £2,000. Prior to the due date for installation, *B* states that it will not honour its side of the bargain. It has decided to purchase its own larger cinema in which to install the system, with the expectation of making £10,000 profit from so doing. If *A* is entitled to claim for its performance interest it will receive £2,000, being the amount of expected profit; if *A* is entitled to claim for its restoration interest, it will be able to recover the costs of the preliminary and now wasted expenditure of £5,000; if *A* can recover under its restitutionary interest for the gain expected to be made by *B* at its expense it will receive £10,000.

1.37 In fact, it is not always possible to choose a secondary interest in order to increase the value of one's claim, although this may sometimes be permitted. The secondary interests (if any) associated with each obligation are shown in the following diagram:

Type of obligation	Primary interest protected	Secondary interests (if any) protected
Contract	Performance	Restoration Restitutionary
Promise	Performance	Restoration Restitutionary
Delict	Restoration	None[37]
Unjustified enrichment	Restitutionary	None
Negotiorum gestio	Restoration	None

Figure 1.4

1.38 This diagram indicates that in relation to contract and promise, the restoration and restitutionary interests may be protected. As shall be seen in later chapters, however, a contracting party is not automatically entitled to claim for one of the secondary interests rather than its performance interest. There are various reasons for restrictions on the ability to choose to have a secondary interest protected. Where, for instance, it would allow a contracting party to avoid the consequences of a bad bargain, a party will normally be restricted to a claim for its performance interest. On the other hand, where a contract is frustrated, a party can normally claim restitution of any sums paid under the contract for a performance which was not received prior to frustration. Disgorgement of profits made by a contract breaker is, however, not permitted.[38]

1.39 The diagram indicates that in respect of delict, unjustified enrichment, and *negotiorum gestio*, only the primary interest is protected by the available remedies. This is for the following reasons:

(1) In respect of delict, one is not permitted to claim for a performance interest. The law of delict concerns compensation for harm, not fulfilment of an expectation of performance. Damages may, however, include losses which would not have arisen in the future had the harm not occurred. Thus, in a road traffic injury, if the injured party is incapacitated from working, future earnings which he expected to make during the period of incapacity will be recoverable. This, however, is simply preserving his restoration interest— had the delict not occurred, he would have been in a position to undertake the work. Even where an interdict is sought in delict, the performance

---

37 As is discussed at **3.54** and **6.20**, exceptionally a restitutionary measure may be available in delict, for example in relation to breach of confidence.
38 *Teacher v Calder* (1899) 1 F (HL) 39. See further **4.56–4.60**.

interest is not protected—one is simply seeking to preserve the status quo by preventing a diminution occurring. In theory the law could permit disgorgement of the profits of a wrongdoer (ie the restitutionary interest), but as shall be seen below[39] Scots law has been unwilling to allow this, save in very exceptional cases.

(2)　In respect of unjustified enrichment, performance is irrelevant even where the parties may originally have been in a contractual nexus. If contractual remedies are barred only the restitutionary interest may be claimed. In many enrichment actions, a pursuer will be seeking to have a benefit restored to him, and the claim may therefore seem to resemble a restoration claim. Strictly, however, as the measure of recovery is related to the gain made by the defender, it is the restitutionary interest which is being protected in each case.

(3)　In respect of *negotiorum gestio* the *gestor* is only ever entitled to recover its reasonable expenses from the administration. The *gestor* has no expectation of performance, nor can it claim for any enrichment it may have incidentally occasioned to the position of the *dominus*.[40]

TYPE OF LIABILITY IN OBLIGATIONS—PERSONAL AND REAL RIGHTS[41]

1.40　In Scots law, as in classical Roman law, a distinction is made between a personal right (*jus in personam*) and a real right (*jus in rem*). The proper province of personal rights is the law of obligations; the proper province of real rights is the law of property. A personal right is a right exercisable by a party against a specific person or persons, created as the result of a voluntary or imposed legal tie (*vinculum juris*) existing between the party and the other person or persons. A real right is a right in a thing exerciseable against all persons, or, as it is sometimes put, exercisable 'against the world'.[42] A real right may be acquired in a number of ways, including by transfer from an existing holder of the right (for instance, transfer of the right of ownership under a contract of sale), by voluntary creation of a new real right in an existing thing (for instance, the creation of a right of security over land), and by operation of law upon the creation of a new thing (for instance, the right of ownership granted to the creator of a new species of thing made from raw materials).

1.41　In a contract between *A* and *B*, *A* may only exercise his contractual rights against *B*, and vice versa. If *B* fails to perform his contractual duties, *A* may not raise a claim for the breach against anyone other than *B*. The same applies to each

---

39　In chapter 6.

40　The relevance of enrichment as a ceiling in cases of 'impure' *negotiorum gestio* must, however, be noted: see further on this point **5.08**.

41　For a useful treatment of the distinction between personal and real rights, see Kenneth Reid, 'Obligations and property: Exploring the Border' 1997 Acta Juridica 225.

42　Intellectual property rights present a difficulty, as they do not fit neatly into either the real or personal category. It may be better to treat them separately as a third type of right: Reid, op cit, at p 229.

of the other obligations. Thus, where *A* commits a delict against *B*, only *B* is liable in damages to *A*.[43] Where *A* makes a mistaken payment to *B*, only *A* may seek restoration of the payment, and may do so only from *B*.

1.42 By contrast, in the law of property, if *A* owns some property, for instance a house, then he is entitled to vindicate his right of ownership against any party who seeks to interfere with it, for instance by trespassing in the house or by seeking to occupy it without *A*'s permission. It is, however, possible for more than one real right to exist in relation to a piece of property. Thus, in respect of a house, there may exist at the same time the real right of ownership in *A*, the real right of security in *B*, a bank, and the real right of lease[44] in *C*, the tenant. These real rights may all be compatible with each other.[45]

1.43 Although personal and real rights are to be distinguished, the two often interact. This occurs most frequently where a contract is used as the means to transfer a real right. Thus, by a contract of sale between *A* and *B* (creating personal rights between them), the parties can agree that *A* will transfer the right of ownership (a real right) in a book to *B*. The personal rights come into existence when the contract is formed. The real right will be transferred in accordance with the intention of the parties or by application of various statutory provisions.[46] Another interaction of the two types of right occurs where a personal right to seek restoration of a benefit which is being unjustifiably retained is exercised in order to force *B* to restore a thing in *B*'s ownership to *A*. If, however, *A* has not lost ownership of the thing, then strictly *A* is not exercising a personal right of unjustified enrichment. Rather he is vindicating his real right of property by demanding the return of property which belongs to him. The difference is between *A*'s saying, in the first case, 'You are in possession of something which belonged to me in circumstances where you can no longer justify retaining the thing. I am asserting my personal right of unjustified enrichment to compel you to restore ownership of the thing to me' and saying, in the second case, 'You are in possession of something I own. I am asserting my right of ownership in it. Give it back to me.' The first claim appeals to a personal right, the second to a real right.

1.44 In common law systems, the above division of personal and real rights is also recognised. However, one noticeable difference between Scots and English law lies in the English law of restitution, some features of which equate to unjustified enrichment in Scots law. Restitution in English law concerns itself not simply with personal rights but also some proprietary (real) remedies. The reason for this is that the subject of restitution in England is built around the remedy of restitution, rather than the event triggering liability (unjustified enrichment). As restitution is a remedy also found within property law, the topic of restitution in

---

43 Leaving aside the exception of vicarious liability.
44 In Scots law, the right of lease is hybrid right. Lease is a contractual relationship, but the tenant may acquire a real right of occupancy under the lease in certain circumstances.
45 Although not where, for instance, the grant of a lease is in breach of an antecedent right possessed by the security holder: *Trade Development Bank v Warriner & Mason* 1980 SC 74, IH; *Trade Development Bank v David Haig (Bellshill) Ltd* 1983 SLT 510, IH.
46 In the case of goods, under the Sale of Goods Act 1979.

England encompasses both personal rights to seek restitution as the result of unjustified enrichment, but also real rights to seek restitution founded upon a claim to ownership of property.[47] In Scots law, the topic of unjustified enrichment is based upon a cause of action stemming from the creation of a personal right. Proprietary enrichment remedies therefore simply do not exist in Scots law.

1.45 One further aspect of the division between real and personal rights may be noted. In classical Roman law, according to the scheme of the Jurist Gaius,[48] the law was divided into persons, things, and actions. Within the law of things were found both rights in corporeal property and rights deriving from obligations, which Gaius conceived of as incorporeal things. A 'thing' was part of an individual's assets, his patrimony. An individual's assets or patrimony therefore included not just his corporeal property (such as his house and other possessions), but also rights which he might have to receive performance under a contract, or to receive damages for having been injured as the result of a delict. An obligation was thus conceived of as a species of property. If one applies this notion of obligations as part of our patrimony in the modern law, it is possible to talk about owning a contractual right. As an alternative to saying that *A* has a contractual right to receive performance from *B*, one could say that *A* has the real right of ownership in the personal right to receive performance under the contract with *B*.

1.46 It is therefore possible to talk about having real rights in personal rights. Doing so is not always helpful, however. To describe my rights under a contract as my right of ownership of contractual rights is a convoluted way of expressing matters. Ordinarily therefore it is not helpful to theorise in this way. However, on occasion it may make sense to talk of rights in rights. If, for instance, one were drawing up an inventory of a deceased person's estate, it would be important to list any rights the deceased had to receive payment under a contract as part of the assets forming his estate. One might in that situation helpfully talk of the deceased having owned the right to receive performance at the time of his death. In the context of this work, however, the description of personal rights as assets and thus as property is an unnecessary complication, and the simple distinction between personal and real rights that was explained above will be maintained for the purposes of exposition.[49]

OBJECTIVE AND SUBJECTIVE PERSPECTIVES ON LIABILITY

1.47 In assessing whether an obligation exists at law, it is possible to adopt either an objective or a subjective approach. An objective approach considers whether an obligation has been formed by asking whether a reasonable person, having

---

47 Burrows, *Understanding the Law of Obligations* (Hart Publishing, 1998), comments (at p 7) on the English law view: 'the independent law of restitution is a division not only of the law of obligations but also of the law of property. That is, it is concerned not only with personal remedies but also with proprietary remedies'.
48 See Gaius *Institutes* 2,12–14; Justinian *Institutes* 2,2.1–3.
49 For a discussion of the concept of rights in rights, see Kenneth Reid, 'Obligations and Property: Exploring the Border' 1997 Acta Juridica, at pp 230–233.

regard to the conduct manifested by the parties (or in the case of unilateral promise, the party), would conclude that the necessary requirements for formation of the obligation have been met. A subjective approach asks whether the parties (or party) thought that they were bound by the obligation regardless of the impression they may have given by their conduct.

Voluntary obligations

1.48 In many cases whether one applies the subjective or objective approach, the same result is obtained. However, this is not invariably the case, and it is especially in relation to the voluntary obligations, contract and unilateral promise, that different answers may be obtained depending upon the approach taken. As voluntary obligations are said to flow the intention of the party or parties undertaking them to be bound to the obligation, determining whether an obligation exists in a particular case, may be said (on one approach) to depend upon whether the requisite intention to undertake the obligation was in fact present in the mind of the party concerned at the relevant time. To undertake such an investigation is to approach the matter of formation of the obligation from a 'subjective' or 'will' based standpoint. One asks 'Did A intend to contract' or 'Did A intend to undertake a unilateral promise?'. Alternatively, one may approach the question of liability from an 'objective' or 'declaration' standpoint. Such an approach asks whether a party by its whole conduct reasonably manifested an intention to contract (or undertake a promise), or, to put it another way, reasonably declared its intention to be bound. This might be said to be the case even though, upon further examination, it is determined that at the relevant moment in time the party did not subjectively intend to be bound by the obligation.

1.49 Either approach applied strictly, without any concession to the alternative viewpoint, can be productive of injustice. A wholly subjective approach provides no protection for B who claims that he had no means of knowing the subjective intention of A, especially where A's conduct was at odds with its claimed subjective intention. The subjective approach provides a high level of protection to A, who claims to have acted in error, but a low level of protection to B, who acts in response to the reasonable impressions conveyed by A. On the other hand, a wholly objective approach, whilst providing a high level of protection for B, who acts in response to the reasonable impressions conveyed by A, might conversely be said to fail to protect A from the consequences of reasonable errors made by it (eg those made by it of which B was aware and of which unfair advantage is being taken).

1.50 For this reason, it is common for legal systems to temper one or the other approach and to adopt a position somewhere along a line between the two extremes. In relation to contract, Scots law, whilst acknowledging that contract is based upon the agreement of the parties, begins from an objective position, which it then moderates in certain circumstances. By the time of Stair at least, there was a recognition that mere subjective intentions were an insufficient basis for assessing voluntary obligations. While Stair defined contract as based upon mutual consent,[50] a party was required to move beyond mere internal desire and will to contract, and had to demonstrate an external manifestation of such desire and will, a stage Stair called 'engagement'.[51] Without such an external manifestation of consent there could be no contract. A requirement for such engagement demonstrates that, already by the late seventeenth century, Scots law recognised the importance of objectivity in the constitution of contractual obligations.

1.51 Unlike other jurisdictions,[52] there has, however, been little discussion of the subjective-objective debate by the Scottish judiciary. The first comment of any note was made by Lord President M'Neill in *Thomson v James*,[53] the case which settled the question of the postal rule in Scotland. Competing appeals to a subjective or objective approach to formation of contract were made by counsel in the case. The Lord President made the following comment:

'In a great many cases the maxim that there must be a concurrence of will at the moment of completion of the contract cannot be rigidly or literally applied. The very opposite may be the fact. Although one cannot, by accepting an offer, bind a dead or insane person, he may bind an unwilling person, one who has altogether changed his mind.'[54]

1.52 Whilst this comment might be interpreted as supporting a modified subjective approach (or, as it may be referred to, a 'quasi-mutual assent'[55] approach), a preference for objectivity as the starting point gained ascendancy as a result of the comments of Lord President Dunedin in the later case of *Muirhead & Turnbull v Dickson*,[56] which concerned a dispute as to the nature of a contract relating to a piano. The Lord President analysed the parties' differences thus:

'[The seller] thought he was selling on the hire-purchase system, and the other person thought he was buying upon some instalment plan. But commercial contracts cannot be arranged by what people think in their inmost minds. Commercial contracts are made according to what people say.'[57]

1.53 This comment is frequently cited as the seminal Scots approach. Objectivity is thus preferred as the starting point in Scots law, although a recognition that some errors may vitiate consent ensures that the law adopts a modified objective view (or, as it may be referred to, a *'justus error'* approach).[58] In practice, it may be

---

50 Stair, I.3.2.
51 Stair, I.10.1,2.
52 South Africa being a good example, where the subjective-objective debate has been engaged in enthusiastically by academics and judges. For comparison of the Scottish and South African discussion, see M Hogg and G Lubbe, 'Formation of Contract', in *Mixed Legal Systems in Comparative Perspective: Property and Obligations in Scotland and South Africa* (Oxford University Press, due 2004).
53 (1855) 18 D 1, IH.
54 (1855) 18 D at 11.
55 This term is adopted in the South African jurisprudence.
56 (1905) 7 F 686, IH.
57 (1905) 7 F at 694.
58 The term also derives from South African jurisprudence. It refers to the question of whether *A* has been misled by *B*'s behaviour, and has thus made a *justus error* (reasonable error) as to *B*'s intention. Such a *justus error* requires that *A* is held to the contract despite not having subjectively agreed to it.

found that whether a system begins from an objective or subjective stance which it then modifies, the result in individual cases is often the same whichever of the two approaches is chosen.[59]

Imposed obligations

1.54 In relation to imposed obligations, Scots law adopts an objective assessment. Thus, one does not for the most part[60] ask—'Did A subjectively intend to harm B?', but 'Did A in fact harm B?'; not 'Did A subjectively intend to benefit from an enrichment conferred *sine causa* by B?' but simply 'Did A benefit from an enrichment conferred *sine causa* by B?'. This is so because imposed obligations are not held to arise as a result of the will of the party on whom they are imposed, and thus an assessment of the subjective state of mind of such a party is prima facie irrelevant. It should not (and indeed does not) matter whether A, the driver of a motor vehicle, intends to undertake delictual liability towards B, a pedestrian, when A's car hits B while the latter is crossing the road. The obligation is imposed by virtue of A's conduct, and the state of A's mind is irrelevant.[61]

1.55 The advent of cases which impose delictual liability for negligent conduct on account of the defender having 'voluntarily assumed a responsibility' towards the pursuer might be thought properly to give rise to an examination of the state of mind of the defender. What if it could be shown that A, a solicitor, had no subjective intention of assuming any responsibility towards B, his deceased client's daughter, when A was preparing the client's will? Would this negate any such liability on the part of A as was imposed by the House of Lords in *White v Jones*[62] and subsequently by the Inner House of the Court of Session in *Robertson v Watt*?[63]

1.56 If one were to take the phrase 'assumption of responsibility' at face value, such a negation of liability should be possible. The comments of Lord Jauncey in *Smith v Bush*[64] in relation to the liability of a negligent surveyor would seem to lend credence to this view. His Lordship characterised the facts of the case as giving rise to:

'a situation in which the individual concerned, albeit under no obligation in law to assume a responsibility, elected to do so'[65].

The reference to an 'election' of responsibility suggests an active, subjective assent to liability. However, such an approach, treating assumption of tortious liability

---

59 See Hogg and Lubbe, fn 52, for a comparison of various scenarios in Scots and South African law.
60 A clear exception is in relation to the intentional delicts recognised by Scots law, such as assault, trespass, passing off.
61 The only relevant consideration might be whether A was acting involuntarily at the time of the injury, for instance because he was suffering a heart attack at the wheel.
62 [1995] 2 AC 207, [1995] 1 All ER 691, HL.
63 4 July 1995, IH (unreported).
64 [1990] 1 AC 831, [1989] 2 WLR 790, [1989] 2 All ER 514, HL.
65 [1990] 1 AC at 870.

as if it were a voluntarily assumed obligation, seems plainly to contradict the characterisation which has already been given to delict (or tort) in this work as an imposed obligation. With respect to Lord Jauncey, it seems dangerous to treat His Lordship's comments as an accurate characterisation of the nature of tortious liability imposed via the test of assumption of responsibility.[66]

1.57   It is suggested that Lord Griffiths put the matter more accurately when he said of assumption of responsibility:

'The phrase can only have any real meaning if it is understood as referring to circumstances in which the law will deem the maker to have assumed responsibility to a person who acts on advice.'[67]

In a similar vein, in more recent decisions of the House of Lords, in *Henderson v Merrett Syndicates Ltd*[68] Lord Goff described assumption of responsibility as 'an objective test', and in *Williams v Natural Life Health Foods*[69] Lord Steyn remarked:

'[T]he touchstone of liability is not the state of mind of the defendant. An objective test means that the primary focus must be on the things said or done by the defendant or on his behalf.'[70]

These comments affirm the orthodox approach that liability in delict (or tort) is indeed to be imposed objectively, even where recourse is had to the largely fictional test of assumption of responsibility.

1.58   As to unjustified enrichment, is the objective-subjective debate of relevance when considering whether the obligation ought to be imposed? Broadly speaking, in assessing whether the requirements for unjustified enrichment liability are made out, subjective considerations are irrelevant. There are some issues, however, where consideration of the state of mind of the parties may be relevant. These include: (1) assessing whether a mistaken transfer was made as the result of a culpable error, where one may need to assess the state of mind of the payer; (2) assessing whether a benefit received has been consumed in good faith, where the state of mind of the recipient may be at issue; (3) assessing whether the recipient of a benefit has been enriched at all, where the recipient's view of what constitutes an enrichment may need to be considered; and (4) in the case of recompense, where the law stipulates that the obligation to restore will lie where there was 'no intention of donation', where one must therefore consider whether the pursuer did indeed have any such intention.

---

66 However, it might be argued that a surveyor who has prepared a survey report on which he knows the purchaser of a house will rely ought, in Scotland at least, to be seen as having promised unilaterally to the purchaser that the contents of the report are accurate. In Scotland, where consideration is not an issue as it was before the House of Lords in *Smith v Bush* , this might well be a preferable analysis to a delictual one.

67 [1990] 1 AC at 862.

68 [1995] 2 AC 145, [1994] 3 All ER 506, HL.

69 [1998] 2 All ER 577, HL.

70 [1998] 2 All ER at 582f–g. One may also note the approach of the English Court of Appeal in *Electra Private Equity v KPMG* [2001] 1 BCLC 589, CA, which disapproved of the approach of the judge at first instance for requiring a 'conscious' assumption of responsibility.

1.59   Issue 3 from the foregoing list raises the question of whether a benefit is to be subjectively valued by the recipient or objectively valued by the judge acting as the reasonable person. Consider the following example: an individual builds upon land in the bona fide but mistaken belief that it is his own, but it transpires that he does not have title to the land. Has the landowner been enriched? If the landowner is permitted to take a wholly subjective view, he may agree that he has been enriched; on the other hand, he may take the view that he has not been enriched, saying 'I had no desire to have this building erected upon my land. Indeed, the construction of this building has destroyed the beauty of the site. I do not consider myself in any way to have been enriched.' If a court were to take an objective view, such a remark from the landowner would be unlikely to persuade the court. The court might well say to the landowner: 'While you may not have desired the building, you are now in a position to rent or sell it. You are therefore enriched.'

1.60   It is suggested that the starting point for a Scottish court in an enrichment case is likely to be (as with contractual obligations) an objective approach, tempered by reasonable considerations advanced by the recipient as to devaluation of the benefit received.[71] Support for this may be found in the comments of Lord Chancellor Loughborough in *York Buildings Co v Mackenzie*.[72] In an action for reduction of the transfer of an estate to the defender, where the defender had made improvements to the estate, and the pursuer sought to exclude these improvements from any adjustment to be made between the parties, Lord Loughborough commented:

> 'It would be singular indeed if these were to be deemed no permanent improvement. It is not according to the fancy of the owner or of the builder, that the improvement upon the estate is to be estimated. ... The only question is the *quantum*. ... If it had been referred to a jury, the proper question would have been, whether or not the buildings were proper for the estate?'[73]

1.61   Clearly arguments as to subjective devaluation are unlikely to feature in those enrichment cases where the defender has received a sum of money or some moveable property, as in such cases the enrichment will usually be clear.[74]

INTERFACE OF OBLIGATIONS

1.62   Thirty years ago, anyone asked to provide a pictorial representation of the law of obligations might, with a reasonable degree of confidence, have suggested the following:

---

71   In the example cited, for instance, if the bona fide builder had erected a building on land which was planned as a nature reserve to be open to the paying public, the erection of an unwanted building might conceivably injure the landowner's economic interests.

72   3 Paton 579, HL.

73   3 Paton at 584–585. Despite such comments, no doubt some improvements could be subjectively devalued. Hume commented: ''tis essential ... that the improvements are not of a fanciful sort, or suited only to particular taste and humour of the late possessor' (*Lectures*, vol III, at p 171, reprinted as volume 15 of the Stair Society Collection).

74   Leaving to one side any question of a change of position defence being raised.

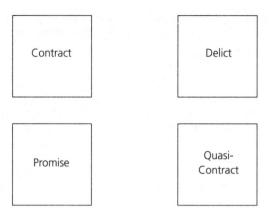

Figure 1.5

The categories of obligation were largely seen as separate and distinct, and fact situations were conceived as giving rise most naturally to one type of obligation, with little thought as to whether there was also the possibility of defining the situation in terms of another obligation.[75] There were some recognised scenarios where two obligations might co-exist—such as the promise contained within a contract—but these were exceptions to the general view that the existence of one obligation was conclusive of the exclusion of any of the others. Even the now burgeoning topic of concurrent liability in contract and delict was in its infancy.

1.63 If one were asked to draw a pictorial map of the law representing its current state, one might tentatively suggest the following[76] (where 'P' represents unilateral promise and UE unjustified enrichment):

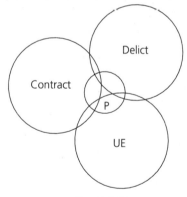

Figure 1.6

75 The separateness of the obligational groupings in the map is a slight exaggeration: as far back as the time of Stair, there was an appreciation that there might be interaction between the groupings, if not a developed notion of concurrent liability.

76 This map makes some minor omissions. Thus, *negotiorum gestio* is not included (and how one might include it is debatable). One might also have added Stair's distinction between obediential and consensual obligations: Stair I.3.2.

1.64 The overlapping areas of this Venn diagram (a graphic form which many readers may recall with mixed feelings from their schooldays) are intended to represent several aspects of what may be termed the 'interface' between the different parts of the law of obligations:

(1) *Concurrency of obligations.* It is now recognised that the same fact situation may give rise to more than one obligation. Concurrency of obligations has blossomed primarily in the contract/delict interface. The topic is addressed in chapter 3. Its permissibility across other divides, such as delict/unjustified enrichment remains controversial, as will be seen from the discussion in chapter 6.

(2) *Availability of remedies to protect an interest other than the primary interest associated with the obligation.* As was seen earlier, it is possible with some obligations to seek protection of an interest other than the primary interest associated with the obligation.

(3) *Problems with identification of the nature of the obligation or remedy.* There are some circumstances where ascertainment of the obligation intended by the parties is problematic. This issue is considered in relation to promise/contract in chapter 2. As for remedies, an interesting debate has arisen in relation to *restitutio in integrum*,[77] which it is now argued by some should be seen properly as an enrichment remedy rather than as a contractual one.

(4) *Emergence of new sub-groups.* Some types of liability have developed (or re-emerged) which exhibit elements of more than one obligational group. Among these may be counted *culpa in contrahendo* (if it exists in Scots law), liability for pre-contractual expenditure, and disgorgement of profits for invasion of rights, grounds of liability which are discussed in more depth in chapters 3, 5 and 6 respectively. Where one might precisely fit these into the diagram is debateable however.

1.65 These are topics of great importance not only for the student of the law but also for the legal practitioner. A party who has suffered financial loss as the result of the negligent provision of professional services may have the option of suing in contract or delict;[78] a party who has tendered services negligently may be able to claim some payment in enrichment even if an action for payment in contract is barred due to his or her breach of contract;[79] and a party who is unable to plead factual circumstances in defence in a contractual action may find that they can be pled in defence in a delictual one.[80] These are all issues of which legal practitioners must be aware if they are fully to protect the interests of their clients.

RISE OF CONCURRENT LIABILITY

1.66 Concurrent liability, particularly between contract and delict, is not a new phenomenon.[81] T B Smith recognised the possibility of contractual and delictual

---

77 This, however, would more properly be represented by moving the remedy from one distinct circle to another, rather than looking at the overlap between the circles.
78 As to which, see chapter 3, passim.
79 As to which, see chapter 4.
80 As to which, see chapter 3.
81 See further on this topic, Hogg, 'Concurrent Liability in the Scots Law of Contract and Delict' 1998 JR 1.

concurrence in his *Short Commentary on the Law of Scotland* published in 1962.[82] *Junior Books Ltd v Veitchi Co Ltd*[83] is a case of concurrent liability, since the defender was held not only to owe a duty arising under contract but also to the pursuer in delict. In addition, it has been recognised for some time that a lawyer may owe a duty to his or her client concurrently in both contract and delict,[84] and a doctor treating a patient privately may come under both a contractual and delictual duty in respect of diagnosis and treatment.[85] It is only in the last ten years or so, however, that the topic has blossomed, with an increasing number of claims being made in situations of concurrent liability.

1.67 Concurrency of liability arises where a defender incurs liability in respect of the same matter (normally breach of duty) in more than one obligational group. The liability under each obligational group may be owed to the same person or to a different person, for instance to a direct contracting party in contract and to a third party in delict, but so long as the liability concerns the same act or omission then it is said to be concurrent. The paradigm situation is, as already noted, concurrency between contract and delict. The recent judicial interest in such liability was sparked by the English cases of *Henderson v Merrett*[86] and *White v Jones*[87] and the prevailing view as a result of these cases is that concurrency between contract and delict will be held to exist for breach of duty unless there is some good reason to deny it.[88] The same considerations exist in relation to concurrency of promise/delict.

Permissible concurrencies

1.68 The contract/delict and promise/delict interfaces aside, the possibility of concurrency between other obligational groups is more doubtful. The remaining potential concurrencies are as follows:

Contract/promise

1.69 No reported cases of concurrent liability exist where a breach of contractual duty by *A* towards *B* has also been classified as a breach of promise to *B*. This accords with the nature of the obligations: a unilateral promise implies that the

---

82 T B Smith comments (*Short Commentary*, at p 282): 'Though contract may, as between the parties, modify the duties which the law would otherwise impose, unless they are so modified, they are not superseded merely because parties have entered into a contractual relationship. A person sustaining damage as a result of *culpa* or fault may elect to base his action on reparation rather than on contract'.

83 1982 SC (HL) 244, 1982 SLT 492.

84 See for instance *Robertson v Bannigan* 1965 SC 20, IH, and *Kyle v P&J Stormonth Darling* 1994 SLT 191, 1993 SCLR 18, IH.

85 *Edgar v Lamont* 1914 SC 277, 1914 SLT 80, IH.

86 [1995] 2 AC 145, [1994] 3 WLR 761, [1994] 3 All ER 506, HL.

87 [1995] 2 AC 207, [1995] 2 WLR 187, [1995] 1 All ER 691, HL.

88 Denial of concurrency is usually for policy reasons, such as exist in building chain cases, where the English courts have consistently denied tortious liability between distant parties in a contractual chain.

promisee can come under no duty to the promissor, whereas contract implies (save in the case of gratuitous contract) that the other party incurs a duty also. Concurrent liability in contract/promise towards *B* in respect of a particular obligation would thus be theoretically inconsistent.

1.70 It is of course possible for a promise to be attached to a contract. An option given to a tenant within a lease to purchase the subjects at the expiry of the lease is a clear example. Here, however, the option is a clear unilateral promise, and so breach of it is a breach of promise alone and not also a breach of a contractual obligation (unless so under a further free-standing contractual clause).

1.71 A party may also within a contract undertake an obligation to a third party who is not one of the contracting parties. Such an obligation can be characterised as promissory in nature, although it is usually referred to as a third party right or *jus quaesitum tertio*. Its exact location on the map of the law of obligations is uncertain, some writers seeing it as pure promise,[89] some as promise modified,[90] some as contractual in nature,[91] and some as *sui generis*.[92] A promise between *A* and *B* that *B* will pay *C* £500 on a specified date could be seen as giving rise to concurrent liability should the promise be breached, because such breach would allow *A* an action for breach of contract, or *C* an action of specific implement for breach of the promise to pay. On the other hand, if one were to classify the right in favour of *C* as contractual in nature, no issue of concurrency would arise.

Contract/enrichment

1.72 The received view is that no concurrency of action is possible between these two obligations. That is not to say that where a contract is void, avoided, or frustrated, enrichment remedies will be unavailable, for, as shall be seen later, they may well be in some cases.[93] But where a contractual obligation exists it is to be enforced by contractual remedies alone, and where a fact situation discloses a breach of contract the pursuer may in general exercise contractual remedies only and not enrichment ones.[94] This is because enrichment is held to be a subsidiary remedy, postponed to the operation of contract. If a contract has provided for certain ends, then not only is the achievement of these ends justified by the

---

89 Such as Stair (see I.10.5).
90 Such as H L MacQueen, with which view the author concurs. See MacQueen, *Stair Memorial Encyclopaedia*, vol 15, paras 827–828.
91 Such as Gloag. See *Contract* at pp 234-235.
92 Such as McBryde who states (at p 242) 'It may be better to treat *ius quaesitum tertio* as an independent right which shares some of the characteristics of other contractual rights but also has special features'. McBryde adopted a slightly more pro-promise approach in his comment in *Promises in Scots Law* (1993) 42 ICLQ 48 at 49: 'it might be that the doctrine is not wholly dependent on promises, but nevertheless the existence of a concept of unilateral promise makes it easier to allow the creation of rights in, and enforcement by, persons who are not parties to a contract'.
93 See further the discussion at chapter 4, passim.
94 This statement ignores the difficulties in the classification of *restitutio in integrum*, and also the question of whether a pursuer who has paid a sum of money may recover that sum following breach, or whether he is restricted to a claim in damages: as to which see the discussion in **4.75–4.79** and **4.88–4.106** respectively.

agreement of the parties, but the parties are impliedly taken to have limited themselves to contractual remedies in the event of breach.[95]

Promise/enrichment

1.73 Unilateral promise, like contract, is a voluntary obligation. Thus the operation of enrichment remedies where a promise is extant is governed by the same rule as operates with respect to the contract/enrichment interface, that is, enrichment remedies are unavailable, enrichment being postponed to promise.

Delict/enrichment

1.74 To ask whether concurrence of action exists at this interface is, to put the question in a form in which it is more commonly asked, to ask whether there is any possibility of 'restitution for wrongs'[96]. In other words, can a defender in a delictual action be required not only to compensate the pursuer for loss suffered, but also to disgorge any profits made as a result of the wrongdoing? The answer of Scots law is in the negative. The policy of the law of delict is compensation for loss and not punishment, and enrichment, being a subsidiary remedy, is not permitted to distort this policy by allowing the pursuer to strip the defender of profits made through his wrongdoing.[97]

Rationalising the law's view of concurrency

1.75 As will be obvious from the above, the answer to whether a concurrent action may lie is to be found in a number of enquiries. These include:

The obligational hierarchy

One way in which the hierarchy of obligations may be depicted is as follows:

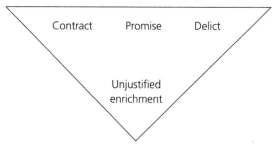

95 See further on this issue, the discussion in chapter 4.
96 The phrase is a borrowing from English law, and should be avoided as being something of a misnomer: see further **6.12**.
97 See further the discussion at **6.10–6.19**. One should note, however, the availability of an account of profits in a breach of confidence action: see **6.20**.

Under this model, contract, promise and delict are viewed as first level obligations, with unjustified enrichment, a postponed obligation, applicable only if none of the other three are operational.[98] For ease of reference this may be referred to as the 3:1 model.

1.76 The 3:1 model, however, is not the only way in which the hierarchy of obligations may be depicted. Another model flows from Stair's analysis of the law. To use Stair's terminology, the obligation to make reparation (that arising from delictual conduct) and restitution (that arising from what is now called unjustified enrichment) are both 'obediential'. They do not depend upon the agreement of the party or parties bound by the obligation, but are obligations imposed externally (in Stair's world view, by God). Contract and promise, per contra, bind parties only if they consent to be so bound, and are thus 'consensual' in Stair's terminology. On this classification, therefore, the obediential obligations are placed at the top of the pile, with the consensual obligations below them. This model, which may be referred to as the 2:2 model, may be depicted thus:

Delict	Unjustified enrichment
Contract	Promise

One would be bound to make reparation, for instance, if a delict were committed, unless contract excluded such a duty,[99] delict being a higher obligation than contract; the same would be the case for the duty to restore property retained without entitlement (the duty of restitution).

1.77 If both models are in some sense accurate, which it is submitted they are, then they are clearly making different points about the interaction of the law of obligations:

(a) *The 3:1 model*: The 3:1 model is making the point that the Scottish courts have recognised that enrichment remedies are postponed to contract and promise by virtue of the fact that these obligations render enrichments justified, and are postponed to delict by virtue of the fact that the purpose of the law of delict is compensation not disgorgement. The affirmation of any of these three obligations thus excludes the operation of enrichment remedies.

(b) *The 2:2 model*: The 2:2 model is making the point made by Stair, namely that delict and enrichment are obligations imposed upon us without reference to our consent, whereas contract and promise must be voluntarily entered into. A result of this view is that delictual or enrichment obligations will operate

---

98 See further on the nature of enrichment as a subsidiary obligation the discussion at **4.52– 4.55**.

99 Stair, I.18.1: 'contrary consent destituteth or extinguisheth any obligation ... not only to conventional, but to natural obligations'.

between parties unless they are excluded consensually, thus giving rise in some cases to the possibility of concurrent liability if they are not.[100]

Policy

1.78 Issues of concurrency are affected by the policy of the law in relation to the remedies appropriate to redress breach of an obligation. For instance, the law traditionally understands the purpose of damages for breach of contract to be the compensation of the pursuer for any loss suffered, by putting him in the position in which he would have been had the contract not been breached. There is therefore no right to disgorgement from the defender of any sums beyond such losses (ie an enrichment remedy). A similar policy of compensation for loss operates to prevent any enrichment claim in respect of a delict.

1.79 Other policy considerations can also operate, for instance the protection of creditors in bankruptcy. This has been a strong policy in preventing indirect enrichment claims against a bankrupt.[101]

Causation

1.80 A causal connection must be shown between the cause of action and the loss suffered. Thus, in some cases where a contract/enrichment concurrency has been at issue, the courts have held that the defender's gain is simply too incidental to found an enrichment action.

1.81 The questions necessary to assess in detail whether a concurrent action may be possible in a particular fact scenario are discussed in detail in chapters 2 to 6.

ROLE OF GOOD FAITH

1.82 If the issue of concurrent liability has exploded before academic and judicial attention in recent years, then no less so has the question of whether or not Scots law recognises a general duty to act in good faith. This issue has been most hotly discussed in relation to the obligation of contract.[102] If such a general duty were to apply across the range of obligations, then the question would arise as to whether, and if so how, such a duty would affect the interaction of the various obligations.

---

100 T B Smith criticised 'the fallacy that, if A owes a contractual duty to B, he cannot owe a duty of care in reparation to C' ('The Common Law Cuckoo', in *Studies Critical and Comparative* (W Green, 1962), at p 106). Similarly, on the English law, Lord Goff of Chieveley commented: 'the law of tort is the general law, out of which the parties can, if they wish, contract': *Henderson v Merrett* [1995] 2 AC 145, HL, at 193B.

101 See further **4.31**.

102 There is now a growing literature on this subject. For Scots law see A D M Forte (ed), *Good Faith in Contract and Property Law*. For English law see Roger Brownsword, *Good Faith in Contract*; M Bridge, 'Good faith in commercial contracts' in *Good Faith in Contract: Concept and Context*; A Mason, 'Contract, good faith and equitable standards in fair dealing' (2000) 116 LQR 66; J Stapleton, 'Good faith in private law' (1999) 52 Current Legal Problems 1. For a European perspective see J Beatson and D Friedmann (eds), *Good Faith and Fault in Contract Law*; A Hartkamp et al (eds), *Towards a European Civil Code*; or Zimmermann and Whittaker (eds), *Good Faith in European Contract Law*.

1.83 It is argued by some that good faith lacks inner coherence and is not susceptible to precise enough definition.[103] The same, however, could be said of the duty to act as would a reasonable person, the standard of behaviour demanded by the law of delict and a standard which the courts do not seem to have experienced any great difficulty in applying. It is suggested that, for instance, in relation to contracting parties a duty to act in good faith might be defined as follows:

> The duty to act honestly and openly in one's dealings with the other party, which includes (but is not limited to) not seeking to take undue advantage of the other party, disclosing all such information to the other party the failure to disclose which would distort an honest and open relationship, and treating the other party not simply as an adversary but as co-operative agent.[104]

If this seems a rather expansive definition, then it is no more so than any definition which might be provided for the delictual duty to act reasonably.

1.84 There is no native authority for the view that a duty to exercise a delictual right to compensation or to exercise an enrichment remedy is subject to a requirement of good faith. However, there has been renewed interest in a contractual duty of good faith at least since Lord Clyde's reference in *Smith v Bank of Scotland*[105] to 'the broad principle in the field of contract law of fair dealing in good faith'.[106] The existence at present, however, of such a general duty is questionable, and while some have used this statement as a springboard for arguing for a revitalised doctrine of good faith[107], Lord Clyde's comments have been interpreted by others as restricted to the facts of *Smith*.[108] The existence of such a duty in relation to unilateral promise must be even more questionable. The strongest argument against the further development of such a general duty to act in good faith when contracting is no doubt that a compelling case has yet to be made out that the law as currently operating is so deficient as to require such a development.

1.85 If a general doctrine of good faith were to develop in the law of obligations, then certain issues concerning the operation of good faith as between the different obligations would arise, among them the following:

(1) If good faith were, for instance, to preclude a pursuer from suing in breach of contract because the party in breach had not been given a fair opportunity to remedy the breach, would good faith also act as a bar upon a concurrent

---

103 Such an argument does not seem to have prevented the courts applying the requirement of good faith specified in the Sale of Goods Act 1979, s 25.

104 Whilst good faith and fair dealing are often conjoined (see Principles of European Contract Law (PECL), art 1:201 for instance), it is suggested that the duty of good faith (as suggested in the main text) may be distinguished from a duty to act fairly.

105 1997 SC (HL) 111; 1997 SLT 1061; 1997 SCLR 765.

106 1997 SC (HL) at 121B–C.

107 See in particular H L MacQueen, in Forte, op cit, fn 102 above.

108 Note for instance L Macgregor, 'The House of Lords "Applies" O'Brien North of the Border', 1998 ELR 90, who opines that 'Lord Clyde on the other hand provided very little guidance on the use of this decision as an authority. However, in view of the emphasis which he placed on the relationship involving cohabitation it is doubtful whether the decision will have an effect on the general principles of misrepresentation' (at p 92) Also C E F Rickett, 'The Financier's Duty of Care to a Surety' (1998) LQR 17 who suggests (at p 22) that *Smith* is confined to its facts, although he does remark in closing that 'Lurking in the background, of course, is the notion of good faith'.

delictual action? It might seem undesirable if a pursuer were able to avoid a duty to exercise a contractual remedy in good faith by suing instead in delict.

(2) It might become possible to rationalise the existence of some obligations or obligational sub-groups as deriving largely from notions of good faith.[109] This might arguably be so, for instance, for *culpa in contrahendo* (were it to be recognised in Scots law) and for aspects of unjustified impoverishment (such as liability for pre-contractual expenditure).[110]

(3) The doctrine of good faith might be recognised as providing a rationale for explaining why some interests are protected by certain obligations, but not by others. For instance, it could be argued that disgorgement of profits is not in general allowed for breach of contract, because, in essentially penalising the party in breach, it is inconsistent with fair dealing in good faith.

EUROPEAN CODIFICATION AND LEGAL DEVELOPMENT

1.86 Many Scots legal practitioners (and indeed students) may be unaware of developments in this respect, but over the past ten years there has been a growing movement in academic circles to rediscover a common European private law, a new *jus commune*.[111] Such development has led to the production of 'soft law', that is to say proposed codes within the law of obligations which do not have the force of law as yet but which are suggested for future codification (whether at national or European level), and, in the meantime, may be adopted by contracting parties should they so wish. One such code is the Principles of European Contract Law (PECL), the first part of which was published in 1995, with further parts added in 1999 and 2003. A similar project is underway in relation to delict.[112] Within Scotland too, a national plan for codification is taking shape. Initially this was a private project of the former law commissioner, Professor Eric Clive, and was restricted to the field of enrichment.[113] At the time of writing, however, a project for a full Private Law Code is taking shape, with the participation of a group of academics envisaged. Such a project will inevitably consider the interface issues with which this work is concerned.

---

109 In a much more general sense, whole areas of the law of obligations may be said to rest upon a principle of fair dealing or good faith—thus the restorative basis of enrichment as a whole can be argued to be based upon principles of good faith and equity, going back to the canon law and beyond.

110 H L MacQueen has argued that liability for pre-contractual expenditure under the line of cases following *Walker v Milne* (1823) 2 S 379, IH, is indeed based upon a requirement of good faith: see 'Good Faith in the Scots Law of Contract: An Undisclosed Principle?', in Forte, op cit, fn 102 above.

111 See, for instance, the collection of papers from diverse European scholars in A Hartkamp (ed), *Towards a European Civil Code*. In this respect, the publication of the first volume of a modern pan-European contract textbook may be noted: H Kötz and A Flessner, *European Contract Law*, vol 1 (1997).

112 See The Common Core of European Private Law Project (commonly called the 'Trento Project'), which is working towards the production of a draft Delict Code. See also Christian von Bar, *The Common European Law of Torts*; Walter van Gerven et al, *Cases, Materials and Text on National, Supranational and International Tort Law*.

113 Reprinted as chapter 25 of Hartkamp (cit fn 111 above).

1.87 While such codes tend to deal only tangentially with interface issues, reflecting the extent to which these issues remain a neglected field of study within obligations, the very existence of such codification projects offers some prospect that more considered solutions may be sought to interface problems, rather than the somewhat haphazard rules which currently prevail. There remain problems, however, particularly for codification at a European level. If a European Code is to tackle interface issues, it will face a large hurdle at the very outset, namely that the subject matter of interface issues differs from jurisdiction to jurisdiction. This is so because while Scots law may treat a particular fact situation as one of delict, French law (for instance) may treat it as one of contract. As the content of each obligational grouping differs between jurisdictions, so does the subject matter of the interface areas. An additional difficulty is that Scots law possesses a discreet obligation, unilateral promise, which is not possessed by other European jurisdictions.[114] Without changing the very divisions between the various obligations, such problems cannot be eliminated. This hurdle is a not insignificant one, and it remains to be seen whether it will prove insurmountable for a pan-European harmonisation of obligations law.

1.88 Even if this initial hurdle is overcome, further difficult issues would need to be resolved, the hierarchy of obligations being one. While, for instance, Scots law (and English law) classifies enrichment as a subsidiary obligation to contract, Dutch law recognises no such subordination.[115] Fundamental issues such as these require to be addressed before one can discuss the detail.

1.89 The foregoing comments may seem overly pessimistic, but they are not intended to be so. At the initial meeting of the Commission on European Contract Law, the participating members may have been doubtful as to the viability of their enterprise. The desire among academics for a new *jus commune* must not be underestimated. This powerful motivation may well overcome the problems of a harmonised approach to interface questions, even if difficult choices require to be made.

EFFECT OF THE HUMAN RIGHTS ACT 1998[116]

1.90 At the time of writing, the provisions of the Human Rights Act 1998 have yet to have a significant impact upon the law of obligations. This may be in large part because the terms of the Act are conceived primarily as operating in relation to public bodies, and many obligations operate solely within the realm of private law. The current state of affairs cannot be considered anything other than a honeymoon period, however, as the horizontal direct effect of the Human Rights Act, as well as obligational cases involving public bodies, is likely increasingly to draw the law of obligations within the scope of the Act's provisions.[117]

---

114 Although the validity of unilateral promises is upheld by PECL: arts 1:107 and 2:107.

115 See further on this issue Hogg, 'Lowlands to Low Country: Perspectives on the Scottish and Dutch law of Unjustified Enrichment', Ius Commune Research School (2001).

116 See, in general, The Hon Lord Reed, *A Practical Guide to Human Rights in Scotland* (W Green, 2001).

117 See further H L MacQueen and D Brodie, 'Private Rights and the Private Domain', in Boyle et al (eds), *Human Rights and Scots Law* (2002).

1.91 Even before the implementation of the Act, the European Court of Human Rights had ruled that the failure of the English courts to allow a damages claim in tort to the plaintiff in *Osman v Ferguson*[118] constituted an infringement of his right to a fair trial under article 6 of the European Convention on Human Rights.[119] More recently, the decision of the House of Lords[120] that a convicted spy must account to the Crown for profits made through breach of his contract is, it is reported, also to be challenged before the European Court of Human Rights on the basis that it restricts his freedom of expression guaranteed by article 10.[121] As the Human Rights Act is increasingly referred to in relation to obligational matters it is likely to be so by reference to the articles of the Convention concerning the right to a fair trial (art 6), the right to a private and family life (art 8),[122] the right to freedom of expression (art 10), and the right to freedom of assembly and association (art 11). In addition, it is likely that articles 1 and 2 of the First Protocol concerning the right to protection of property and to education will be relied upon.

1.92 Since the passing of the Act, the courts have been faced with a number of procedural arguments in relation to obligations actions. In *Gunn v Newman*,[123] a reparation action for personal injury, it was argued before the Inner House that the Court of Session Act 1988, ss 9(b) and 11, concerning proofs and jury trials in civil actions, were incompatible with the defender's right to a fair hearing under article 6. The Inner House was not prepared to make a determination on this matter without first giving the Lord Advocate and Advocate General the opportunity to comment. Such arguments are likely to continue, with inhibition upon the dependence[124] as well as arrestment upon the dependence[125] also having been challenged. Such arguments are in essence procedural, however, and not related solely to obligations cases, and shall not therefore be considered further in this work.

---

118 [1993] 4 All ER 344, CA.
119 See the decision of the ECHR in *Osman v United Kingdom* (2000) 29 EHRR 245.
120 *Attorney-General v Blake* [2001] 1 AC 268. The case is discussed at **4-58–4.60.**
121 See the Daily Telegraph, 16 May 2003.
122 As demonstrated in *Douglas v Hello! Ltd* [2001] 2 All ER 289, CA, actions of breach of confidence may raise issues concerning the right to privacy.
123 2001 SLT 776, IH.
124 *Karl Construction Ltd v Palisade Properties plc* 2002 SLT 312, OH.
125 *Fab-Tek Engineering Ltd v Carillion Construction Ltd*, 2002 SLT (Sh Ct) 113.

Chapter 2

Contract and Unilateral Promise

NATURE OF CONTRACT AND UNILATERAL PROMISE

Theoretical basis

2.01 In theoretical terms, distinguishing between contract and unilateral promise is a simple matter; in practical terms doing so is not without difficulty.

2.02 A contract is an agreement, enforceable at law, between two or more parties in terms of which one or more parties undertakes to do or refrain from doing specified acts.[1] A unilateral promise is an undertaking, binding on one party alone, to do or refrain from doing specified acts.[2] The essence of contract then is that it is bilateral, it binds more than one party to the obligation; promise, per contra, is unilateral, only one party being bound to the obligation.

Agreement

2.03 A promise is not usually described as stemming from an 'agreement', as the ordinary sense of the word agreement suggests that the will of more than one party is operative.[3] To quote Lord President Robertson in *Malcolm v Campbell*:[4]

'The words "I have agreed" set out the fact of an agreement, and an agreement is necessarily a mutual or bilateral arrangement.'[5]

However, it has been suggested that it is possible to define unilateral promise as stemming from the 'agreement' of the obligor to be unilaterally bound. This

---

1   The standard work on contract is W W McBryde, *The Law of Contract in Scotland* (2nd edn, 2001). A shorter treatment is H L MacQueen and J Thomson, *Contract Law in Scotland* (2000).
2   See further on the nature of promise in general, R Black, *Stair Memorial Encyclopaedia*, vol 15, paras 611–618; McBryde, *Contract*, ch 2 and *Promises in Scots Law* (1993) 42 ICLQ 48.
3   In *Macfarlane v Johnston* (1864) 2 M 1210, IH, Lord Neaves was disapproving of the notion of agreement in a promissory context, stating (at 1214): 'The word "agree" is ambiguous, and, strictly ought to be confined to pactions', although he added (at 1214) 'it is also used improperly as a word of unilateral signification'.
4   (1891) 19 R 278, IH.
5   (1891) 19 R at 280.

suggestion was made by Lord President Hope in *Lord Advocate v City of Glasgow District Council*,[6] who commented:

'As a general principle under our law, an obligation will arise from the expression of willingness to be bound. If the obligation is based on a promise, that expression of willingness may be by one party only. If it is based on offer and acceptance the expression of willingness must be by both. ... On either alternative the party who has expressed his willingness to be bound by the obligation can be said to have bound himself to it by his agreement.'[7]

In fact, an expression of 'agreement' had been held to constitute a unilateral promise on at least one prior reported occasion. In *Macfarlane v Johnston*,[8] a statement made by a party that 'we agree to pay you' was held to amount to a unilateral promise.[9]

2.04 Contract, while bilateral, may be gratuitous, consideration not being a requirement of Scots law. A bilateral gratuitous contract is an agreement where although there are two parties bound to the obligation, only one comes under any onerous duty. One party has only rights under the contract, and is thus 'bound' to the obligation in a nominal sense only.

2.05 It is an interesting question whether a creditor under a contract (whether an onerous or gratuitous contract) is bound to receive a contractual performance even if it is no longer wanted. The case of *White & Carter (Councils) Ltd v McGregor*,[10] while suggesting that a party may in certain cases be bound to receive an unwanted performance, does not fully settle the matter, as in the circumstances of the case the debtor was able to perform without the co-operation of the creditor. While it may be unwise to lay down a general rule, there may well be situations where to permit a creditor to refuse performance would be inequitable and unduly prejudicial to the debtor. The performance to be rendered in a particular case might relieve the debtor of an unwanted burden (eg a transfer of property which the debtor cannot afford to maintain, or a transfer for tax purposes), and in such situations it seems equitable that the creditor should be compelled to receive performance.

Promise as gratuitous

2.06 It was seen in chapter 1 that promise is always unilateral. It has been said that promise is also always gratuitous, for at the moment when the obligation is created, the promisee comes under no obligation to the promissor, even although it may be envisaged by the parties that the promise is made with the expectation

---

6 1990 SLT 721, IH.
7 1990 SLT at 725.
8 (1864) 2 M 1210, IH.
9 Lord Justice Clerk Inglis stated ((1864) 2 M at 1213): 'It appears to me that the use of the verb "agree" is of very little consequence ... for the distinction between a promise and an obligation of a different kind does not consist in the use of the word promise.'
10 1962 SC (HL) 1.

of receiving something in return.[11] The opinion that promise is always gratuitous is not universally shared however. Professors MacQueen and Black, W D H Sellar, and the present author have espoused the view that promise is always gratuitous. This was likewise the opinion of the institutional writer Bankton.[12] On the other hand, Professors Thomson and McBryde have adopted the view that a promise may be gratuitous or onerous. There is currently no consensus on this point.

2.07 The crux of the matter lies in the understanding of the term 'gratuitous'. If it denotes an obligation where performance is tendered without the promisee being bound to tender counter-performance, then promise must always be considered gratuitous; if, on the other hand, it denotes an obligation where performance is tendered without the expectation of receiving something in return for the promise, then there may exist onerous promises, for some promises are indeed given with the expectation of receiving something in return (for instance, a conditional promise where the condition involves value being transferred to the promissor). It was suggested in chapter 1 that the first meaning is the correct one, and this accords with the view of the Scottish Law Commission quoted in that chapter.[13]

2.08 Where the promissor has the ability to compel counter-performance, then such a promise is no more and no less than a 'contractual promise', to use the English law's notion of the word promise. Those cases which have been suggested by some authors to be onerous promises are, it will be found upon closer examination, cases where the expected benefit is the counter-performance under a contract related to the promise; the promise itself remains gratuitous.

2.09 Consider the following examples:

Example 1: A grants *B* an option to purchase a house for an agreed sum. This situation is argued by some academics to be one of onerous promise, as the promissor expects to receive the sum of money stipulated. It is suggested however that the correct analysis is as follows. The sum of money is the counter-performance for the transfer of the house, not for the giving of the promise. The promise is therefore gratuitous, as no counter-performance can be compelled for it.

Example 2: A (a bank) grants a promissory note to *B*. *B* transfers the note for value to *C* who presents it for payment at *A*'s offices. Again it is suggested by some academics that as *A*'s promise is issued in exchange for value given by *B*, it is an onerous promise. It is suggested that the better analysis is as follows. *A* and *B* are to be regarded as having entered into a contract, under which *A* has agreed to issue a promissory note to *B* in exchange for an agreed sum. Again therefore the value given by *B* is offered in exchange for *A*'s contractual undertaking. It is not offered in respect of the promise itself. The promise is again gratuitous.

---

11 While it is possible to argue that the qualities of 'gratuitous' and 'unilateral' are synonymous (a view suggested as a possibility by the present author at 1998 SLT (News) 25), the better view is that the two qualities are to be distinguished. This conclusion follows from the recognition that contracts, while always bilateral, may be gratuitous. The 'unilateral contract' does not exist in Scots law, despite the use of the term by English law to mean something akin to Scots unilateral promise, albeit in contractual form.

12 Bankton, I.xi.1.

13 See **1.16**.

Example 3: A promises to pay *B* a sum of money if *B* will recommend *A* to *C*, a business with whom *A* wishes to contract. *A* in this scenario is receiving the services of *B*, a valuable commodity in *A*'s eyes. This might be argued to be an onerous promise. However if *B* makes the recommendation requested then the better analysis is that this situation is contractual, *A*'s offer having been accepted by *B* through the latter's conduct.

Example 4: A promises to pay £100 to anyone who finds his missing dog.[14] Such a public offer of reward is capable of being seen as a unilateral promise in Scotland. In fact, the reported cases have analysed reward cases as contractual in nature.[15] However, if one adopts a promissory analysis, is such a promise onerous? It is not possible, as in the earlier examples given above, to separate the promise here from any underlying contract. This therefore represents one of those hard cases where one must simply decide which of the two definitions of 'gratuitous' discussed above at **2.07** one prefers, and draw the requisite conclusion therefrom.

Example 5: A invites various parties to tender for a construction contract.[16] Each tenderer is required to pay a processing fee to cover the costs of *A*'s administration. *A* gives an undertaking to each tenderer that timeously submitted bids will be considered. Has *A* made an onerous promise? The correct analysis of this situation is somewhat trickier. It is suggested however that one of two analyses should be adopted:

(a)   One could view *A*'s undertaking to consider timeously submitted bids as a unilateral promise made to each tenderer. If one does so, however, it is suggested that the promise ought still to be seen as gratuitous. The fee is submitted as counter-performance for the processing and not for the obligation to consider the bid. The promise remains gratuitous.

(b)   Alternatively, it may be more satisfactory to adopt a contractual route and consider this to be a case where there is a subsidiary bilateral contract in terms of which *A* has agreed to process timeously submitted bids in exchange for a fee.

Under neither route is one forced to conclude that there is an onerous promise.

Example 6: Alter the facts of (5) slightly. Again say that *A* invites various parties to tender for a construction contract. *A* gives various undertakings to each tenderer about the tendering process. In return, in submitting an offer on the prescribed form, each tenderer gives various undertakings to *A*. How is this scenario best analysed? It is suggested that in this situation one must adopt a contractual analysis. There is a subsidiary contract in terms of which the parties have agreed to be bound to particular procedures in the tendering process.

The foregoing discussion demonstrates that some of the examples commonly given by supporters of the view that promise may sometimes be onerous can in fact be explained by means of an underlying contract (as in the first two examples above). There remain difficult cases (such as the public offer of reward) where one is simply forced back on to one's choice of the preferred definition of 'gratuitous'.

2.10   To complete the picture, one cannot overlook the terminology of the Requirements of Writing (Scotland) Act 1995. It may be of assistance to quote a portion of s 1 of the Act at this point:

---

14   This is an example suggested by MacQueen and Thomson (para 2.55) as one which might be an onerous promise.
15   See **2.75–2.82**.
16   Further on the analysis of promises in tendering processes, see **2.34–2.51**.

'(1)   Subject to subsection (2) below and any other enactment, writing shall not be required for the constitution of a contract, unilateral obligation or trust.

(2)   Subject to subsection (3) below, a written document complying with section 2 of this Act shall be required for—

    (a)   the constitution of—

        (i)   a contract or unilateral obligation for the creation, transfer, variation or extinction of an interest in land;

        (ii)   a gratuitous unilateral obligation except an obligation undertaken in the course of business.'

One may note several things about these provisions:

(1)   the Act itself contains no definition of the terms unilateral or gratuitous or their use in conjunction with the word obligation;

(2)   in s 1(1), a contract is distinguished from a unilateral obligation. This supports the view that contract is always a bilateral obligation in Scots law, which is the view which was suggested as the preferable one in chapter 1; and

(3)   the use of the term 'unilateral obligation' in s 1(1) followed by 'gratuitous unilateral obligation' in s 1(2)(a)(ii) suggests that not all unilateral obligations are gratuitous. This therefore adds weight to the Thomson/McBryde position that some unilateral promises may be non-gratuitous.

2.11   The Act is unhelpful in its failure to define essential terms such as unilateral and gratuitous.[17] In failing so to do, it merely adds confusion to the debate as to whether promise is by nature gratuitous. Whilst its terms suggest that that is not always so, this view runs counter to the preferable one, already discussed above. It is suggested that the position it adopts, so far as this can be ascertained, is not to be seen as conclusive by any means.

Promisee ever bound?

2.12   A problem arises if a promise has been given on the faith of a non-binding undertaking by the promisee to refrain from doing certain acts, and, the promissor having fulfilled his promise (eg the payment of a sum of money), the promisee then recommences performance of the conduct in question.[18] One solution is to view this as a contractual arrangement between the parties. If a promissory analysis is maintained, however, it would seem to leave the promissor with no recourse. An alternative solution is to argue that, if the promisee reneges on the understanding, the promissor is entitled to exercise enrichment remedies against the promisee, in the case of a money payment the *condictio ob causam finitam*.[19]

---

17   In this respect see the critique of W D H Sellar, 'Promises', in *A History of Private Law in Scotland*, vol II, at pp 279-282.

18   R Black, writing in *Stair Memorial Encyclopaedia*, vol 15, at para. 613, gives the example of a promise to make a payment of money if the promisee ceases to pay court to the promissor's daughter, something which the promisee then begins to do once more.

19   Further on the *condictio ob causam finitam*, see chapter 4, fn 14.

Conditions

2.13 An offer is made with the intention that it is accepted, and is thus clearly an undertaking to be bound to a contract on the condition of acceptance. Similarly, a promise may be made *sub conditione*, either upon some performance or non-performance by the promisee, or the occurrence of some external event.[20] In this case the promised conduct does not fall to be performed unless and until the condition is fulfilled.

DISTINGUISHING PROMISE FROM CONTRACT

2.14 Allusion has already been made to the practical difficulties of distinguishing promise and contract. A shared feature of offer and promise, that the former is, and the latter may be, made conditionally is the principal reason why contract and promise are hard to distinguish in some cases. It is said that what is crucial is the intention or will of the party: did the person making the statement intend immediately to be bound?[21] If that is the case, the party is held to have intended a unilateral promise. Assessing such intention can be a difficult process, entailing an objective assessment of the meaning to be given to the words used by the party issuing the statement, as well as the surrounding circumstances.

2.15 Consider the following examples:

(1) *A* states that he will pay *B* £500 on a specified date if *A* is still in employment at that date;

(2) *A* states that he will pay *B* £500 on a specified date unless A has changed his mind by that date;

(3) *A* states that he will pay *B* £500 if *B* completes a marathon;

(4) *A* states that he will pay *B* £500 if *B* gives his leather jacket to *A*.

2.16 Ignoring for the moment any issues concerning the form of the undertakings, example (1) is most naturally classified as a conditional promise, the condition being the continuation of a specified state of affairs. Example (2) could also be classified in this way, although as the condition depends wholly upon vagaries of the will of *A*, a serious doubt must be entertained as to whether *A* ever seriously intended to come under any obligation. Example (2) is, for that reason, probably not a promise.

2.17 Examples (3) and (4) reveal the difficulty in distinguishing promise from offer. Example (3) is more likely to be seen as a conditional promise, example (4) as an offer. Why this should be so is not immediately obvious, for both are statements requiring performance by *B* as a condition of his claiming the benefit promised by *A*. In example (4) *A* receives a benefit which directly increases his patrimony, which certainly adds weight to a contractual analysis. It may be,

---

20 See McBryde, paras 2-25–2-27.

21 Stair I.10.4; Black, *Stair Memorial Encyclopaedia*, vol 15, para 613; W G Normand, *Consideration in the Law of Scotland* (1939) 55 LQR 358 at 361. See also *Morton's Trustees v Aged Christian Friend Society of Scotland* (1899) 2 F 82, IH, per Lord Kinnear at 85.

however, that without ascertaining further details of the transactions it is simply not possible to reach a definite conclusion. If we were to add to the facts of example (3) that the promise had been made by *A* on a sponsorship form and that *B* was to undertake the marathon to raise funds for charity, we would feel more confident in concluding that *A* intended his statement to be a promise. The non-mercantile context adds weight to the promissory analysis. If in example (4), *A* were to follow the statement with the query 'Do you accept?', this would almost certainly lead us to conclude that the statement was intended to be an offer.

2.18 Whenever acceptance is the condition, the statement will not be viewed as a promise but as an offer.[22] In *Morton's Trustees v Aged Christian Friend Society of Scotland*,[23] Lord Kinnear referred to the fact that (in his Lordship's opinion) the obligor had anticipated acceptance of his undertaking as an indication that a contractual framework was envisaged rather than a promissory one.[24] However, the mere presence of an acceptance (in the absence of a condition as to such) will not of itself render the initial statement an offer.[25] When the stipulated condition is not voluntary conduct by the party to whom the statement is made (as in example (1) above), it is suggested that the statement will not be classified as an offer but, where the appropriate intention to be bound is present, as a promise.

2.19 These two criteria provide some assistance in distinguishing offer from promise. Others which may assist include whether the context is mercantile, such context being more likely to indicate a contractual analysis, and whether there is a direct benefit to the obligor, the absence of such being more likely to indicate a promissory analysis.[26]

2.20 Does it make a difference whether a statement is classified in promissory or contractual terms? Emphatically yes, as there are issues of form and effect which clearly distinguish the two obligations, amongst them:

(1) *Form*. This is addressed separately at **2.21–2.22** below.
(2) *Lapse of offer*. If the statement is an offer, it will expire after the passage of a reasonable time[27] (if no other time of expiry is stipulated) and will lapse

---

22 Stair, distinguishing promise and offer, describes the conditional nature of offer thus: 'when the condition relateth to the constitution of the obligation, then the very obligation itself is pendent, till the condition be purified, and till then it is no obligation; as when any offer or tender is made, there is implied a condition, that before it become obligatory, the party to whom it is offered must accept' (I.10.3); see further I.10.5.
23 (1899) 2 F 82, IH.
24 (1899) 2 F at 86. Lord Kinnear's statement that an acceptance was expected because 'the offer is made on certain conditions' does not, however, provide an especially helpful test, as it fails to distinguish conditional promises, which are also made on 'certain conditions'. More telling in the case was, one suspects, the fact that the obligee was expected to undertake 'certain things involving the expenditure of time and trouble as well as money' (per Lord Kinnear at 86).
25 An option to purchase, for instance, will most likely be accepted by the promisee, but it will normally be viewed as a promise and not an offer.
26 In *Smith v Oliver* 1911 SC 103, 1910 2 SLT 304, IH, the Lord President, rejecting a contractual analysis of the statements made by Mrs Oliver, said (1911 SC at 111) 'so far as mutual contract is concerned, the lady was getting no benefit except in the sense in which anybody may be said to get something when anything is done in which he is interested'. This statement seems, however, to ignore the possibility of gratuitous contracts.
27 *Thomson v James* (1855) 18 D 1, IH, per Lord President McNeill at 10; Gloag, *Contract*, at p 37.

upon the death of the offeror;[28] a promise does not lapse after a reasonable time, and is enforceable against the executors of a deceased promissor.[29]

(3) *Locus poenitentiae.* A promise cannot be revoked once made. In the case of an oral promise, this is the moment when the promise is uttered, even if the promisee does not hear of it until later;[30] in the case of a written promise, this is when the promissor puts the document out of his possession.[31] An offer may be revoked until acceptance takes effect, unless accompanied by a promise that the offer is to be kept open for a specified time.[32]

(4) *Conduct amounting to acceptance.* Conduct otherwise amounting to an acceptance will not constitute such if it is carried out in ignorance of the terms of the offer;[33] whereas the performance of a condition imposed upon a promisee will oblige the promissor to perform the promised act even if the conduct of the promisee was carried out in ignorance of the promise.[34]

(5) *Assignation.* An offeree cannot assign his right to accept the offer to another party, unless the offeror so consents;[35] a promisee may assign his right to receive the benefit of the promise, without permission of the promissor unless *delectus personae* is present.[36]

FORM

2.21 The required form of contracts and promises is regulated by the Requirements of Writing (Scotland) Act 1995. The general rule for contracts and for unilateral obligations is that they do not require writing.[37] They may therefore be oral, written, or a mixture of the two. However, in order to constitute a contract or unilateral obligation for the creation, transfer, variation or extinction of an interest in land, a written document subscribed by the granter(s) is required.[38] So, missives for the sale of land or for a lease greater than one year in duration[39]

28 Stair I.10.6; Bell, *Principles*, s 79; McBryde, paras 6-69–6-73.
29 *Smith v Oliver* 1911 SC 103, IH; Black, *Stair Memorial Encyclopaedia*, vol 15, para 616; McBryde, para 2-16, 'Promises in Scots Law' (1993) 42 ICLQ 48 at p 50.
30 Stair I.10.4; Black, *Stair Memorial Encyclopaedia*, vol 15, para 618.
31 *Shaw v Muir's Executrix* (1892) 19 R 997, IH; Bell, *Principles*, s 23; McBryde, paras 2-38, 4-01 et seq; Black, *Stair Memorial Encyclopaedia*, vol 15, para 618.
32 See further **2.32–2.33**.
33 McBryde, para 6-35. Note also Lord President McNeill in *Thomson v James* (1855) 18 D 1, IH, who states (at 10): 'An offer is nothing until it is communicated to the party to whom it is made, and who is to decide whether he will or will not accept the offer'. English law concurs on this point: *Taylor v Allon* [1966] 1 QB 304.
34 Black, *Stair Memorial Encyclopaedia*, vol 15, para 616. There seems to be no other authority for this view, but it flows naturally from first principles.
35 Stair I.10.6; McBryde, para 6-109; Black, *Stair Memorial Encyclopaedia*, vol 15, para 616; *J M Smith Ltd v Colquhoun's Trustee* (1901) 3 F 981, IH, per Lord Trayner at 989–990.
36 There is no specific authority on this point. However, there is ample authority that, in general, rights may be assigned without consent where *delectus personae* is absent. Bell, *Principles*, s 1459 and Erskine, *Institute*, III.5.2, cited by Black, *Stair Memorial Encyclopaedia*, vol 15, at para 616, support this general point.
37 Requirements of Writing (Scotland) Act 1995, s 1(1).
38 Ibid, s 1(2)(a)(i), s 2(1).
39 Ibid, s 1(7) excludes from the definition of 'interest in land' a tenancy or right to occupy land for a year or less.

require to be constituted by subscribed writing. Such a document is also required for the constitution of a gratuitous unilateral obligation, other than one undertaken in the course of business.[40] So, a promise by a father to provide financial support to his daughter whilst she is at university would require to be in writing, whereas a promise by the partner of a firm to a company director that documents will be delivered by a certain date would not.

2.22 A question arises over whether a unilateral gratuitous obligation made in a non-business context and which was contained within a contract would be exempted from the requirement of writing because the contract was so exempt. An example would be a contract between two parties not undertaken in the course of business containing a gratuitous option in favour of one of the parties to purchase property. As the Act contains no provision exempting such a unilateral promise from the requirement of writing merely because of its containment within a contract, it is to be presumed that the promise at least would require to be subscribed (which, in practice, would mean the whole contract would be subscribed).

GIVING EFFECT TO AN ACCEPTANCE OR A PROMISE

Acceptance of an offer

2.23 Before an acceptance of an offer is effective, the general rule is that the offeree must communicate the acceptance to the offeror.[41] Exceptions to this rule include cases where the offeror has waived the need for communication of the acceptance, and where (unless forbidden by the terms of the offer) the offeree indicates acceptance through his conduct. This is consistent with Stair's requirement that a contracting party must move beyond the stage of will to the stage of engagement.[42]

2.24 The general rule stated in the preceding paragraph—that the offeree must communicate an acceptance to the offeror—may be expressed in a slightly different manner, by stating that an offeree must take steps to indicate to the offeror that he has irrevocably accepted the offer.[43]

2.25 Is there a distinction between the two expressions of the rule? The first expression of the rule (that the acceptance must be communicated), places an emphasis upon *receipt* of the acceptance. The second expression of the rule (that the offeror must take steps to indicate his acceptance) suggests that what is crucial is *transmission* of the acceptance. In many cases, it will not matter which expression of the rule is favoured—an acceptance will be transmitted and received

---

40 Ibid, s 1(2)(a)(ii), s 2(1).
41 See McBryde, paras 6-112–6-125.
42 See **1.50**.
43 See McBryde, who states (para 6-114): 'Instead of saying that acceptance must be communicated, it may be more accurate to state that the offeree must go beyond the deliberative stage. What is required is (1) intention to accept, followed by (2) actions showing the intention to be irrevocable.'

without dispute. However, the distinction will matter where either (a) the acceptance is transmitted but for some reason not received by the offeror, or (b) the transmission and receipt do not occur instantaneously or at the same place, in which cases there may be a dispute as to the time and/or place of contracting. The two expressions of the rule will produce different results in these two cases.

2.26 Except in the case of the postal rule (discussed below), what Scottish authority there is on acceptance of offers is not conclusive as to whether the transmission or receipt view is to be preferred. However, there appears to be a majority of academic opinion in favour of the receipt view. English law adopts the view that receipt of an acceptance is required.[44] The recommendation of the Scottish Law Commission[45] that the postal rule be abolished similarly favours a receipt view. The offeror may of course stipulate which of the two, receipt or transmission, is to prevail, and such a stipulation will supplant the common law.

Oral acceptance

2.27 In the case of an oral acceptance, an acceptance is communicated when the offeror utters the words of acceptance, either in the presence of the offeror or at a distance by some means allowing for them to be heard by the offeree, for instance the telephone.[46] It is suggested that where an acceptance is left on a telephone answering machine, the acceptance is effective when the message is spoken and recorded, and not when it is played back.

Written acceptance

2.28 In the case of a written acceptance, the acceptance must be delivered into the hands of the offeror or his agent to be effective. Putting the written acceptance through the offeror's letterbox would be sufficient to constitute acceptance. The exception to this is the so-called postal rule (or mailbox rule) which holds that the posting of the letter in a public post box or otherwise transmitting it into the hands of the postal authorities will constitute an acceptance at the moment of posting/transmission.[47] Committing the letter to a private agent (for instance, a private postal courier) to deliver will arguably not effect an acceptance until the offeree has lost the power to recall the delivery, which may not be until some time after the letter has been transmitted to the agent. A written acceptance which is still in the hands of the offeree, even though it has been signed by him, is not yet effective to indicate an irrevocable intention to accept the contract.[48] This is

---

44 *Brinkibon Ltd v Stahag Stahl etc* [1983] 2 AC 34, HL.

45 Scottish Law Commission Report No 144 (1993), *Formation of Contract: Scottish Law and the United Nations Convention on Contracts for the International Sale of Goods.*

46 See the comments of Lord Denning in *Entores Ltd v Miles Far East Corporation* [1955] 2 QB 327, [1955] 3 WLR 48, [1955] 2 All ER 493, CA, who opined that the offeror must actually hear the words of acceptance.

47 *Thomson v James* (1855) 18 D 1, IH.

48 See the comment of Lord President M'Neill in *Thomson v James* (1855) 18 D 1, IH, at 11: 'It is not enough that [the offeree] commits his acceptance to writing and locks it in his own repositories.'

consistent with the general rule of Scots law that, to be effective, writing must be delivered.[49]

Other forms of acceptance

2.29 In the case of an acceptance in a form other than writing or words the position is as follows. Acceptance by conduct[50] is effected when the conduct is performed, or begun to be performed. Acceptance may also be made (unless stipulated otherwise) by telex, telegram, facsimile, email, or any other form capable of indicating irrevocable acceptance. There are no clear rules in Scots law as to when acceptance is effected when one of these technological means is used. If the view that what is crucial is transmission of the acceptance is correct, then as soon, for instance, as the 'send' button is pressed to transmit an email acceptance, the contract is concluded at that point, for the offeree will have done all that is necessary to indicate his unequivocal acceptance of the contract. However, if the alternative and more widely held view, that receipt of the acceptance is necessary, is correct, then the acceptance will not be effective until it is received by the offeror. As with a telephone answering machine, it is suggested that receipt occurs when the acceptance is 'delivered' to the offeror rather than when he peruses it. Thus, an email acceptance is effected when it is downloaded into the 'inbox' of the offeror's computer even if it is not opened and read until later.

Unilateral promise

2.30 A promise committed to writing is not effective until delivered to the promisee, or to someone empowered to receive delivery of the promise on the promisee's behalf. Again this is consistent with the general rule that writing to be effective must be delivered.[51]

2.31 What of an oral promise: when does it take effect? Common sense dictates that it is effective when the promissory words are uttered. What of a promise uttered by the promissor without anyone else being present? Working from first principles, it would seem that in such a case the promissor has not done sufficient to commit himself unilaterally to being bound. There requires to be at least one other person present in order that the promissor is held to exhibit sufficient intention to be bound. The promisee need not be present when the words of promise are uttered for the promise to be effective, thus communication to the promisee is not a requirement of the constitution of a promise.[52] In practical terms of course, the promisee will have to become aware of the existence of the promise in order to enforce it.

---

49 See McBryde, chapter 4, passim.
50 The conduct may simply be conduct indicating an acceptance, for instance, raising one's hand at an auction, or it may be performance of an obligation under the contract, for instance payment of the contract price. See further McBryde, paras 6-76–6-80.
51 As to which general point, see McBryde, chapter 4, passim.
52 See *Stair Memorial Encyclopaedia*, vol 15, para 618.

PROMISES ATTACHED TO INVITATIONS TO TREAT AND OFFERS

2.32 A unilateral promise may be attached to an invitation to treat or to an offer. A familiar example is the promise that an offer will be kept open for acceptance until a specified time.[53] Such a promise is effectual in Scotland, but not in England (unless given for some consideration by the offeree). An interesting question arises as to the interaction of the promise to keep open an offer, with the rule that a qualified acceptance kills the offer. Consider the following problem:

> *A* makes an offer to *B* for the purchase of *B*'s house. *A* states that the offer is open for acceptance until 1 July. On 20 May, *B* responds with a qualified acceptance of *A*'s offer. On 25 May, *B*, having heard nothing more from *A*, withdraws its qualified acceptance and purports to accept *A*'s original offer. *A* replies that the making of *B*'s qualified acceptance has had the effect of cancelling *A*'s original offer, but *B* replies that *A* promised to keep the offer open until 1 July. Can *B* validly accept *A*'s original offer?

The rule in *Wolf & Wolf v Forfar Potato Co*[54] is that a qualified acceptance kills the original offer, which cannot then be accepted, unless the original offeror is willing to reissue that offer. Can the promise to keep open the offer be viewed as operating as an automatic reissue of the original offer, should the qualified acceptance be withdrawn? It is suggested that this would be inequitable to the original offeror, and contrary to what was intended by the promissor, and thus that the better view is as follows. The promise is accessory to the offer; when, therefore, the offer is rejected by the qualified acceptance, the promise is also to be seen as having being rejected, and the original offeror released from the obligation to keep open the offer.

2.33 A further example of such conjoined promises is those contained within invitations to tender. A party inviting tenders may make various promises to the tenderers, such as: (1) a promise that all tenders submitted timeously will be considered, or that those submitted after a specified date will not be considered;[55] (2) that the highest tender will be accepted;[56] or (3) that the party inviting tenders will abide by the conditions of tender. Such undertakings are most naturally considered as unilateral promises in Scots law. They may be enforceable, if appropriate, by an unsuccessful tenderer. Thus, a tenderer who submits the highest bid to a party who has bound himself to accept such bid may, upon discovery that another bid was accepted, seek reduction of the contract concluded in breach of the promise made to him and declarator that a valid contract exists between himself and the party inviting tenders.

---

53 Commonly found in missives for the purchase of heritable property.
54 1984 SLT 100, IH.
55 See discussion of *Blackpool and Fylde Aero Club v Blackpool Borough Council* [1990] 3 All ER 25, CA, at **2.37–2.44**.
56 See the discussion of *Harvela Investments Ltd v Royal Trust Co of Canada* [1986] AC 207, HL, at **2.34–2.36**.

Harvela Investments

2.34 In England, in the absence of a doctrine of unilateral promise, the courts have sought to employ the device of 'unilateral contract' to hold parties to conditions of tender. The first of two important English cases in this area was *Harvela Investments Ltd v Royal Trust Co of Canada*:[57]

> Royal Trust invited tenders for the sale of a controlling block of shares in a company. Bids were submitted from Harvela and the second defendant, Sir Leonard Outerbridge. One of the conditions to which Royal Trust bound themselves was that 'if any offer made ... is the highest offer received by us we bind ourselves to accept such offer'. Harvela submitted a timeous bid of C$2,175,000, Sir Leonard a bid of C$2,100,000 'or C$101,000 in excess of any other offer which you may receive which is expressed as a fixed monetary amount, whichever is the higher'. Royal Trust accepted Sir Leonard's referential bid. The House of Lords held that the implied intention of the conditions of tender was to exclude referential bids and to invite only fixed price bids. Sir Leonard's referential bid thus being invalid, Harvela's fixed price bid was the highest and Royal Trust were bound to sell to Harvela. The House of Lords ordered the shares to be transferred to Harvela upon payment by them of the purchase price together with interest thereon.

2.35 Of interest for present purposes is the analysis given by Lord Diplock to the communications between the parties. The invitation given to both Harvela and Sir Leonard was seen by Lord Diplock as an offer to sell the shares to the highest bidder (and not merely an invitation to treat), such offer being capable of acceptance only by the highest bidder. In addition, the invitation constituted a 'unilateral or 'if' contract'[58] made with both bidders. These unilateral contracts were made, said Lord Diplock, 'at the time when the invitation was received by the promisee to whom it was addressed by the vendors'.[59] They were unilateral contracts because 'under neither of them did the promisee, Harvela and Sir Leonard respectively, assume any legal obligation to anyone to do or refrain from doing anything'[60]. It was Royal Trust alone who undertook any duty under the unilateral contracts, namely 'to enter into a synallagmatic contract'[61] with the highest bidder. These circumstances may be represented as follows:

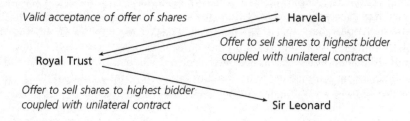

Valid acceptance of offer of shares — Harvela

Royal Trust

Offer to sell shares to highest bidder coupled with unilateral contract

Offer to sell shares to highest bidder coupled with unilateral contract — Sir Leonard

57 [1986] AC 207, HL.
58 [1986] AC at 224, per Lord Diplock.
59 [1986] AC at 224, per Lord Diplock.
60 [1986] AC at 224, per Lord Diplock.
61 [1986] AC at 224, per Lord Diplock.

2.36 Note how the 'unilateral contract' in this case (the promise to accept only the highest bid) is, in effect, the equivalent of a Scottish unilateral promise. Note how it binds without even being accepted by the offeree. The English courts, unable to use the doctrine of unilateral promise, adapt the obligation of contract to fit the circumstances, although it is hard to see what consideration is given for Royal Trust's undertaking given that Lord Diplock admits that neither bidder undertook to do anything under the unilateral contracts.[62]

Blackpool Aero Club

2.37 The second important English case concerning 'unilateral contract' is *Blackpool and Fylde Aero Club v Blackpool Borough Council*.[63] On the face of it, the exchanges between the parties appear similar to those in *Harvela*. The analysis provided by the court is somewhat different however:

> The defendants, a local authority, wished to grant a concession for the use of an airport owned by them. The plaintiffs, along with two other tenderers, submitted a tender for the use of the airport for the purpose of providing pleasure flights over the Blackpool area. The invitation to tender issued by the council contained, inter alia, the following condition: 'The council do not bind themselves to accept all or any part of any tender. No tender which is received after the last date and time specified shall be admitted for consideration.' The Aero Club submitted their tender prior to the stipulated time and date, by posting it through the town hall letter box. However, due to an administrative error on the part of the council, the letter box was not opened until the next day, and the tender was erroneously rejected as a late tender. The council awarded the contract to one of the other two tenderers. The plaintiffs brought an action against the defendants claiming damages for breach of contract or, in the absence of contract, for negligence. In relation to the contractual argument, the Court of Appeal agreed that there had been a breach of contract and awarded the plaintiffs damages.

2.38 The Aero Club had argued that, even although their tender had not been accepted, a contract had existed between them and the council at least to the extent that the council was bound to consider timeously submitted tenders, having (impliedly) undertaken to do so in the conditions of tender. Whilst the council had expressly stated only that later tenders would not be considered, the Court of Appeal held that this must also be taken to amount to an implied undertaking that timeously submitted tenders would be considered.[64] Bingham LJ put the matter thus:

> 'where, as here, tenders are solicited from selected parties all of them known to the invitor, and where a local authority's invitation prescribes a clear, orderly and familiar procedure ... the invitee is in my judgment protected at least to this extent: if he submits a conforming tender before the deadline he is entitled, not as a matter of mere

---

62 It would be wrong to see the share price as the consideration for the unilateral undertaking to sell to the highest bidder. The share price is rather the consideration for the obligation to transfer the shares.

63 [1990] 3 All ER 25, CA.

64 [1990] 3 All ER at 31a–b, per Bingham LJ.

expectation but of contractual right, to be sure that his tender will after the deadline be opened and considered in conjunction with all other conforming tenders or at least that his tender will be considered if others are.'[65]

2.39   This contractual right to have a tender considered is clearly separate from any contract which may or may not eventually ensue between tenderer and employer. It is also clearly an implied contract. The offer of this subsidiary contract, as it may be called, was made when the invitation to tender for the main contract (the airport concession) was issued by the council; it was accepted when a tenderer submitted an offer for the main contract. It was enforceable against the council even by a tenderer whose offer for the main contract was never accepted. The analysis of the court may be portrayed thus:

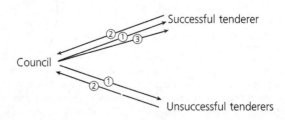

2.40   Arrow 1 represents the invitation to treat for the main contract along with the (implied) offer of the subsidiary contract (the contract whose sole term was that a timeously submitted offer for the main contract would be considered). Arrow 2 represents an offer for the main contract together with an (implied) acceptance of the subsidiary contract. Arrow 3 represents the acceptance by the council of the successful tender.

2.41   Although the term 'unilateral contract' is not referred to in the judgments, it is clear that the contract implied is of the same type as that in *Harvela*, that is one which imposes a duty on only one party (in this case the council). The analysis differs in that (1) in *Harvela* there was only one party who could fulfil the requirement of the unilateral contract, by submitting the highest bid, whereas in *Blackpool*, because of the nature of the undertaking, the benefit accrued to any tenderer submitting a bid on time; and (2) in *Blackpool* the subsidiary contract required to be accepted (albeit with no obvious consideration on the part of the acceptor), whereas in *Harvela* the unilateral contract was held to exist by mere declaration of one of the parties. In this respect the analysis in *Harvela* comes closer to the Scottish notion of unilateral promise. The effect of the two cases is substantially the same, however: the reliance of a tenderer upon a condition of the tender is protected.

2.42   Had the facts of *Blackpool* arisen in Scotland, it is highly likely that promissory analysis would have been the chosen avenue of redress. The council would have been held to have promised to consider timeously submitted bids. One problem from a Scots law point of view, however, might have been with the

---

65   [1990] 3 All ER at 30h–j, per Bingham LJ.

implication made: could a party which had stated that late tenders would not be considered be impliedly held to have promised that it would consider timeously submitted tenders? The implication made in *Blackpool* seems questionable. There is, in any event, a reluctance to construe a statement as a promise.[66]

2.43 Where undertakings about the tendering process are given by a party inviting tenders in exchange for undertakings about the process given by a tenderer (as may well be the case), then it may well be better to view the situation as one where there is a subsidiary bilateral contract between the parties governing such process.

2.44 The phenomenon of a 'unilateral contract' is essentially an English creation, and the absence of such a phenomenon in Scots law is discussed at **2.84** below.

Obligations between tenderers

2.45 A question arises as to whether a tenderer may ever be held to have undertaken an obligation to a fellow tenderer. To take an example: the invitation to tender for a works contract contains a condition that tenderers will not enter into agreements with each other to the effect that a party to whom an invitation to tender is issued agrees not to submit a bid. As such a condition will normally become a term of the contract between employer and successful tenderer, its breach would be remediable by the employer. What of any remedy available to other tenderers? There are three possibilities:

(1) All tenderers who submit bids are held to have given unilateral promises to each other that they have abided by the conditions of tender. In other words:

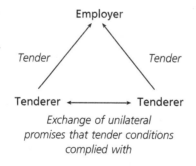

*Exchange of unilateral
promises that tender conditions
complied with*

(2) The contract between employer and successful tenderer is held to include a *jus quaesitum tertio* in favour of the unsuccessful tenderers, the *jus quaesitum tertio* being a warranty that the conditions of tender have been complied with. In other words:

---

66 See McBryde, para 2-04.

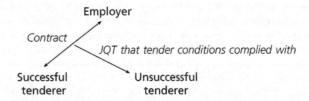

2.46

(3) The tenderers could be held to have entered into a contractual relationship with each other. Such a contract would be ancillary to any contract that was eventually entered into between the party inviting tenders and the successful tenderer. An English decision which demonstrates some similarities to this situation is *Clarke v Earl of Dunraven*:[67]

> The case concerned a yacht which, in breach of the rules of a race, had damaged another yacht. A question arose of whether there was any contractual means available to the owner of the damaged yacht to recover damages from the owner of the offending yacht. All entrants of the race had signed an entry form which contained the undertaking that 'while sailing under this entry, I will obey and be bound by the sailing rules of the Yacht Racing Association and the by-laws of the club.' One such rule was that 'If a yacht, in consequence of her neglect of any of these rules, shall foul another yacht ... she shall forfeit all claim to the prize, and shall pay all damages.' The English Court of Appeal held that the owner of the yacht which had fouled the other was obliged to compensate the owner of the damaged yacht in damages, a decision upheld on appeal to the House of Lords.

2.47 The Court of Appeal asked the question 'Was there any contract between the owners of those two yachts?'[68] or, put another way, 'Did the owner of the yacht which is sued enter into any obligation to the owner of the other yacht, that if his yacht broke the rules, and thereby injured the other yacht, he would pay damages?'[69] The decision in the case was that yacht owners did owe each other such a contractual obligation, although it is not made clear from the opinions delivered how such contractual obligations were formed and what the consideration was. The difficulty, however, with applying this decision to a tendering scenario is that unsuccessful tenderers do not make it to the next stage of the process, unlike yacht owners who submit entries for a race—in competing with each other they interact in a way that can be described in contractual terms.

2.48 There is no native authority on the liability of tenderers to each other in respect of the rules of the tendering procedure, and none of the three solutions noted above would be unproblematic if pled before a Scottish court. As for the promissory argument, communication of a promise is not strictly required before the obligation can come into existence, thus this would not be a bar to the existence of a promise in favour of other tenderers. The difficulty with the promissory argument, however, is that any such promise to fellow tenderers must be implied. Promise is construed strictly in Scots law, and there is little, if any, authority as to when a promise may be implied.

67 [1897] AC 59, HL.
68 [1895] P 248, CA, at 255, per Lord Esher MR.
69 [1895] P at 255, per Lord Esher MR.

2.49 If the promissory analysis were to be accepted by a Scottish court, then any collusion between tenderers would be in breach of a promise to the unsuccessful non-colluding tenderers. It is submitted that any of them would be entitled to raise an action for breach of promise against the successful contractor and to sue for damages. A difficulty would arise in the calculation of loss, for it is unlikely that any one unsuccessful tenderer could show that his bid would have been successful. Damages may be available, however, for the loss of a chance of winning the contract.[70] In the absence of a *jus quaesitum tertio* in favour of other tenderers, it is unlikely that the contract between employer and successful tenderer could be undone.

2.50 The second possibility (*jus quaesitum tertio*) avoids difficulties surrounding implication, as a *jus quaesitum tertio* may be implied from the terms of a contract. Moreover, delivery or an equivalent of the *jus quaesitum tertio*, if one does exist, may be said to have occurred, as each tenderer has been given notice of the conditions of tender. However, it is hard to see how the employer and successful contractor may be said to have intended to confer any benefit upon unsuccessful tenderers through the use of a non-collusion condition. On the contrary, such a clause seems designed to protect the interests of the employer.

2.51 The third possibility, that of viewing tenderers as entering a preliminary contract with each other (and perhaps also the party inviting tenderers) is a possibility, but as with the promissory route, one might struggle to find any intention to be bound to a contract. It would certainly be difficult in most cases to point to any offer and acceptance made by the various tenderers each to the others. Indeed, in most tendering procedures tenderers will not be permitted to communicate with each other. Any contractual solution would require to be of an implied, and highly fictional, nature.

OPTIONS

Two types of option

2.52 The word 'option' is not a term of art, and it is possible to attach to the word varying definitions. However, the sense in which it is used most frequently is to describe a right given to a party which may be exercised to secure some benefit for that party.

2.53 There are two alternative ways of characterising such an option in Scots law:

(1)   the option may be seen as a firm *offer*; or
(2)   the option may be seen as a *unilateral promise.*

It is debatable whether, as a third possibility, an option may, prior to the exercise thereof, be considered *contractual* in nature. It is suggested that the better view is

---

70 See **3.83–3.88** for discussion of loss of a chance.

that, while an option may be contained within a contract, as the option binds one party alone, the nature of the option itself is best described as unilateral, and not therefore as contractual in nature.

2.54 In England options to purchase real estate have been characterised as 'unilateral' or 'if' *contracts*, which may be transformed into bilateral contracts by the party in whose favour the option is granted by taking up the option. This was the analysis adopted by Lord Diplock in *Sudbrook Trading Estate Ltd v Eggleton*:[71]

> Sudbrook Trading Estates were lessees of four adjacent commercial premises. In terms of each lease they were given the right to purchase the premises at a price to be agreed upon by two valuers, which failing, by an umpire appointed by the valuers. When Sudbrook sought to exercise such right, the landlords refused to appoint a valuer. The landlords argued that the options disclosed merely an 'agreement to agree', something which was not enforceable at law. The House of Lords disagreed, holding that the lessee was entitled to enforce the option to purchase the properties. By failing to appoint a valuer, the landlord was in breach of contract. An assessment of a fair and reasonable price for the sales was ordered to be conducted by an independent valuer.

2.55 Lord Diplock made the following comments on the nature of the option granted to the lessee:

> 'In modern terminology, it is to be classified as a unilateral or "if" contract. Although it creates from the outset a right on the part of the lessees, which they will be entitled, but not bound, to exercise against the lessors at a future date, it does not give rise to any legal obligations on the part of either party unless and until the lessees give notice in writing to the lessors, within the stipulated period, of their desire to purchase the freehold reversion to the lease. The giving of such notice, however, converts the "if" contract into a synallagmatic or bilateral contract, which creates mutual legal rights and obligations on the part of both lessors and lessees.'[72]

This is an imaginative explanation by the House of Lords of the nature of an option, faced as it was with only contract to solve the problem.[73] Scots law, possessing the obligation of unilateral promise and not recognising unilateral contracts, does not adopt such an analysis of options. Of course, if the option is in the form of a firm offer, then the exercise thereof will amount to an acceptance and a contract will be constituted.

2.56 Parties may specifically state that an option is to be a firm offer or, on the other hand, a unilateral promise. In the event that the nature of the option is not specified clearly by the parties, a court will require to consider the parties' dealings as a whole as well as the language used in order to ascertain the intention of the parties.

2.57 It is worthwhile bearing in mind the following points in relation to each possibility:

---

71 [1983] 1 AC 444, HL.
72 [1983] 1 AC at 477A–B.
73 Lord Diplock was to return to these ideas in his speech in *Harvela Investments Ltd v Royal Trust Co of Canada*, discussed earlier at **2.34–2.36**.

Option as an offer. It is possible to say that every offer, whether firm or not, gives the offeree the 'option' (in a loose sense) of whether or not to contract. However, because an offer may, unless made firm, be withdrawn at will, an offeree has no concluded right to the benefit offered in a simple offer. The term option, where used to describe an offer, is best reserved for firm offers, that is to say, those offers which are guaranteed to remain open for a specified period of time. Such guarantee operates by way of a unilateral promise to keep the offer open.[74] In such cases, the exercise of the option is an acceptance of the contract offered. If the option relates to a matter which requires to be in formal writing (eg the transfer of ownership in land), then the offer and acceptance must be in the required form. In complex transactions, however, the parties may have envisaged that more detailed missives will follow on from this preliminary offer and acceptance,[75] and the initial contract may simply amount to an agreement to enter into a more detailed contract.[76]

Option as a promise. If the option is a promise *simpliciter* (rather than one attached to an offer), then it will only require to be in formal writing if it is a unilateral gratuitous promise not undertaken in the course of business.[77] Whether or not such a promissory option requires to be in writing, subsequent fulfilment of the option may require formal writing if, for example, the option is to purchase heritable property.[78] The exercise of the option may be seen as the offer of a subsequent contract[79] or as a stage preliminary to such. However, as a promise cannot impose any duties upon the promisee, a question arises as to what is to happen where an option is 'accepted', so to speak (ie exercised), but the promisee subsequently revokes the exercise of the option.[80] In such a case, the promissor may have incurred considerable expense in preparing to fulfil the conduct required by the option. Is the promisee to be allowed to cancel the transaction without compensating the promissor? Under strict promissory analysis the answer must be yes. However, the promissor may make one of several arguments in opposition to this: (a) if the promisee never had any genuine intention of exercising the option, this may constitute the delict of misrepresentation; (b) if the promisee has exercised the option then it might be argued that the 'acceptance' of the option converts the obligation

---

74 *Littlejohn v Hawden* (1882) 20 SLR 5, OH, per Lord Ordinary (Fraser) at 7.

75 As to possible problems surrounding the conclusion of such detailed missives, see **2.69–2.71**.

76 Whilst it is sometimes said that a contractual agreement binding parties to enter into a subsequent, more detailed agreement, is not enforceable, being a mere 'contract to contract', this is not so. Short-form missives of lease are regularly concluded which oblige the parties to enter into a more detailed lease in due course, the terms of the more detailed lease being attached to the missives in draft form. There is no doubt that such an arrangement is perfectly enforceable. However, the terms of the subsequent contract to be entered into must be capable of ascertainment, whether by virtue of an attached draft or by reference to a third party for determination in case of dispute, or else the agreement to contract may be struck down as void from uncertainty. This issue arose for decision in *McCall's Entertainments (Ayr) Ltd v South Ayrshire Council* 1998 SLT 1403, OH.

77 Requirements of Writing (Scotland) Act 1995, s 1(2)(a)(ii).

78 *Stone v Macdonald* 1979 SC 363, OH.

79 H L MacQueen, 'Offers, Promises and Options' 1985 SLT (News) 187 says (at p 190): 'The notice may be regarded as an offer to enter a contract which the promissor is bound to accept ... or as the acceptance of a firm offer of a contract constituted by the option.'

80 See on this point H L MacQueen, 'Offers, Promises and Options' 1985 SLT (News) 187 at p 189.

from a unilateral one to a bilateral one.[81] This seems a rather inelegant solution, however, and it is neither clear whether parties would be presumed to have intended such a course of action nor whether it is possible in Scots law.[82]

Example of an option by way of firm offer

2.58 The classic example of an option is one for the purchase of heritable property.[83] Whilst a firm offer is not usually characterised as an option in Scots law, in *Hamilton v Lochrane*[84] a firm offer was so described:

> Hamilton was a builder who entered into a memorandum of agreement with Mrs Lochrane in which Hamilton undertook to build a house which Mrs Lochrane would have the option for a certain period of purchasing. In due course Mrs Lochrane intimated that she did not want to exercise the option. Hamilton raised an action for payment of £150, being the cost of making certain alterations to the house during its construction, alterations which Hamilton alleged had been made at Mrs Lochrane's request. The Inner House of the Court of Session was sympathetic to Hamilton's claim, and allowed him a proof of his averments.

2.59 Whilst the option in this case was not exercised by the party to whom it was offered, Lord Trayner commented on its nature as follows:[85]

> 'It appears to me that the writing I have referred to [the memorandum of agreement], although represented, and in some respects accurately represented, as an agreement between the parties, comes, in effect, to nothing more than this—an offer on the part of the pursuer to sell the house to the defender, binding on the pursuer for a certain time, within which the defender had the option to accept or decline the offer. But the exercise of

---

81 This was the approach taken by Lord Diplock in *Sudbrook Trading Estate v Eggleton* [1983] 1 AC 444, HL, discussed above at **2.54–2.55**.

82 McBryde states (at para 2-33) that 'There is no rule of law that an obligation once created is immutable'. Presumably a promisee who wished to become a contracting party would have to indicate by some means an intention to be bound. Would such a situation not, however, be better analysed as a separate contract following on from the original promise? Contra McBryde, Professor Black states: 'The juristic nature of the obligation and its character as onerous or gratuitous is determined once and for all when it first comes into existence: if at that stage the content of the obligation is not the product of the agreement of the parties there is not then, and there will not subsequently be, a contract between them in relation to the promised performance.' (*Stair Memorial Encyclopaedia*, vol 15, para 613). Also contra McBryde on this point is the dictum of Lord President Dunedin in *Smith v Oliver* 1911 SC 103, IH, at 111: 'a party cannot turn what is, in its nature, a mere promise into a contract, so as to be allowed to prove it by parole, by simply averring that on the faith of the promise certain things were done by him', although McBryde (1st edn) doubted the authority for Lord Dunedin's proposition (see McBryde, *Contract* (1st edn), paras 2-43–2-46).

83 This will (until the abolition of the feudal system comes into effect) normally be the option to acquire ownership of the *dominium utile* via disposition of the same. However, there is at least one recorded case of an option (given to a tenant) to acquire ownership through subinfeudation: *Bissett v Magistrates of Aberdeen* (1898) 1 F 87, IH.

84 (1899) 1 F 478, IH.

85 (1899) 1 F at 482.

the option, which was just the acceptance of the offer, to be effectual and binding on either party required to be in writing, or proved by the oath of the party who was said to have accepted.'

In Lord Trayner's view, therefore, the option was a firm offer, requiring acceptance in the appropriate form to conclude a contract of sale. In relation to the sale of heritage this approach is not entirely unproblematic, for the concluded contract of sale which Lord Trayner envisaged would have been concluded had Mrs Lochrane exercised the option would have been a contract with very little content indeed, requiring the common law to fill in many gaps. Nonetheless, such problems are not insurmountable. A standard form of missive or disposition, for instance, could have been attached to the firm offer, thereby avoiding any problems which might be occasioned by a terse contract of sale. If such a course were to be adopted, there is no reason why an option should not be constituted as a firm offer, although there may be advantages in particular cases of constituting the option as a unilateral promise instead.

Examples of promissory options

2.60   Whilst it is possible to embody an option as a firm offer, it is also possible and perhaps preferable to use the form of unilateral promise *simpliciter*. Doing so will usually avoid any problems of form in relation to the exercise of the option.

2.61   Examples of promissory options to purchase heritable property have been found in missives of sale,[86] feu dispositions,[87] leases,[88] and other agreements,[89] as well as being constituted as free-standing promises.

2.62   An example of a promissory option to purchase heritable property is found in *Stone v Macdonald*:[90]

> The owner of a field disponed it to a farmer but retained an option to purchase back three acres of the field, such option to be exercisable within a ten-year period. The landowner's successors gave notice by letter within that period that they wished to exercise the option, but, while the farmer acknowledged receipt of the letter, following his death his executors refused to dispone the land. The Lord Ordinary held that the option was a validly created unilateral obligation to convey the land, and that this option had been duly exercised by the party in whose favour it had been granted.

The benefit of this approach is that the exercise of the option does not require formal writing, something which had not been used when the option was exercised.

---

86   See for instance *Stone v Macdonald* 1979 SC 363, OH.
87   *Banff and Buchan District Council v Earl of Seafield's Estate* 1988 SLT (Lands Tr) 21 (right of pre-emption given to superior in feu charter).
88   *Davidson v Zani* 1992 SCLR 1001, Sh Ct. It is, however, not entirely clear from the opinion of the court whether this option was seen as promissory.
89   For an example of an option within a contract, where the subject matter of the contract was the option alone, see *Miller Homes Ltd v Frame* 2000 GWD 11-388, OH.
90   1979 SC 363, 1979 SLT 288, OH.

2.63 A further example of an option to purchase heritable property is found in the more recent case of *McCall's Entertainments (Ayr) Ltd v South Ayrshire Council*.[91] The facts of the case are narrated at **3.26**. In his decision in the case, the Lord Ordinary (Lord Hamilton) was not explicit in stating that the option was promissory in nature, although his brief reference to the form of the tenant's exercise of the option suggests that he was of that opinion. The terms of the option made it clear that, if it was exercised, a separate contract of sale of the subjects was to be concluded between the parties. Whilst there was no draft form of missives for such a subsequent sale, an omission which gave rise to some of the matters at issue between the parties, there was reference in the option clause to various matters which the contract of sale was to include. Lord Hamilton concluded that the option to purchase the subjects had been validly exercised by notice sent to the landlords, and that the obligation of sale was sufficiently precise and unambiguous to require the landlords to proceed with the sale.

2.64 It is suggested that the constitution of an option in promissory form is to be recommended. Where the exercise of the option will require a subsequent contract to be entered into by the parties, a draft of the contract should be agreed[92] together, in the case of the transfer of heritable property, with a draft disposition. Where the exercise of the option will entail expense on the part of the party granting this, consideration should be given as to who is to pay for such costs, particularly if there is any danger that the party exercising the option may subsequently renege on such exercise.

Requirements of form

2.65 The required form of an option depends upon its nature as a firm offer or unilateral promise, and whether or not the option relates to the transfer of an interest in land. These matters are governed by the relevant provisions of the Requirements of Writing (Scotland) Act 1995.[93] If the option is a gratuitous unilateral obligation then, unless it has been undertaken in the course of business, it will require to be in writing complying with the Requirements of Writing (Scotland) Act 1995, s 2.

2.66 A requirement of form applicable to the constitution of the option does not necessarily entail that the exercise of the option need be in a similar form. Thus, while an option to purchase shares constituted as a gratuitous unilateral promise and not given in the course of business would require to be in formal writing, the exercise thereof would not (unless so specified by the parties) require to be in formal writing. This is so because such exercise would not constitute a contract or unilateral obligation relating to land or a gratuitous unilateral obligation, nor would it create, transfer, vary or extinguish an interest relating to land. On the contrary, the exercise of the option would merely bring into operation rights

---

91 1998 SLT 1403, OH.

92 Omission of a draft form of contract can lead to uncertainty. As Lord M'Laren noted in *Malcolm v Campbell* (1891) 19 R 278, IH, at 281: 'One must, in deference to the authorities, admit that a unilateral obligation to convey land for a price is a legal obligation, but I must say that to my mind it is not a very intelligible obligation, because one does not know how the contract is to be worked out.' A draft contract clearly resolves this difficulty.

93 See **2.10** above.

already constituted.[94] Parties may of course agree among themselves that a specified form is to be required for the exercise of an option. If an option relating to an interest in land were constituted as a firm offer, then the option as well as the exercise thereof would require to be in formal writing.

Problems for performance of the option

2.67 An option may involve the performance of a simple act by the obliged, for instance the transfer of a sum of money. Failure to complete such transfer will automatically render the obliged to be in breach of promise (or contract, should the option have been a firm offer, accepted by the exercise of the option). The transfer of heritage for value, however, is normally preceded by an exchange of missives. The question arises of whether, in particular circumstances, such a missive stage was envisaged as part of the exercise of an option to acquire heritage.

2.68 Consider the following possibilities:

(1) an option states that A shall have the option, exercisable before a specified date, to require the disposition by B to A of agreed subjects for an agreed price (or for no value);

(2) an option states that A shall have the option, exercisable before a specified date, of purchasing agreed subjects from B for a specified price; or

(3) an option states that A shall have the option, exercisable before a specified date, of purchasing agreed subjects from B at a price to be agreed between the parties.

It is submitted that in scenario 1, the disponee (A) is not entitled to request missives of sale. All that is necessary is that a disposition be tendered in exchange for payment of the agreed price. In the absence of any agreement as to the terms of such disposition, an argument might arise as to whether the lack of such agreement would render the obligation void from uncertainty. This is unlikely, however, as the common law could fill any gaps. The safest course of action of course would be for the parties to agree that the disposition is to follow the style as nearly as possible of an agreed draft.

2.69 It is unlikely, however, that the parties will wish merely to provide for an agreed form of disposition, unless the transfer of the property is to be a gift (which may be the case for instance where the exercise of the option is made conditional upon a specified event such as the marriage of A). The parties are more likely to envisage that missives will precede any disposition, which is the case in scenarios 2 and 3 above. Again, the attachment of an agreed draft form of missive is advisable. If this is not done, then the obligation to sell should still be enforceable so long as determination of the subjects and price is possible.[95] If, as in scenario 3 above, the price is to be subject to negotiation, then clearly there is the possibility

---

94 See on this point *Stone v Macdonald* 1979 SC 363, OH, in particular the comments of Lord Ross at 368–369. This case was decided under the old law relating to *obligationes literis* (ie the law in operation prior to 1 September 1995), but it is submitted that it still offers support to the position stated.

95 See *McCall's Entertainments (Ayr) Ltd v South Ayrshire Council* 1998 SLT 1403, OH.

that agreement on this matter may not be reached. In such a case, it is essential that provision is made for determination of the price by a third party valuer, acting either as an arbiter or arbitrator. In English law, a failure by one party to co-operate with the appointment of a valuer has been held to amount to a breach of contract, with the result that the court sent the matter to an independent valuer for determination of a fair and reasonable price.[96] Such a course of action by the court may reasonably be described as interventionist, and a similar reaction by the Scottish courts should not be relied upon. The safest course of action is to seek to provide for all eventualities in the contract terms.

2.70 Where an agreed style of missive is not provided, then the possibility exists that the parties may fail to agree other common terms of the missives. What then? Again, it may be possible for determination of such matters to be made by a third party or by the common law. If this is not possible, however, the risk is run that, the parties being held to have failed to reach agreement, the exercise of the option may be thwarted. Could such a failure to reach agreement be deemed culpable behaviour on the part of the party who had granted the option?[97] As there can be disagreement between reasonable parties as to acceptable terms within missives, it would be difficult to argue that a party was acting in bad faith, and that any claim should lie. Even if it could be shown that the granter of the option was acting in bad faith in failing to reach agreement, it is doubtful that this alone could ground an action of damages (or implement) against him.

2.71 Given the foregoing, it is highly recommended that an option to transfer heritable property be granted subject to an agreed style of missive of sale and disposition. This recommendation applies equally to other cases where performance of the option will require the parties to enter into a subsequent contractual relationship. In every such case a draft of the contract should be attached to the option. Such cases would include those where the option was to purchase moveable property (both corporeal and incorporeal) of any value, to enter into a lease, or to be assumed as the partner of a business.

LETTERS OF INTENT

2.72 Letters of intent are in common commercial use[98] in circumstances where it is desired to award a contract to a party but the detailed contractual terms have yet to be agreed. Their purpose is to reassure the other party that it is intended to award the contract to it, and, in some cases, to encourage that other party to begin preparation and performance even though the contract has yet to be concluded. In general, such letters of intent are not seen as giving rise to any concluded obligation, whether contractual or promissory, but are merely indicative of future

---

96 *Sudbrook Trading Estate Ltd v Eggleton* [1983] 1 AC 444, HL.

97 In some cases a failure to co-operate to agree terms may be held to amount to breach of contract, as it was in *Sudbrook Trading Estate Ltd v Eggleton* [1983] 1 AC 444, HL.

98 For two examples of cases where letters of intent featured prominently in the facts see *Wescol Structures Ltd v Miller Construction Ltd*, 8 May 1998, OH (unreported) and *Kaiser Bautechnik GMBH v GA Group Ltd*, 24 March 1995, OH (unreported); in English law see *British Steel Corporation v Cleveland Bridge Engineering* [1984] 1 All ER 504, QB.

intention. There are evident risks therefore for the contractor in commencing performance solely on the basis of a letter of intent. In the event that no contract follows, for instance because contractual negotiations break down, any part or full performance may be compensated for in unjustified enrichment,[99] although preliminary expenditure will in general be irrecoverable.[100]

2.73 In cases where a contract is eventually concluded, work undertaken prior to conclusion of the contract may be recoverable by retrospective effect of the contract. This occurred in the English case *Trollope & Colls Ltd v Atomic Power Constructions Ltd*:[101]

> In February 1959 Trollope & Colls tendered as subcontractor for certain construction work on a nuclear power station. The tender authorised the main contractor, Atomic Power Construction, to make specified variations to the contract work, which variations were to be taken into account in ascertaining the contract price. In June 1959 a letter of intent was issued to the plaintiffs requesting them to begin construction work, which they did. In April 1960 outstanding contractual issues were settled and the contract was concluded. The question arose for consideration whether the contract might retrospectively apply to work done before April 1960. The Queen's Bench Division held that the work undertaken prior to the conclusion of the contract was covered by the contract terms, either on the basis of an implied term that it should be held to do so, or on the basis that, as the tender permitted variations to the works, this extended to variations which might already have been undertaken prior to acceptance of the tender.

2.74 It has been suggested that it may be possible to view some letters of intent as promissory in nature.[102] The suggestion is that the letter of intent may be viewed as a promise to pay for work undertaken before the formation of the main contract. The difficulty with this view may, however, be with the language used in the letter of intent, as statements of intention have traditionally been distinguished from promises in Scots law,[103] and it must surely be the exceptional letter of intent that will disclose a desire unilaterally to be bound.

OFFERS OF REWARD[104]

2.75 Reported cases concerning offers of reward are numerous. In English law, they are generally viewed as so-called 'unilateral contracts', Treitel citing the offer

---

99 As in *British Steel Corporation v Cleveland Bridge Engineering* [1984] 1 All ER 504, QB. Compensation for wasted pre-contractual expenditure might be available in cases where the other party had represented that a valid contract existed between them, but, for reason of a defect, it did not: see **5.11–5.18**.

100 For discussion of a restricted remedy for the reimbursement of pre-contractual expenditure, see **5.11–5.18**.

101 [1963] 1 WLR 333, QB.

102 See H L MacQueen, 1986 SLT (News) 1 at 4.

103 See *Ricthie v Cowan and Kinghorn* (1901) 3 F 1071, IH.

104 The discussion under this head encompasses cases both of offers of reward by *A* for performance of a certain act by *B*, and also offers by *A* to make payment of a specified sum to *B* upon the happening of some event independent of the will or conduct of *B* (for instance, the death of *B* in accidental circumstances). 'Offer' is used, for the most part, in a general sense and does not necessarily denote offer *stricto sensu* unless the context so indicates.

of a reward offered to one who agrees to walk from London to York as the traditional example of a unilateral contract.[105] The party offering the reward is, states Treitel, offering to enter into a unilateral contract.[106] Such cases are thus seen as distinct from ordinary offer and acceptance scenarios.

2.76 With respect to Treitel and to other English commentators, such reward scenarios appear to be no different from other cases where an offer is made with the expectation that the acceptance will take the form of conduct rather than a verbal or written acceptance. In such cases the offeree may choose to accept by performing the stipulated conduct should he so desire.[107] It seems that such cases are described by English lawyers as unilateral contracts because the offeree appears to have no obligations imposed upon him other than performance of the stipulated conduct should he choose to accept. But how is this in essence any different from an offer to sell goods should the offeree be willing to pay a sum of money in exchange for them? Such an offeree is not obliged to pay, but he may decide to do so and, having paid, his obligation has been performed. Such a sale of goods contract would not be described as a unilateral contract, however, but as a perfectly ordinary example of a bilateral contract. Genuine unilateral contracts in English terms are of the type discussed in **2.34–2.44**.

2.77 The English notion of unilateral contract is muddled, and Scots lawyers should avoid reference to English authorities in this area as they are likely to confuse. Inevitably, however, reference has been made to English authority in relation to offers of reward, and one needs to be aware of it. The starting point is the most famous English case of reward, that involving Mrs Carlill and her smoke ball:[108]

> Mrs Carlill read an advertisement for an anti-influenza medicine called 'The Carbolic Smoke Ball'. The advertisement stated inter alia that '100 pounds reward will be paid by the Carbolic Smoke Ball Company to any person who contracts the increasing epidemic influenza, colds, or any disease caused by taking cold, after having used the ball three times daily for two weeks according to the printed directions supplied with each ball. 1,000 pounds is deposited with the Alliance Bank, Regent Street, shewing our sincerity in the matter.' In reliance upon this advertisement, Mrs Carlill purchased a smoke ball, used it as directed, and subsequently caught influenza. The Carbolic Smoke Ball Company refused to pay her the 100 pounds promised in their adver-

---

105 Treitel, *The Law of Contract*, (11th edn), at p 38.

106 Treitel, op cit, at pp 37–38. As we saw earlier, however, views differ as to how a unilateral contract is constituted in English law. Treitel takes the view that an acceptance of some kind is required. However, as seen in the discussion of *Harvela* (at **2.36** above), another view is that a unilateral contract may be concluded by mere force of will of the offeree and binds from the moment the offer is made.

107 The fact that the acceptance will not in every case be communicated to the offeror would not, in Scots law at least, pose a problem, as an offeror may be held to have waived the need for communication of acceptance if his words or conduct so indicate: *Hunter v General Accident Corporation* 1909 SC 344, 1908 SLT 656, IH, affd 1909 SC (HL) 30, 1909 2 SLT 99; *Stair Memorial Encyclopaedia*, vol 15, para 641. See also *Carlill v Carbolic Smoke Ball Co* [1893] 1 QB 256, CA.

108 [1893] 1 QB 256, CA. Those with a passion for the case or for legal *memorabilia* in general may be interested to know that it is possible to purchase a reproduction of the advertisement for the smoke ball from a company specialising in legal gifts, appropriately named the Carbolic Smoke Ball Co (no connection is claimed to the original company). Their internet address is http://www.carbolicsmokeballco.com.

tisement. The English Court of Appeal, however, awarded her the money, analysing the promise of reward as an offer: 'In point of law this advertisement is an offer to pay £100 to anybody who will perform these conditions, and the performance of the conditions is the acceptance of the offer.'[109]

2.78 There has been much debate in English law as to whether the offeror may revoke the offer once the offeree has begun, but not yet completed, performance of the condition stipulated.[110] This problem is avoided in Scots law if it is possible to view offers of reward (or indeed offers to pay a sum of money upon the occurrence of any event) as unilateral promises, binding once made and thus irrevocable. However, ignoring for one moment problems as to form if a promissory analysis is adopted, does Scots law view the case of an undertaking to pay money upon a specified event as one of unilateral promise?

2.79 At **2.17–2.18**, some suggestions were made as to criteria which might help to distinguish offer from promise. Amongst them was included whether the party giving the undertaking had envisaged an acceptance, whether he expected to benefit to any extent, and whether the context was a mercantile one. It was suggested that an affirmative answer to these enquiries would add weight to an offer analysis. These factors may help to explain why the reported Scots cases have followed the *Carlill* approach and adopted an offer analysis.[111]

2.80 The question of offers of reward was considered in the Scottish case *Hunter v General Accident Corporation*:[112]

The pursuer's husband was killed in an accident at a railway station. At the time of his death he had in his possession a diary in which was printed an advertisement of the defender's, offering insurance in respect of death caused by railway accident. The deceased had previously returned a tear-off slip from the diary to the defender as he was required to do to effect the insurance. The terms of the insurance were that £1,000 would be paid by the General Accident Corporation to the representative of any person killed or fatally injured in a railway accident while travelling as an ordinary paying passenger.[113] The Inner House held that the insurance advertisement was not merely an invitation to treat, but was an offer,[114] one which had been accepted by the deceased by return of the tear-off slip.

2.81 In the Inner House, Lord Kinnear described the situation in the following terms:

'It is suggested that this is making a contract by an advertisement, but it is none the worse for being an advertisement if it is a distinct and definite offer unconditionally accepted. The instances of such a contract are familiar. They are to be found in the books, and perhaps the most common example is a contract made by advertisement undertaking to give a definite reward for the

109 [1893] 1 QB at 262, per Lindley LJ.
110 See discussion of the case law in Treitel, *The Law of Contract* (11th edn), at p 39.
111 It is possible to construe an earlier reward case, *Petrie v Earl of Airlie* (1834) 13 S 68, IH, as promissory in nature, but the opinions of the court not being reported in the Session Cases, its status as an authority for this position is dubious.
112 1909 SC 344, 1908 SLT 656, IH, affd 1909 SC (HL) 30, 1909 2 SLT 99, HL. See also *Hunter v Hunter* (1904) 7 F 136, IH.
113 See narration of the facts by the Lord Ordinary, Lord Johnston, at 1907 15 SLT at 570–571.
114 The Lord President described it as an 'open offer' (1909 SC at 353).

performance of certain services. It is held that the offer is accepted by the person who performs the services, and thereupon makes a claim, in respect of his having done so, to the reward in terms of the offer. But the principle is quite clear - that when a general offer addressed to the public is appropriated to himself by a distinct acceptance by one person, then it is to be read in exactly the same way as if it had been addressed to that individual originally.'[115]

It is clear that the wording and direct nature of the advertisement, together with the promise to pay a specified sum, was influential in the court distinguishing this case from the case of an ordinary advertisement.

2.82 There are clear differences if the offer of reward is viewed as a promise rather than as a standing offer. Apart from the ability of the offeror to revoke the offer until acceptance occurs, there are also issues of:

(1) *Form*. If one views an offer of reward as a unilateral promise, then the question arises of whether it requires to be in writing. This depends upon whether one views such a promise as gratuitous. A reward is clearly offered on the condition that some conduct be performed. However, such conduct may not always directly benefit the promissor. If a reward is offered for finding the promissor's lost dog, then clearly the promissor benefits if the dog is returned; per contra a reward offered to the first person to prove a mathematical hypothesis, such as the prize offered in respect of Fermat's Theorem, does not benefit the promissor in any direct sense. Even in the case of the lost dog, one returns to the thorny issue of whether such a promise is gratuitous or not.[116] If it is not, then such a promise, not being made in the course of business, would require to be in subscribed writing before it could be constituted. Such rewards, if they are placed in newspapers or distributed via printed notice, are unlikely to be so. The only recourse for an individual seeking to enforce such an offer of reward would be to plead personal bar against the promissor.[117] As this would require actual knowledge of the claimant's reliance by the promissor, such a plea would be unlikely to succeed;

(2) *Knowledge of the claimant*. One claiming a reward which is construed as an offer must have performed the conduct having been aware of the offer, if such conduct is to constitute an acceptance;[118] a promisee, per contra, may perform without even being aware of the reward, and is still entitled to claim the reward.

SPECIFIC EXAMPLES OF PROMISE IN SCOTS LAW

2.83 Various circumstances may be amenable to promissory analysis, amongst them the following:

115 1909 SC at 353.
116 See the earlier discussion at **2.06–2.11**.
117 Requirements of Writing (Scotland) Act 1995, s 1(3), (4).
118 There is no native authority on this point, but it is supported by the Australian case of *R v Clarke* (1927) 40 CLR 227.

Prize competitions. Most prize draws require entrants to purchase tickets, and such are likely to be analysed as contracts. However, it has become common for newspapers to indicate in prize draws that 'no purchase is necessary' and that entrance to the draw may be gained merely by submission of one's name and address. While it is still possible to view this as a gratuitous contract, it may in the alternative be viewed as a situation of conditional promise, the promise being to award the prize to whoever is randomly or otherwise selected.

Negotiable instruments. Included within the class of negotiable instruments are privately issued banknotes. Three Scottish clearing banks issue bank notes which include a promise on the face of the note, for instance: 'The Governor and Company of the Bank of Scotland promise to pay here to the Bearer on Demand Ten Pounds Sterling' followed by a reproduction of the signature(s) of company officers, and the date and place of issue. This is a promise to pay in legal tender in sterling (which in Scotland would be a promise to pay in coinage[119]) to the bearer of the note on condition of presentation thereof and is thus a unilateral promise. Documentary credits can be viewed as unilateral promises.

Cheque guarantee cards. Current practice by the Scottish clearing banks is to include on the reverse of current account plastic cards a box typically containing the words '£100 Cheque Guarantee'. Does this phrase constitute a promise to a merchant or other person accepting a cheque presented together with the card that the issuing bank will honour such cheque up to the value of £100?[120] The statement, if it is a promise, is a terse one. However, it is submitted that the correct inference of such statement is that it is indeed intended as a unilateral promise by the issuing bank to honour the cheque up to the stated limit.

Guarantees offered in respect of goods or services. It is common for goods to be sold with an accompanying manufacturer's guarantee. As these are often offered without any payment by the customer to the manufacturer, they can be viewed as promissory in nature.[121]

Cautionary obligations.[122] The undertaking to stand as cautioner (guarantor) for the debt or the obligations of another (the principal debtor) may take one of various forms. A cautioner may make an offer of caution to the third party (the creditor); the cautionary undertaking may be exercisable as a *jus quaesitum tertio*

---

119 No banknotes are legal tender in Scotland (see Currency and Bank Notes Act 1954, s 1(2)), consequently only coinage constitutes legal tender (see Coinage Act 1971, s 2 as amended by Currency Act 1983, s 1(3)).

120 There are typically conditions attached to such guarantee, for instance that the number of the card bearing the guarantee is written on the reverse of the cheque and that the person accepting the cheque verifies that the signatures match. Such conditions are imported by reference on the card. Thus the Bank of Scotland Autoteller card currently in use bears the words 'Refer to Issuer for Conditions of Use'.

121 However, where the guarantee is offered at no consideration to a consumer purchasing the goods under a sale of goods contract, the guarantee is deemed to be contractual in nature: Sale and Supply of Goods to Consumers Regulations 2002, reg 15.

122 See further on cautionary obligations Wilson, *The Scottish Law of Debt*, chapter 10.

by the third party; or the obligation of caution may take the form of a unilateral promise. In all cases the obligation of caution is accessory to the principal, usually contractual, debt or other obligation.

Offers of reward. These are discussed at **2.75–2.82** above.

Options, for example to purchase property. These are discussed at **2.52–2.71** above.

Promises to keep offers open. These are discussed at **2.32–2.33** above.

Promises between neighbours. For instance, a neighbour might promise to cease using his property in a fashion that had been causing nuisance.

Promises to waive contractual rights. A party may promise not to enforce a contractual right or not to do so for a period of time. Whilst this may be described as waiver of contract, it may be analysed as a unilateral obligation.

IOUs. It is possible to categorise a written undertaking to repay a debt as a unilateral promise.[123] Such an analysis is particularly apposite in relation to private debts (eg a loan between friends), where the debt is unlikely to have been constituted contractually.

Promises to pay money (for whatever reason). Unless the promise to pay is embodied in a mutual contract, then an undertaking to pay a sum of money may be constituted as a unilateral promise. Thus a father may promise to pay his daughter an annual allowance while she is undertaking a course of study at university. This obligation would be a unilateral promise.

Requirements 'contracts', that is, an undertaking to supply goods when required by the other party, often referred to as a 'standing offer'. These are seen as contractual in English law, but may be considered as promissory in Scots law. Although the matter is not settled, such an obligation (whether contractual or promissory) is likely to be considered to contain an implied term permitting the promissor to terminate the obligation by the giving of reasonable notice.

There is of course a requirement of subscribed writing for gratuitous unilateral promises in non-business settings which may prove problematic for some of the above (for instance, promises between neighbours in the list), unless personal bar may be relied upon.

UNILATERAL CONTRACTS IN SCOTS LAW?

2.84 The foregoing discussion in this chapter has made the case that:

(1)　contract is always bilateral in Scots law, meaning that two parties are bound to the relationship, promise being always unilateral, only one party being bound to the relationship;[124]

123　See *McTaggart v MacEachern's Judicial Factor* 1949 SC 503, OH.
124　See **2.04** and **2.06–2.11**

(2)   contract, while bilateral, may be gratuitous, that is one party's duties may be offered for no counterpart duties of the other party;[125] and

(3)   what is described in English law as a 'unilateral contract' equates approximately to the Scots unilateral promise[126].

There is no reliable authority which supports the view that unilateral contracts exist in Scots law.

THE PRINCIPLES OF EUROPEAN CONTRACT LAW

2.85   Unilateral promises are brought within the ambit of the Principles of European Contract Law. Article 1:107 states that:

'These Principles apply with appropriate modifications to agreements to modify or end a contract, to unilateral promises and to other statements and conduct indicating intention.'

This statement is potentially of far-reaching importance for unilateral promise. It means that the whole conceptual framework for contract set out in the Principles may be applied *mutatis mutandis* to unilateral promises, except in so far as this would be incompatible with the nature of unilateral promise. What the 'appropriate modifications' might be that would require to be made to the Principles in applying them to unilateral promise is not fleshed out. The task of analysing this would require to be undertaken by anyone wishing to apply the Principles to a unilateral promise.

The commentary to article 1:107 indicates that a unilateral promise is not treated, as in Scots law, as a distinct type of obligation, but as contractual in nature.

2.86   The Principles go on to state (in art 2:107) that:

'A promise which is intended to be legally binding without acceptance is binding.'

The use of the term 'promise' here encompasses more than the unilateral promise of Scots law (and of article 1:107). The article is intended to apply not merely to such unilateral promises, but also, as the commentary to the article makes clear, to 'promises which do not need acceptance', this category of promise being distinguished from unilateral promises. It appears that this category would include cases where, for instance, parties had reached an understanding that an offer would be binding without the need for an acceptance.[127]

---

125   See **2.04**.

126   See **2.41–2.43**.

127   This appears to be so as the commentary conceives of offers as a species of promise, albeit normally promises requiring consent before they become binding.

Chapter 3

Contract and Delict

NATURE OF THE OBLIGATION OF DELICT

3.01   The obligation flowing from the commission of a delict[1] is the obligation to compensate another for harm (*damnum*) caused to him or his property as a result of wrongful behaviour[2] (*injuria*). The notion of delict in Scots law is neatly encapsulated by the maxim *damnum injuria datum*, that is to say, loss caused wrongfully.

3.02   The Scots law of delict has its historical roots in the *actio injuriarum*[3] and *actio legis aquiliae*[4] of classical Roman law, although the structure of the modern law derives essentially from the institutional writers. In modern Scots law there is a general action for the reparation of harmful conduct.[5]

3.03   One who commits a delict is referred to as a wrongdoer.[6] The wrongdoer is obliged to compensate the party harmed by paying monetary damages in an amount judged by the court to adequately represent, in so far as money can, the loss suffered by the party harmed. The obligation to pay damages is styled the obligation to make reparation.

Wrongfulness and fault

3.04   The wrongful behaviour will normally be the commission of a positive act, although there are some circumstances where an omission may constitute wrongful conduct. At common law, for conduct to be wrongful it must exhibit fault on the part of the wrongdoer. Fault may be demonstrated by intentional conduct (*dolus*) or careless conduct (*culpa*).[7] Before a defender's fault gives rise to liability under the general action, it is now commonplace to insist that the defender be shown to have breached a duty of care owed to the pursuer.[8] In

---

1   From the classical Latin *delictum* meaning fault, offence, or crime. The common law uses the term tort for its cognate obligation, from the medieval Latin meaning wrong or injustice.
2   The behaviour may be the commission of a positive act or, in some cases, an omission to act.
3   This action redressed insults to one's personality, honour or reputation.
4   This action redressed wrongful damage to property (and later persons also).
5   Scots law also recognises a number of nominate delicts.
6   The English term 'tortfeasor' is not used in Scots law.
7   Some commentators use the term *culpa* as a synonym for fault in general, not simply careless fault: see for instance Thomson's use of the term (*Delictual Liability*).
8   See further on this **3.07** below.

respect of the nominate delicts, having their own specific criteria for liability, a duty of care is not insisted upon.

3.05 In South African jurisprudence, the requirements of fault and wrongfulness are treated as separate substantive requirements.[9] Wrongfulness in South African law is something more than fault. Wrongfulness is not constituted unless a recognised interest of the pursuer has been injured. In Scotland, there is no tradition among academic writers of insisting upon a separate notion of wrongfulness. However, it may also be said of Scots law that unless a specific interest protected by the law has been harmed, then culpable conduct will not give rise to liability. Thus, there is no generally recognised interest in Scots law in the protection of one's own image.[10] This means therefore that one cannot generally prevent one's image being exploited in an advertising campaign, unless infringement of privacy, breach of confidence or copyright, or some other nominate delict can be made out. Scots law would benefit from a clearer explanation of the role of wrongfulness in our law, whether it is to be considered a separate component part of the delictual action, and, if so, what this means in practice.

3.06 By statute, some delicts may be committed without any fault on the part of the wrongdoer.[11] The wrong is constituted by commission of the relevant behaviour, regardless of the culpability of the wrongdoer. Such liability is called strict liability.

The duty of care

3.07 This concept is fully addressed in the standard texts on delict,[12] and so only a brief résumé of the main issues follows here. The foundational authority on the duty of care is the case of *Donoghue v Stevenson*,[13] in which liability was imposed in delict upon a manufacturer for causing personal injury to a consumer through consumption of the manufacturer's product (ginger beer). As the diagram below indicates, the injured party, Mrs Donoghue, had no contractual link with the other parties:

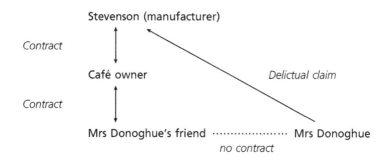

9   See for instance the treatment in Boberg, *The Law of Delict*.
10 Unlike in other jurisdictions, such as Germany.
11 For instance, strict liability for defective products under the Consumer Protection Act 1987.
12 See for instance Thomson, *Delictual Liability*, chapters 3 and 4; *Stair Memorial Encyclopaedia*, vol 15, paras 255–272.
13 1932 SC (HL) 31, 1932 SLT 317, HL.

It will be appreciated that the case in fact involves concurrent liability in contract and delict, as the manufacturer was already under a contractual duty to the café owner in respect of the defective goods (the bottle of ginger beer) which had caused Mrs Donoghue to suffer personal injury after she drank it. It is well known that the House of Lords was willing to allow the manufacturer to be concurrently liable for the injuries suffered by the consumer on the basis that the manufacturer ought reasonably to have had the consumer in contemplation at the time he was performing the careless act in question as a party likely to be injured by the carelessness. This became the basis of the test for the so-called 'duty of care', a mechanism used to establish a limit on those injuries which were considered wrongful (*injuria*) for the purposes of liability, and those which were not. Unless a 'duty of care' owed to the pursuer has been breached, there will be no liability under the general action for reparation of delict in Scotland.

3.08 The duty encompassed by *Donoghue* has, since the case, been extended to relationships other than that between manufacturer and consumer, and has been recognised as covering property damage as well as personal injury. Whilst the law of Scotland need not have used this concept of 'duty of care' as the means to restrict the category of wrongful behaviour,[14] and might conceivably have continued to develop the limiting mechanisms developed in the case law prior to this date, the duty of care analysis is the one that was adopted and extensively developed in the years following the *Donoghue* decision.

3.09 Before any delictual liability will be imposed for breach of a duty of care, the following three criteria must be met: (1) the type of injury and the party injured must have been reasonably foreseeable to the defender at the time of the breach, (2) the parties must be in a 'proximate' (close) relationship, and (3) it must be fair, just and reasonable to impose a duty of care. This tripartite test was laid down by the House of Lords in *Caparo Industries plc v Dickman plc*.[15] The third criterion in particular allows specific policy concerns to be brought into play by the courts. However, it is also worth bearing in mind that the second requirement, the concept of 'proximity', is also sometimes used to embody policy considerations. In *Caparo Industries*, a case involving a claim for economic loss against auditors of a company, Lord Oliver said:

> ' "[P]roximity" in cases such as this is an expression used not necessarily as indicating literally "closeness" in a physical or metaphorical sense but merely as a convenient label to describe circumstances from which the law will attribute a duty of care. It has to be borne in mind that the duty of care is inseparable from the damage which the plaintiff claims to have suffered from its breach. It is not a duty to take care in the abstract but a duty to avoid causing to the particular plaintiff damage of the particular kind which he has in fact sustained.'[16]

---

14 See for instance Douglas Brodie's analysis of W A Wilson's critique of delict in *Scots Law into the 21st Century*. Wilson had argued that the existing concepts of *culpa* and remoteness of damage could adequately delimit liability in Scots law: see Wilson, 'The Analysis of Negligence', in *Introductory Essays on Scots Law* (W Green, 1984).

15 [1990] 2 AC 605, [1990] 1 All ER 568, HL.

16 [1990] 2 AC at 651E, per Lord Oliver.

As will become apparent with regard to claims involving pure economic loss in particular, the courts have on occasion allowed policy considerations to influence their understanding of whether parties are in a proximate relationship.

3.10 In cases involving physical damage—that is, personal injury to the pursuer or damage to the pursuer's property—the requirement of proximity is usually considered to be established merely by establishment that the injury was reasonably foreseeable. In other words, the fact that a pursuer could reasonably foresee that its negligence would cause physical damage to a party is sufficient to bring the pursuer and defender into a close relationship. Nothing further need usually be established. This was recognised by Lord Oliver in *Murphy v Brentwood District Council*[17] who said:

> 'In the straightforward case of the direct infliction of physical injury by the act of the plaintiff there is, indeed, no need to look beyond the foreseeability by the defendant of the result in order to establish that he is in a "proximate" relationship with the plaintiff. The infliction of physical injury to the person or property of another universally requires to be justified. The causing of economic loss does not.'[18]

For pure economic loss—that is, a diminution in the value of the pursuer's economic assets—something more beyond foreseeability of the loss must be shown. The 'something more' may be constituted by varying factors, including reliance by the injured party upon a misrepresentation of the pursuer, or other close contact between the parties such as to give rise to an expectation on the part of the injured party that the wrongdoer would take reasonable care not to cause economic injury to the former.

Harm

3.11 It is generally accepted that harm or damage to the pursuer or his property is a necessary element before a delict can be said to have been committed under Scots law. Are there any exceptions? It might be argued that, for instance, the delict of trespass is often committed in circumstances where no physical harm is caused to the subjects on which the wrongdoer has trespassed. In such cases the only avenue open to the lawful occupier of the subjects is to seek an interdict to prevent a repetition of the trespass. Has the trespasser who causes no physical damage therefore not committed a delict? He has. The correct interpretation of this situation is that the trespasser's presence is itself considered harmful, diminishing as it does the occupier's use and enjoyment of his property, particularly his right to privacy. It is safe to conclude that harm or damage is an essential element in the commission of a delict.

---

17 [1991] 1 AC 398, [1990] 2 All ER 908, HL.
18 [1991] 1 AC at 468H–487B, per Lord Oliver.

Delict a bilateral obligation

3.12 It was stated in chapter 2 that delict is a bilateral obligation. Does this make sense when one considers that where a wrong has been committed by *A* against *B* it would appear that *A* has a duty imposed upon him (to make reparation) but no rights, and *B* has a right (to receive reparation) but no duty?

3.13 It is possible to explain the nature of delict as a bilateral obligation in two ways:

First, if one adopts the modern terminology of 'duty of care' to explain the basis of the general action in delict, it may be said that we all owe duties of care to each other not to behave in a manner that we can reasonably foresee will injure others. In other words, the duties of care which are imposed on us by the law are reciprocal, and can thus be said to give rise to bilateral obligational relationships. However, the weakness of this argument is that it only refers to the position before a harmful act has been committed. Once harm occurs the obligation to make reparation crystallises, at which point the delictual relationship can appear to be much more one-sided. We must therefore look to a second, more convincing explanation.

The second explanation examines the obligation of delict at the point at which it is proper to consider its nature, that is, at the point after the harm has occurred. While there may exist duties of care before this point, a duty of care is merely a term which the law uses to state that we must act carefully towards each other. These duties are no doubt imposed by the law and are considered part of the subject matter of 'delict' in a general sense. However, these duties to act carefully are not the same as the obligation to make reparation for loss caused to another, which was the definition of the obligation of delict given at the beginning of this chapter. This obligation is bilateral. It requires the interaction of two parties, the wrongdoer and the injured party, before the obligation can come into existence. Two parties are bound to the obligation, even if the party harmed is bound only in a nominal sense (in the same way that the party benefited by a gratuitous contract may be said to be nominally bound into the contractual relationship).[19] This second explanation reassures us therefore that in Scots law delict is not to be considered a unilateral obligation.

---

19 As noted at chapter 1, fn 17, it is not generally considered that the injured party has a 'duty' to mitigate his loss, although whether or not he has done so will be considered by a court when calculating the damages due; cf the comments of Viscount Haldane in *SS Baron Vernon v SS Metagama* 1928 SC (HL) 21, HL, at 25–26: 'the burden lies on the negligent ship to show by clear evidence that the subsequent damage arose from negligence or great want of skill on the part of those on board the vessel damaged. *It is their duty to do all they can to minimise the damage*, but they do not fail in this duty if they only commit an error of judgment in deciding on the best course in difficult circumstances' (emphasis added). These comments would appear to support a view that there is a duty to mitigate incumbent upon the injured party.

GENERAL ACTION FOR REPARATION OF WRONGFUL BEHAVIOUR

3.14 It was stated at **3.01** that Scots law derives its law of delict from a general principle of loss wrongfully caused, *damnum injuria datum*. This principle finds its most natural expression in our law in a general action for the reparation of wrongful behaviour. In addition to the general action of reparation, Scots law also recognises a number of nominate delicts. These may be seen as specific, crystallised examples of the general principle of *damnum injuria datum* upon which the law rests. One might portray the position thus:

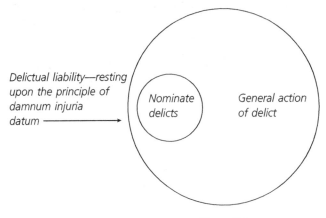

Figure 3.1

3.15 What does this conception mean in practice? It means that where loss has been caused wrongfully in Scots law, a right of action will prima facie lie. If the pursuer's claim relates to an interest which is addressed by means of a specific nominate delict, the pursuer will be required to have regard to the requirements enumerated by the law in relation to that delict. If, on the other hand, no specific delict addresses protection of the interest at issue, the pursuer will simply frame his claim with regard to the requirements of the general action of reparation. Within this realm of the general action the law is continually developing, with new fact situations being held to give rise to delictual liability.

3.16 English law by contrast, does not recognise a general principle underpinning its law, nor a general action for the reparation of harm. It has a law of torts, not a law of tort. The whole of the English law is composed of individual nominate torts. The largest of these, in terms of reported cases, is the tort of negligence. By contrast, in Scots law negligence is merely a specific type of fault in the law.

3.17 What *Figure 3.1* above does not indicate is where statutory liability is to be located on this map. Is it within the category of nominate delicts, within the general delictual action, or somewhere else? Where for instance should one place statutory occupiers' liability (fault based), or the liability imposed upon manufacturers in respect of dangerous products (strict liability, which is an exception to the standard requirement of fault)? Statutory liability is not traditionally

73

conceived of as falling within nominate delicts, neither is it placed satisfactorily as part of the general action of delict, which is based upon the common law. It is best to conceive of statutory liability as occupying a separate sub-category of delictual liability:

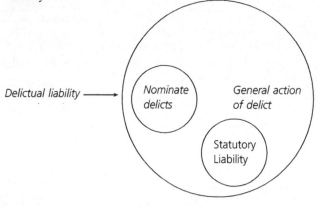

Delictual liability ⟶ *Nominate delicts* · *General action of delict* · Statutory Liability

Figure 3.2

3.18 It is not intended to explore further in a general way the requirements for delictual liability. This topic is treated satisfactorily in other works, to which reference is made.[20] Having considered briefly the nature of delict, it is now intended to consider the interaction between the obligations of delict and contract in the law. The relationship between delict and enrichment is addressed in chapter 6.

RELATIONSHIP BETWEEN CONTRACT AND DELICT

3.19 In chapter 1[21] the hierarchy of obligations was discussed, and it was noted that (under the so-called 3:1 model) contract, promise and delict may be viewed as first level obligations, with unjustified enrichment a postponed obligation, applicable only where none of the other three are. It was also noted that under the other equally applicable model (the 2:2 model), delict and unjustified enrichment may be seen as 'higher' obligations, because, being imposed by law, they may only be excluded from situations where they would otherwise apply if parties so agree. The hierarchy of obligations affects the relationship between the obligations of contract and delict, the precise nature of the relationship often being determined by whichever model of the hierarchy is emphasised in particular circumstances.

3.20 Certain basic propositions may be stated about the relationship between contract and delict:

(1) Parties negotiating a contract, but who have not yet reached *consensus in idem*, may (in general) break off negotiations at any point prior to contractual

20 See Thomson, *Delictual Liability; Stair Memorial Encyclopaedia*, vol 15, Obligations.
21 At **1.75–1.81**.

engagement. However, negotiating parties may still incur delictual (but not contractual) liability towards each other if the requisite elements of a delict are made out.

(2) Parties in a contractual relationship are in general terms free to structure their relationship as they wish. They may include, or omit, whichever matters in the contract they see fit. If they choose to omit certain matters, for instance the matter of damages for breach, the 'gaps' may be filled by common law contractual rules.

(3) Parties in a contractual relationship may choose to exclude delictual liability between themselves.[22] If they do not, then delictual liability may arise between them. This may operate alongside any liability for breach of contract (concurrent liability).

(4) A party in a contractual relationship may incur contractual or delictual liability to a third party. Contractual liability to third parties arises only under the doctrine of *jus quaesitum tertio* (third party rights). Delictual liability may exist towards a third party if the contracting party is held to owe a duty of care not to cause loss of the kind in question to that third party. The extent of such delictual liability to third parties may (subject to any applicable restrictions imposed under Unfair Contract Terms Act 1977) in some cases be limited or excluded by a term of the contract, but not in others. The presence of a contractual chain which includes the wrongdoer and the party harmed, where these parties are not in a direct contractual relationship with each other, may mitigate against the imposition of delictual liability between wrongdoer and victim.

These basic points form the subject matter of much of the more detailed commentary in the remainder of this chapter.

3.21 In theory, a breach of contract could be conceived of as culpable wrongful conduct and thus be denoted as a delict. Scots law has chosen not to take such a view, however. As breach of contract and its consequences depend inherently upon a contractual matrix, Scots law has chosen to define breach of contract as a contractual rather than a delictual matter. That is not to say, however, that conduct which amounts to a breach of contract cannot additionally amount to a delict—it may, so long as the component requirements of the delictual action are made out.[23]

LIABILITY WHILE NEGOTIATING

3.22 Parties negotiating a contract are generally free to break off negotiations without incurring any liabilities towards each other. Liability may arise, however, if during the negotiating period a delict has been committed by one of the parties.[24]

---

22 Subject to restrictions imposed by statute, for instance the Unfair Contract Terms Act 1977, and the Unfair Terms in Consumer Contracts Regulations 1999 (SI 1999/2083).
23 Further on this topic, see the treatment of concurrent liability at **3.59** ff.
24 As to which, see **3.33** ff.

3.23 While Scots law does not yet recognise a general common law duty to negotiate in good faith, the presence of *bad faith*—for instance, actings amounting to fraud—may constitute a delict. Consider the following example:

> A leases commercial premises in a shopping centre from B. A's lease is due to expire in six months. A is negotiating with B for the renewal of the lease. B has indicated to A that B is, in principle, willing to re-let the premises. In fact, B has no intention of re-letting the premises to A, and is negotiating with A only to assist B's negotiations with C, who wishes to purchase the property for its letting potential. Shortly before the expiry of the notice period of the lease, B informs A that B is unwilling to re-let. A is forced to find new premises at a substantially higher rent than if A had begun to look for them six months earlier.

The foregoing circumstances would amount to fraudulent misrepresentation[25] on the part of the landlord, entitling the tenant to damages.

3.24 As parties are generally free to break off negotiations without explanation or for any reason without incurring liability, a negotiating party must take care if acceding to requests by the other party to undertake preparatory expenditure which will provide no benefit to the other party should negotiations be broken off. Consider the following example:

> A is proposing to build a new shopping centre. B is interested in taking up a tenancy in the shopping centre as the flagship store. A and B enter into negotiations for a lease. B gives no indications that it definitely intends to take up the tenancy, but asks A to make certain expensive design modifications to the shopping centre to accommodate B's requirements should a lease be concluded. After these modifications are made, B settles on a more favourable location for a store and breaks off negotiations with A.

In a situation like this, there seem to be no grounds for arguing that the prospective tenant comes under any liability towards the landlord in respect of the expensive modifications which the landlord has made in the expectation of securing the tenant's occupation of the site. Whilst the nineteenth century authority of *Hamilton v Lochrane*[26] might support such liability, the line of cases of which it forms part has been interpreted recently by the Court of Session in a restrictive fashion.[27] A landlord, concerned at the possibility of failure to recover such costs, should reach a separate undertaking with the tenant in relation to such matters, if such an agreement is practicable in the circumstances.

Obligations to negotiate (or negotiate in good faith)

3.25 A specific contractual undertaking that a party will negotiate a contract, or negotiate in good faith, is unlikely to be upheld by the Scottish courts. English law is against the enforceability of such contracts, following the decision in *Walford v Miles*:[28]

---

25 Misrepresentation is discussed more fully at **3.34** ff.
26 (1899) 1 F 478, IH. This case, and the line of cases of which it forms part, are discussed more fully at **5.11** ff.
27 Namely, *Dawson International plc v Coats Paton plc* 1988 SLT 854, OH; affd 1989 SLT 655, IH.
28 [1992] 2 AC 128, HL.

Parties were negotiating for the sale of a business. The sellers agreed to deal exclusively with the prospective buyers and to terminate any negotiations with competing parties (ie a lock-out agreement). The prospective buyers alleged in addition that it was an implied term of the lock-out agreement that the sellers would continue to negotiate in good faith with the prospective buyers. When the sellers broke off negotiations with the prospective buyers, the prospective buyers sued for breach of contract.

The House of Lords, whilst acknowledging that a lock-out agreement for a definite time was perfectly valid in English law,[29] reaffirmed the existing English law view that an agreement to negotiate is not enforceable in law. Lord Ackner stated:

'[T]he concept of a duty to carry on negotiations in good faith is inherently repugnant to the adversarial position of the parties when involved in negotiations. Each party to the negotiations is entitled to pursue his (or her) own interest, so long as he avoids making misrepresentations.'[30]

3.26 *Walford v Miles* would be highly persuasive in Scots law as to the un-enforceability of a contract (or a term of a contract) to negotiate in good faith. At first glance, the decision in *McCall's Entertainments (Ayr) Ltd v South Ayrshire Council (No 1)*,[31] in which *Walford* was cited to the court, appears to take a different approach:

A term of a lease of heritable subjects granted to the tenants an option to purchase the subjects. The option clause obliged the landlords 'to enter negotiations for the sale to the Tenants of the subjects and to so sell the subjects, at a price to be agreed between the parties and failing agreement within three weeks, at a price to be fixed by an Arbiter'. When the tenants sought to exercise the option, the landlords argued, inter alia, that the language used indicated that this was a mere agreement in principle and not an enforceable option. The Lord Ordinary disagreed, holding the clause to be enforceable.[32]

3.27 It would, however, be going too far to suggest that the decision in *McCall's Entertainments* is authority for the proposition that all clauses or agreements obliging parties to negotiate (or to negotiate in good faith) will be enforced by the Scottish courts. A crucial factor in the case was that if the parties did not, following negotiations, reach agreement on price, the matter was to be settled by an arbiter. The clause therefore did not lack specification or certainty, as it

---

29 See the comments of Lord Ackner, [1992] 2 AC at 140.
30 [1992] 2 AC at 138.
31 1998 SLT 1403, OH.
32 Whilst the clause, on the face of it, appears to be a clause obliging the parties to negotiate a contract of sale should the option be exercised, Lord Hamilton took the view that 'on intimation to the landlords by the tenants within the specified timescale of their intention to exercise the option, the tenants would become obliged to purchase as the landlords would become obliged to sell the subjects' (1998 SLT at 1409H) which suggests rather that a concluded contract of sale would then have been in existence. Lord Hamilton explains the reference to 'negotiation' as follows: 'The parties certainly envisaged that they would enter negotiations but, having made provision against failure to agree essential elements by such means, their bargain is complete' (at 1409H). Lord Hamilton thus took the view that the reference to negotiation did not render the contract uncertain, as the fall-back reference to an arbiter in the event of disagreement would allow for ascertainment of the price.

provided for a fall-back mechanism to ascertain the crucial matter of the price. Such clauses in leases, providing for negotiation on matters subject to a reference to an arbiter in the absence of agreement, are common. This is clearly a different type of obligation to negotiate than an alleged open-ended obligation to negotiate all or many of the terms of a contract where provision has not been made for a third party determination should agreement fail to be reached.[33] The attitude of the Scottish courts to an open-ended agreement to negotiate is likely to be that adopted by the House of Lords in *Walford*.

3.28 Whilst general undertakings to negotiate in good faith are unlikely to be upheld in Scotland, a lock-out agreement, to the effect that for a prescribed period a party will not negotiate with any other persons except the other party to the lock-out agreement, is perfectly valid in Scots law.[34]

3.29 In contrast to the position in Scots law, the Principles of European Contract Law provide for liability where negotiations are broken off contrary to good faith. Article 2:301 of the Principles states:

'(1) A party is free to negotiate and is not liable for failure to reach an agreement.

(2) However, a party who has negotiated or broken off negotiations contrary to good faith and fair dealing is liable for the losses caused to the other party.

(3) It is contrary to good faith and fair dealing, in particular, for a party to enter into or continue negotiations with no real intention of reaching an agreement with the other party.'

This article would provide for liability in the example given at **3.23** above of the lease negotiations undertaken in bad faith.

Culpa in contrahendo

3.30 Proposition 1 above[35] was to the effect that parties negotiating a contract might incur delictual but not contractual liability.[36] In other jurisdictions, most notably Germany, a party negotiating a contract may be liable in *contract* for damage caused to the other negotiating party, such liability being known as *culpa in contrahendo*. The liability has been explained thus:

'Once parties enter into negotiations for a contract, ... a relationship of trust and confidence comes into existence irrespective of whether they succeed or fail. Thus, protection is afforded against blameworthy conduct which prevents the consummation of a contract. A party is liable for negligently

---

33 In theory parties who were at arm's length and negotiating a contract could bind themselves to negotiate a contract in good faith and agree that any, or all, of the terms which were not agreed could be settled by a third party. It is uncertain whether a Scottish court would enforce such an agreement, although if one takes the view that the arbiter would in essence be acting as an agent for both parties, there would seem to be no theoretical objection to it.

34 *Dawson International plc v Coats Paton plc* 1988 SLT 854, OH; affd 1989 SLT 655, IH.

35 See **3.20**.

36 As discussed in chapter 5, there also exists a distinct category of pre-contractual liability in Scots law, based upon the line of cases following *Walker v Milne*: see **5.11** ff.

creating the expectation that a contract would be forthcoming although he knows or should know that the expectation cannot be realized. Furthermore, the parties are bound to take such precautionary measures as are necessary for the protection of each other's person or property.'[37]

3.31 Such liability is classified as contractual, although the measure of recovery in general protects the restoration interest, not the performance interest, damages being designed (as in delict) to restore the party to the position he would have been in had not the blameworthy conduct occurred. In a famous German case,[38] the doctrine was employed to award damages to a woman who had been injured in a carpet store when a roll of linoleum fell upon her as a result of the carelessness of an employee of the store who had moved it. In a more recent case,[39] a girl whose mother was shopping for groceries was compensated under the doctrine when the girl slipped on a lettuce leaf and was injured. In Scotland, liability for the negligence of the vendor in such cases would have been imposed in delict, either at common law or under the Occupiers' Liability (Scotland) Act 1960. Liability in *culpa in contrahendo* would also arise where, for instance, the vendor of a house, having arranged a visit to the property with a prospective purchaser, omitted to inform the prospective purchaser that the house had been sold, thus causing the prospective purchaser wasted travelling expenses.[40] This example is less likely to give rise to a remedy under Scots law.

3.32 Scots law does not recognise a contractual doctrine of *culpa in contrahendo*. Where parties have yet to reach a contract, there is no possibility of contractual liability arising. Scots law, however, has a more developed law of delict which provides answers to many of the cases which arise in Germany under the head of *culpa in contrahendo*. Additionally, in cases where parties have been negotiating a contract, and one of the parties has given the impression that a valid contract has been concluded, but due to some defect no contract exists, liability for the other party's wasted expenditure may be imposed on the basis of the doctrine established in *Walker v Milne*. Such liability is discussed further in chapter 5.[41]

Liability in delict while negotiating

3.33 A party negotiating a contract may incur liability in delict towards the other party. This may arise in one of several ways:

(1) where a negotiating party makes a misrepresentation to another negotiating party, whether or not a contract is concluded;
(2) where negotiations are broken off, and one of the parties uses or discloses confidential information which was provided to him during the negotiating process; or

---

37 Friedrich Kessler and Edith Fine, 'Culpa in Contrahendo, Bargaining in Good Faith and Freedom of Contract: A Comparative Study' (1964) 77 Harvard LR 401 at 404.
38 *Reichsgericht*, 7 December 1911, RGZ 78, 239.
39 *BGH* 28 January 1976, BGHZ 66, 51.
40 This example is cited by Kessler and Fine, op cit, fn 37, at 405.
41 At **5.11** ff.

(3)   any other type of conduct by a negotiating party, not falling within either of the above two heads, may be argued to amount to an actionable delict, whether or not a contract has been concluded.

In theory, the ability to raise a delictual claim under any of the above heads does not depend upon whether any resulting contract has been avoided, nor on whether a contractual claim may also lie.[42]

MISREPRESENTATION

Nature of misrepresentation

3.34   A misrepresentation is an untrue or misleading statement of fact[43] which induces a contract between the person making the statement (the representor) and the person who relies upon it (the representee). The misrepresentation must be relied upon before it is relevant. A misrepresentation may be classified as fraudulent, negligent or innocent. A fraudulent misrepresentation is one made by a party knowing or believing it to be false, or who is reckless as to whether it is true or false.[44] A negligent misrepresentation is one made without the due level of care required by the law. An innocent misrepresentation is one made neither fraudulently nor negligently, but in the careful though erroneous belief that it is correct.

3.35   The term 'misstatement' is also encountered, and it is sometimes used interchangeably with the term misrepresentation. There is, however, a tradition (particularly in England) of reserving the term misrepresentation for cases where the misleading statement has induced a contract between the representor and representee, and the term misstatement for circumstances where no contract has been formed between representor and representee (even if it has induced a contract between the representee and a third party). The distinction between misrepresentation and misstatement is more than mere semantics however. If the complaint relates to a misstatement which has not induced a contract between pursuer and defender, the nature of the statement complained of may range beyond mere untrue or misleading statements of fact, and may in addition encompass misleading statements of opinion. Thus, misleading professional advice may ground a claim for misstatement. Indeed, the comments of the defendants in *Hedley Byrne & Co v Heller & Partners*[45] were mere opinion, but would certainly have founded a valid claim in tort but for the presence of the

---

42 As to concurrent liability between contract and delict, see **3.59** ff below.
43 Misrepresentation does not encompass untrue or misleading statements of opinion, law, or intention. However, it is a misrepresentation to state that one holds a particular opinion, if in fact one does not.
44 If the maker of the statement honestly believes it to be true, the misrepresentation cannot be fraudulent: *Western Bank of Scotland v Addie* (1867) 5 M (HL) 80, HL; *Boyd & Forrest v Glasgow & South Western Railway Co* 1915 SC (HL) 20.
45 [1964] AC 465, [1963] 2 All ER 575, HL.

exclusion clause. English law takes the view that misstatements of intention may also ground a tortious action.[46]

3.36 Despite the foregoing distinctions between misrepresentation and misstatement, the use of the former term is more widespread and it is proposed in what follows to employ the term misrepresentation alone, although the context in which it is used will be sufficiently explained to enable the distinctions made in the previous paragraph to be borne in mind.

3.37 Given the foregoing, it may be asserted that a misrepresentation can be made:

(1) in circumstances wholly unconnected to any contract contemplated or undertaken by the representee;

(2) in circumstances in which a contract is contemplated between the representor and the representee, or between the representee and a third party, but where no such contract has been concluded;

(3) in circumstances where a contract has been concluded between the representee and a third party; or

(4) in circumstances where a contract has been concluded between the representor and representee.

In circumstance (1), (2) or (3), any action by the representee will be for damages and will lie in delict alone.[47] In circumstance (4), where a misrepresentation has induced a contract between the parties, the representee may seek to have the contract avoided (a contractual remedy) and in addition (or in the alternative)[48] may seek damages for loss (classified as a delictual remedy).[49]

Reliance upon the representor's skill or knowledge

3.38 Where the misrepresentation forms the background to a contract between representor and representee, avoidance of this contract by the representee will require proof that the contract was induced (at least in part) by the misrepresentation. In order to demonstrate the necessary causal link, the representee will normally seek to show that he reasonably relied upon the skill or knowledge of the representor, disclosed in the representation.[50] Where, however, the represen-

---

46 See for instance *Esso Petroleum Co v Mardon* [1976] QB 801, CA; *Edwards v Lee* [1991] NLJR 1517, QB.

47 See further in respect of delictual damages for negligent misrepresentation: Thomson, *Delictual Liability*, at pp 79–85.

48 That is to say, the innocent party need not seek to have the contract reduced, but may merely seek an award of damages in delict (see MacQueen and Thomson, para 4.64). Such damages are not classified as contractual, because they are not for breach of contract (which would be the case if the misrepresentation had become a term of the contract), but merely for the wrongful behaviour of having induced the contract by misrepresentation.

49 For a detailed discussion of misrepresentation inducing contract, see McBryde, paras 15-27–15-30, 15-44–15-93, and chapter 14 passim, and MacQueen and Thomson, paras 4.57 to 4.66.

50 See for instance *M'Lellan v Gibson* (1843) 5 D 1032, IH, and the comments of Lord Justice Clerk Hope at 1034: 'the alleged false statement must have been relied on and formed the reason for the pursuer entering into the transaction'.

tee himself possesses sufficient skill or knowledge in relation to the matter in question, he cannot be said to have reasonably relied upon the representation.[51] If the representations are blatantly incorrect or misleading, any reliance placed on them will be held to have been unreasonable.

3.39 In cases where the misrepresentation is made to a party with whom the representor does not contract, reasonable reliance upon the skill or knowledge of the representor will certainly require to be present before an action for damages will lie.[52]

3.40 Where A, lacking expert knowledge, obtains information from C, an expert in the matter concerned, and A then transmits this information to B, A is entitled to rely upon C having competently provided it.[53] Thus, if the information is erroneous, it is unlikely that A will be held to have acted negligently. It is possible that A may be held to have made an innocent misrepresentation, although if B knows that the information originates from C, and C knows that the information was to be provided to B, B may have a direct delictual claim against C.[54]

Avoidance of contract for misrepresentation

3.41 Where circumstance (4) in **3.37** pertains, and a contract has been induced between representor and representee as a result of a misrepresentation, the contract may be avoided. This presupposes that the nature of the misrepresentation has been such as to render the contract voidable. Most cases of misrepresentation today are pled on the basis of the voidability of the contract, although it is conceivable that the nature of an error in a particular case might be argued to be 'essential error' in the classical sense of the term, such as to render the contract void.[55] Before a contract may be avoided for misrepresentation, *restitutio in integrum* must be possible, that is to say, it must be possible to restore the parties to their pre-contractual positions.[56] If it is not, then the only remedy will be for damages (unless the misrepresentation is innocent, when damages will not be available).

---

51 *G Percy Trentham Ltd v Beattie Watkinson & Partners* 1987 SLT 449, OH. Note also the comments of Lord Justice Clerk Hope in *M'Lellan v Gibson* (1843) 5 D 1032, IH, at 1034: 'If the pursuer relied upon his own judgment, there is no case under the second issue [ie misrepresentation]'.

52 *Hedley Byrne & Co v Heller & Partners* [1964] AC 465, [1963] 2 All ER 575, HL.

53 This follows from the general rule that a party who engages a skilled professional is not liable for that professional's negligence, so long as the former reasonably believed the latter to be competent: see the comments of Salmon J in *Clayton v Woodman & Son (Builders) Ltd* [1962] 2 QB 533, QB, at 539 (decision at first instance overturned on the facts).

54 See *Smith v Eric S Bush* [1990] 1 AC 831, [1989] 2 WLR 790, [1989] 2 All ER 514, HL.

55 For a discussion of the classical notion of essential error, and of the relationship between essential error and misrepresentation, see McBryde, chapter 15 passim.

56 *Boyd & Forrest v Glasgow & South Western Railway Co* 1915 SC (HL) 20. The House of Lords has suggested that *restitutio in integrum* need not be required to be made in every case *in forma specifica*: *Spence v Crawford* 1939 SC (HL) 52.

Damages for misrepresentation

3.42   An action of damages for a misrepresentation (whether or not a contract has been concluded between representor and representee) is classified as delictual.[57] If fraudulent misrepresentation is alleged, then the requisite elements of fraud must be made out, including proof by the innocent party that the guilty party intentionally or recklessly deceived him. If negligent misrepresentation is alleged, then the innocent party will have to prove that the guilty party has failed to take the requisite degree of care.

3.43   Additionally, if the parties are not in a contractual relationship, then a duty of care will require to be made out. For a duty of care to exist, the parties must be in a sufficiently proximate relationship, injury to the innocent party must have been reasonably foreseeable, and it must be fair, just and reasonable to impose the duty. Where the parties are in a contractual relationship, and damages are sought for negligent or fraudulent misrepresentation, there is no need to aver or prove a special relationship giving rise to a duty of care.[58] This is because the closeness of the relationship is presupposed, in the case of negligent misrepresentation by virtue of the statutory provision giving rise to the entitlement to claim damages for negligent misrepresentation.[59]

3.44   In some cases, a causal connection between the misrepresentation and the loss will not be made out, and a damages claim will fail. For instance, where it is clear that the innocent party would have entered into the contract regardless of the misrepresentation, where the innocent party himself possessed such skill that any reliance upon the representation was not reasonable, or where the representation was so patently erroneous that any reliance by the innocent party was unreasonable, then damages will not be claimable. In cases where the misrepresentation was only one causal factor amongst others, only a proportion of damages will be recoverable from the representor.[60]

3.45   It is clear from the case law, that the fact that *A* is in a contractual relationship with *B* in terms of which *A* is to provide goods or services to *B*, will not preclude *A* from incurring liability in damages to *C* in respect of a misrepresentation made by *A* to *C* in the course of *A*'s performance of his contractual obligations with *B*. Such situations may or may not give rise to questions of concurrent liability.[61] An example of such a misrepresentation by *A* to *C* arose in the English case of *Independent Broadcasting Authority v EMI Electronics and BICC Construction*:[62]

---

57   See Thomson, *Delictual Liability*, at p 85, and MacQueen and Thomson, para 4.63.

58   See in this respect the comments of Lord Carloway in *Hamilton v Allied Domecq plc* 2001 SC 829, OH, at 836G: 'I am of the view that ... there is no need to enter into the field of *Hedley Byrne* type "special relationships" and whether a duty of care is owed'.

59   The relevant provision in Scotland is s 10(1) of the Law Reform (Miscellaneous Provisions)(Scotland) Act 1985; in England it is s 2(1) of the Misrepresentation Act 1967.

60   See the comments of Lord Carloway in *Hamilton v Allied Domecq plc* 2001 SC 829, OH, at 838–839.

61   Whether the circumstances may give rise to concurrent liability will depend upon whether the making of the misrepresentation by *A* to *C* also constitutes a breach of contract by *A* towards *B*.

62   (1980) 14 BLR 1, HL.

BICC were subcontractors in a construction project for the erection of a television transmitter mast. The employers, the IBA, who owned a similar mast to the one under construction, were concerned about the oscillation of the existing mast, and asked BICC to investigate the problem in order that the new mast would not suffer similar problems. BICC informed the IBA that the former was 'well satisfied that the structures will not oscillate dangerously'. After construction of the new mast, during extremely cold weather conditions, the mast broke and collapsed. The IBA sued the main contractor in contract, and BICC in tort for negligent misstatement. In relation to the misstatement claim, the House of Lords affirmed the trial judge's findings that BICC had been negligent in not considering certain cold weather conditions in relation to the design of the mast, and that the statement to the IBA had therefore been made negligently.

This case exemplifies the point that the mere presence of a contractual relationship A–B will not prevent A from incurring liability in delict for a misrepresentation made to C.[63]

3.46　In such circumstances A may have attempted to exclude or restrict any potential liability towards C through the use of a specific disclaimer directed towards C. The effectiveness of such a disclaimer will depend upon its enforceability under the Unfair Contract Terms Act 1977 ('UCTA').[64] Alternatively, A may have stipulated in its contract with B that delictual liability towards any party other than B is excluded. Can A rely upon the effectiveness of such an all-parties disclaimer? Apart from challenges to the validity of such a disclaimer under UCTA,[65] it might be thought that such disclaimers of delictual liability to third parties ought generally to be unacceptable. This topic is considered later in this chapter.[66]

The interest protected by a damages claim

3.47　In all damages claims for misrepresentation, the remedy lying in delict, the measure of recovery will be such as to put the injured party in the position in which he would have been had the misrepresentation not occurred.[67]

Relevant types of damage

3.48　The damage caused as the result of a misrepresentation may be personal injury, property damage, or pure economic loss, as well as secondary (or subsequent) economic loss. All the foregoing are of relevance for a damages

---

63　The result may of course be otherwise in circumstances where A has directly excluded or limited liability when making the representation to C, or has done so in its contract with B.

64　For an unsuccessful attempt to exclude liability towards a third party in a contractual chain, see *Smith v Bush* [1990] 1 AC 831, [1989] 2 WLR 790, [1989] 2 All ER 514, HL.

65　Unfair Contract Terms Act 1977, s 16(1).

66　See **3.201–3.214.**

67　This was succinctly affirmed (so far as misrepresentation inducing contract is concerned) in *Hamilton v Allied Domecq plc* 2001 SC 829, OH, at 838C, per Lord Carloway.

claim. Where the damages claim is by one contracting party against the other, the spectre of indeterminate liability is unlikely to arise, thus rendering a claim for pure economic loss more likely to succeed.

Misrepresentation by omission

3.49 In general, an actionable misrepresentation is not constituted merely through failure to inform another person of some matter. This is the case whether or not the parties concerned are contemplating a contractual relationship:

(1) Scots law has not yet imposed upon parties negotiating a contract a general obligation to negotiate in good faith. Thus, failure by *A* to disclose information which might be relevant to *B*'s decision on whether to contract with *A*, or whether to do so on the terms offered, will not generally be actionable in Scots law.

(2) The position in (1) also applies where parties are at arm's length or are not considering a contractual relationship. Thus, where *A* relies upon an erroneously believed state of affairs, in circumstances where *B* knows of this erroneous belief and where *B* might have corrected it, *B* will in general not incur any delictual liability for failing to do so.

3.50 If a party contemplating entering a contract wishes to be provided with information in order for it to assess the desirability of undertaking the contract or in order for it to estimate the cost of its contractual performance, such information should be requested specifically from the other contracting party or its agents. In the absence of such a request, the other party is not obliged to volunteer such information. Thus, an employer under a construction contract is not required to provide information about site conditions unless this has been agreed with the contractor. Where such information is provided, its inaccuracy may be held to amount to a misrepresentation. However, the provision of some information does not necessarily entail that the failure to provide full and complete information will be actionable, unless such failure may be said to render the information provided inaccurate.[68] In the Australian case *Dillingham Construction Pty Ltd v Downs*,[69] the provision by the defendant of certain information in a specification under the heading 'Special Site Conditions' was held not to constitute a warranty that complete information about site conditions had been given. Furthermore, failure to disclose underground mine workings beneath the site was held not to be actionable in tort.

3.51 If an employer knows of site conditions which will materially alter the nature and costs of work contemplated by the contract, but does not inform the contractor, the contractor may be released from any contractual price that might otherwise have been payable for the work, and may be entitled to remuneration on a *quantum meruit* basis for the work done.[70] While this is not the same as a

68 *Boyd & Forrest v Glasgow & SW Railway Co* 1915 SC (HL) 20, 1915 1 SLT 114.
69 (1972) 13 BLR 97.
70 *G Mackay & Son v The Lord Advocate* 1914 1 SLT 33, OH.

damages claim for a misrepresentation by omission, by awarding a *quantum meruit* for work done, substantially the same result may be achieved.

3.52 There are various exceptions to the rule that an omission does not amount to a misrepresentation. An omission by A will constitute a misrepresentation in any of the following circumstances:

(1) where a fiduciary relationship exists between A and B such as to require disclosure of certain facts;[71]

(2) where A and B are negotiating or have entered a contract which is *uberrimae fidei*, that is, of the utmost good faith;[72]

(3) where surrounding circumstances for which A is responsible have created a false impression in the mind of B—eg non-antique goods are displayed in the window of A's antiques shop, thus giving the misleading impression to B that the goods are antique;[73] and

(4) where A has made a representation which was true at the time when made, but which has since become untrue.[74]

USE OR DISCLOSURE OF CONFIDENTIAL INFORMATION OBTAINED DURING NEGOTIATIONS[75]

3.53 The delict of breach of confidence is committed where a party uses or discloses information which it knows or ought reasonably to know is confidential information pertaining to another party. While this obligation is often constituted as a contractual obligation (for instance, in employment contracts), it will arise in any event *ex lege* unless contractually excluded by parties.[76]

3.54 Whilst many breaches of confidence occur in situations where parties are not related by contract or are not negotiating a contract, breach of confidence may also be relevant during the stage of contractual negotiation. Where parties are negotiating the conclusion of a contract, one or both may provide confidential information to the other. Where the contract is not concluded, then the use or disclosure of such information without the relevant party's permission may amount to the delict of breach of confidence:

> *Example 1: A*, a franchisor, is negotiating with *B*, a potential franchisee, concerning the opening of an enterprise in B's locality. During the negotiations *A* discloses

---

71 Fiduciary relationships include trustee and beneficiary, agent and principal, and solicitor and client.

72 A clear example is a contract of insurance: see the comments of Lord President McNeill in *Broatch v Jenkins* (1866) 4 M 1030, IH, at 1032; *The Spathari* 1925 SC (HL) 6.

73 See the obiter comments of Lord Kyllachy in *Patterson v Landsberg & Co* (1905) 7 F 675, IH, at 681: 'the appearance of age and other appearances presented by these articles constituted by themselves misrepresentations'.

74 *Shankland & Co v Robinson & Co* 1920 SC (HL) 103.

75 See further on breach of confidence, Thomson, *Delictual Liability*, at pp 30–33; *Stair Memorial Encyclopaedia*, vol 18, paras **1451–1500**. As to an account of profits for breach of a contractual obligation of confidence, see *Attorney-General v Blake* [2001] 1 AC 268, discussed at **4.58–4.60**. There is some uncertainty as to whether the older remedy of delivery up and destruction of offending material is still available.

76 *Lord Advocate v Scotsman Publications Ltd* 1989 SLT 705, HL; 1988 SLT 490.

information as to its client base in order to impress *B*. *B* decides not to accept *A*'s franchise offer, but subsequently sets up in business for itself and uses the client information provided by *A*. This constitutes a breach of confidence.

Example 2: A, a company producing microelectronic equipment, wishes to enter a contract with a manufacturer for the production of a new type of microchip. It approaches *B*, a potential manufacturer. As part of the negotiations, *A* discloses details of the design of the microchip in order for *B* to ascertain whether it can produce it and at what price. *B* provides an estimate which *A* is unwilling to accept. Subsequently, *C*, a competitor of *A*, approaches *B*, offering to pay for details of *A*'s new design. *B* provides the details known to it to *C*. This constitutes a breach of confidence.

Example 1 constitutes breach of confidence through use, example 2 through disclosure. In each case *A* can sue *B* in delict for damages. In addition to damages, a further two remedies are available: (1) interdict is available to prevent unauthorised use or disclosure of the information, where appropriate; (2) an account of profits may be required of the wrongdoer, that is to say, the wrongdoer may be required to disgorge any profits he has made from the unauthorised use or disclosure of the confidential information.[77] This is a rare case where the restitutionary interest may be protected by a delictual remedy. As was seen at **1.38**, it is usually only the pursuer's *restoration* interest that may be protected by delictual remedies.

3.55 It is a matter of fact whether information has the necessary quality of confidence. Inherent in the notion of confidentiality is primarily the fact that the information is regarded as confidential by the party to whom it relates, but also the number of persons to whom the information is disclosed. Information concerning *A* which it tells to *B* alone will not be confidential if it is disclosed without any requirement that it be kept confidential or without any reasonable expectation on *B*'s part that it is intended to be confidential. On the other hand, information disclosed by *A* to one person or to a limited number of people will be confidential if *A* requests that it be kept so. What of information regarded by *A* as confidential which it discloses to a larger group of people—can this give rise to the obligation of confidentiality? Take the following example for instance:

A, a large public company, invites tenders for the provision of its information technology requirements. In the invitation to tender documentation *A* discloses certain information about itself which is not in the public domain. The invitation to tender is sent out to 500 potential tenderers.

Can the information disclosed be considered confidential given the size of the group to whom disclosure is made? Without any statement that the obligation is to be treated as confidential, this is doubtful, and it may be that disclosure to 500 persons constitutes disclosure to the public at large.[78] However, if the invitation to tender had included a specific statement that the information was confidential and a request that it be kept so, we might wish to reconsider this view. There is as yet no clear answer to this dilemma.[79]

77 *Attorney-General v Guardian Newspapers Ltd (No 2)* [1990] 1 AC 109, [1988] 3 All ER 545, HL. See further **6.20**.
78 But note the comments of Gurry, *Breach of Confidence*, at p 76: 'the communication of a secret for limited business purposes will not destroy its confidentiality'.
79 See H L MacQueen, 'Breach of Confidence', in *Stair Memorial Encyclopaedia*, vol 18, para 1460.

OTHER DELICTUAL ACTIONS DURING CONTRACTUAL NEGOTIATIONS

3.56 Parties who are negotiating a contract may commit delicts against each other in a number of ways other than those already discussed. It is not proposed to go into any great detail on these matters, but brief reference to some potential delictual situations may be useful:

(1) A party who is negotiating with another party may induce the latter to break an existing contract it has with a third party. Inducing breach of contract constitutes a delict.[80]

(2) Fraud may be committed by a party negotiating a contract other than by means of a misrepresentation.[81] Fraud may in addition be constituted by fraudulent concealment.[82] Because, however, as has already been noted, there is in general no duty to disclose information to another contracting party, fraud constituted by concealment operates in only a few recognised scenarios.[83] Fraud may also be constituted by any other types of behaviour which exhibit that quality of conduct identified by Erskine as a 'machination or contrivance to deceive'.[84] For instance, where A, the seller of goods at an auction, persuades B to make bids at the auction which it had no intention of honouring in order to drive up the bidding to A's benefit.[85] This is a fraudulent scheme, and the buyer would be entitled to avoid the contract.

(3) A party negotiating a contract may undertake preliminary or preparatory works which might conceivably cause physical or economic harm to the other party.

WRONGFUL INTERFERENCE WITH PERFORMANCE OF CONTRACT

3.57 Economic delicts are constituted by interference with a person's economic interests by illegal or illegitimate means.[86] There are of course many legitimate means by which one may interfere with another's economic interests. Setting up in business in competition with someone is the most obvious legitimate means of so doing. One illegitimate type of interference has already been discussed, the

---

80 *British Motor Trade Association v Gray* 1951 SC 586, 1951 SLT 247, IH. See Thomson, *Delictual Liability*, at pp 36–39; *Stair Memorial Encyclopaedia*, vol 15, para 576. It should be noted that this delict does not operate only where parties are negotiating a contract: it will apply wherever A procures a breach of a contract between B and C.

81 Misrepresentation is discussed at **3.34–3.53**.

82 Fraudulent concealment is to be distinguished from fraudulent misrepresentation which is constituted by, for instance, deliberately disguising defects in goods. As McBryde has noted (para 14-17) it is hard to define the distinction.

83 See McBryde, paras 14-17–14-25.

84 Erskine, Inst, III,i,16.

85 See the comments of Lord President Inglis in *Shiell v Guthrie's Trustees* (1874) 1 R 1083, IH, at 1089.

86 As Lord President Dunedin put it in *Mackenzie v Iron Trades Employers' Insurance Association Ltd* 1910 SC 79, IH, at 83: 'you are not entitled to interfere with another man's method of gaining his living by illegal means'. See further, *Stair Memorial Encyclopaedia*, vol 15, paras 574–575.

delict of inducing breach of contract[87]. It has been held by English law that a further economic tort with links to contract is that of wrongfully interfering with performance of a contract.[88] This was first recognised as a tort in *Torquay Hotel Co Ltd v Cousins*.[89] In this case, the defendant had not induced a breach of contract, as the non-performance which he had procured was covered by an exemption clause in the relevant contract and was thus not a breach. However, the English Court of Appeal held that the defendant had, by encouraging non-performance, wrongfully interfered with the contract, something it held to be tortious.

3.58 The *Torquay Hotel* decision has yet to come before a Scottish court for a decision on whether it is also the law of Scotland. However, with a general principle of recovery for loss wrongfully caused in Scots law, it is likely that the decision would be applied by the Scottish courts. The Scottish courts might also on such occasion have the opportunity to decide whether inducement of breach of contract and wrongful interference with performance of a contract (together with the further English economic tort of wrongful interference with an individual's right to enter into a contract) are, as has been suggested in English law, simply manifestations of a more general tort of wrongful interference with business. This suggestion has been made most recently by the Court of Appeal in *Lonrho plc v Fayed*.[90] If this approach is to be followed in Scotland, then it will require to be developed over time. The interest an individual has in protecting and increasing his economic assets is not accorded the same high level of protection as that accorded to an individual's interest in his health or property. Part of the difficulty is that competition is inherent in a free market society, and such competition runs the risk that some individuals will profit at the expense of others. It is therefore important that a legal system ponder carefully which sorts of activity are to be permitted, and which deemed illegitimate.

CONCURRENT LIABILITY[91]

3.59 Of all the issues concerning the interface between contract and delict, that of concurrent liability is the one which has aroused the most judicial interest in recent years. 'Concurrency', as it is used in relation to the contract/delict divide, is not a term of art, and it is possible to give to it one or more of several different meanings. It may refer to situations where:

(1) a party who suffers an injury has the choice of suing a number of parties in either contract or delict in respect of the injury, eg *A* suffers personal injury and has the option of suing *B* in contract or *C* in delict in respect of it, because *B* and *C* both broke independent duties which contributed to the injury;

(2) a party incurs liability in respect of a specific action or inaction to a single party in both contract and delict, eg *A* suffers economic loss because its

87 See **3.56**.
88 See Thomson, *Delictual Liability*, pp 39–40.
89 [1969] 2 Ch 106, [1969] 1 All ER 522, CA.
90 [1990] 2 QB 479, [1989] 2 All ER 65, CA (affd in part [1992] 1 AC 448, [1991] 3 All ER 303, HL).
91 See further Hogg, 'Concurrent Liability in the Scots Law of Contract and Delict' 1998 JR 1.

contracting party *B* negligently performs the contractual services to the injury of *A*. *A* may have the option of suing *B* in contract or delict; or

(3) a party incurs liability in respect of a specific action or inaction to several parties, to one or more in contract and to another one or more in delict, eg *A* negligently fails to perform contractual duties it owes to *B*, a failure which also injures *C*. The question arises of whether *A* may be liable to *B* in contract and *C* in delict.

In chapter 1, in relation to the issue of concurrencies in the law of obligations as a whole, concurrency was given a broad meaning, and was used to encompass the idea of the same factual circumstances giving rise to two or more obligations at the same time. It is possible, however, to give to concurrency a more restricted meaning, corresponding to that of scenarios 2 and 3 above. That is to say, concurrency in a narrower sense may be used to refer to cases where it is in relation to one specific defender that the question of remedies in more than one obligation may arise. In what follows, it is proposed to concentrate on the narrower sense of concurrency. However, some of the policy issues at work in relation to the narrower sense of the word also operate in relation to the broader cases corresponding to scenario 1 above, and so some of these cases are also touched on.

3.60 A proper understanding of the hierarchy (or hierarchies) of obligations discloses that the concurrency of a contractual and a delictual obligation is one of the permitted concurrencies. Whilst Stair did not expressly address the issue of concurrency in his *Institutions*, his conception of the nature of delict as a prior, obediential obligation is consistent with a view that delictual obligations will be owed by parties unless and to the extent that they are excluded by contract,[92] a view which would also admit of the possibility of a concurrency of delictual and contractual obligations.

3.61 The bald statement that the contract/delict concurrency is permitted in Scots law is not without its difficulties, as shall be seen. In particular, cases where pure economic loss is at issue and where the pursuer and defender are not in a direct contractual relationship are problematic.

Reasons for choosing contract or delict

3.62 An important preliminary question is: why bother with the issue of concurrency? Does it matter whether a party who might have a claim in either contract or delict in respect of the same facts chooses one or the other? The following matters may affect the choice:

(1) *Measure of damages.* As discussed in chapter 1, contractual damages are designed to protect a party's performance interest, whereas delictual damages protect its restoration interest. It would be sensible therefore for a party to consider whether it might receive a greater award of damages using contract or delict. In addition, the tests for remoteness of damage are different for the two obligations, and the availability of damages for distress in contract is limited.

---

92 See further Hogg, op cit, at pp 5–6.

(2) *Operation of prescription.* There may be cases where one of the contract or delict claims has prescribed but not the other. Clearly in such a case the party wishing to raise a claim will be forced to rely upon the imprescribed claim. This was the reason for some of the plaintiffs in *Henderson v Merrett Syndicates Ltd*[93] choosing to raise an action in tort. It should be added, however, that as Scots law operates the same quinquennial prescriptive period for contract and delict, and provides for a discoverability delay[94] in respect of damages claims under both obligations, this issue is less likely to arise in our system. In English law, which has differential periods, and provides for a discoverability delay only for tort, it has been suggested that these differences should be removed.[95]

(3) *Availability of defences.* Traditionally, certain defences have been considered to operate only in respect of a delictual claim, and others only in respect of contract. Thus, contributory negligence has traditionally been seen as a defence solely applicable to a delictual action, whereas 'compensation' (or 'set-off') has been seen as applying only to a contractual claim. For contributory negligence, however, this restriction was always an uncertain one. The terms of the Law Reform (Contributory Negligence) Act 1945 are arguably wide enough to cover contractual situations which involve 'fault' on the part of the party raising the claim for breach of contract. The opinion has been judicially expressed that a defence of contributory negligence may in some cases be available to a party sued for breach of contract:

> Accountants were sued for breach of contract in respect of having negligently audited the accounts of a company. The accountants pled that the company had been contributorily negligent and should bear some of the losses. The company argued that the defence was irrelevant in a contract claim. The Lord Ordinary (Dawson) held that the plea was not irrelevant in a case such as the one before him where the breach of contract was co-extensive with a duty of care founded upon negligence.[96]

It may be asserted that the current position is that in a breach of contract claim, where a delictual claim might have been pled in respect of the matter at issue, the defence of contributory negligence will be available.[97]

---

93 [1995] 2 AC 145, HL.

94 By 'discoverability delay' is meant the provision of s 11(3) of the Prescription and Limitation (Scotland) Act 1973, which provides that where the creditor under an obligation was not aware, and could not with reasonable diligence have become aware, that loss had occurred, then the obligation to pay damages only commences when the creditor became so aware or could with reasonable diligence have become so aware. It should be noted that this provision applies only to the obligation to pay damages however. It would not, for instance, apply to an action for payment of a monetary obligation.

95 See Burrows, *Understanding the Law of Obligations*, at pp 18-19; see also the judicial criticism of Mustill LJ in *Société Commerciale de Réassurance v ERAS (International) Ltd* [1992] 2 All ER 82, CA, at 85a-c.

96 *Concrete Products (Kirkcaldy) Ltd v Anderson & Menzies* 1996 SLT 587, OH. Contributory negligence has been taken into account in an English concurrent contract/tort action: *Barclays Bank v Fairclough Building (No 2)* 76 BLR 1, [1995] IRLR 605, CA.

97 The Scottish Law Commission has recommended that in all breach of contract actions account should be taken of the extent to which the aggrieved party's conduct contributed to the loss or harm: SLC Report No 174 on Remedies for Breach of Contract at para 4.13.

(4) *Restrictions affecting the availability of a contractual or delictual remedy.* The contract may contain provisions restricting or excluding contractual liability towards the pursuer, but not delictual liability.[98] In such circumstances, a delictual claim will be preferred. On the other hand, as a pursuer may rescind a contract for material breach without the necessity of showing loss, a party which has suffered such material breach might choose to rescind and then sue for nominal damages if it so wished, whereas a delictual claim would not be available for mere nominal loss.

(5) *Matters affecting the likelihood of recovering damages from the defender.* If it is known, for instance, that a third party has issued an indemnity in respect of a delictual claim which might be made against the defender, such a claim may be preferred if there is any likelihood that the defender will be unable to meet the claim out of its own assets.

3.63 Whilst Scots law in general permits concurrent delictual claims, policy considerations play an important role. There is seldom one clear policy at work, and the difficulty for a court lies in knowing where the balance between differing policy considerations is to lie. Furthermore, the balance between policies shifts over time, as the overruling of *Anns v Merton London Borough Council*[99] for one indicates. The cases disclose that the following, among others, are policy considerations currently at work in the area of the contract/delict interface,[100] and indeed in the law of delict in general:

(1) a policy against allowing negligently caused pure economic loss claims in delict, save in established exceptional circumstances. The current stance of the courts in Scotland and England is one of caution so far as extension of liability into new situations is concerned. Claims in respect of defective goods or buildings are considered pure economic loss and are in general irrecoverable;

(2) a policy in favour of allowing physical loss claims in delict;[101]

(3) a policy of protecting parties who reasonably rely upon another from damage caused by the other;[102]

(4) a policy against finding 'peripheral parties' liable in delict where there is a party who may be considered to have caused more directly the loss;[103]

---

98 For a case where a contractual exclusion was construed not to exclude delictual liability, see *Golden Sea Produce Ltd v Scottish Nuclear plc* 1992 SLT 942, OH.

99 [1978] AC 728, [1977] 2 All ER 492, HL, overruled by *Murphy v Brentwood District Council* [1991] 1 AC 398, HL.

100 The policies noted operate both in relation to cases where C is an independent third party, but also to cases where C is linked via contractual chain.

101 This policy may be outweighed by other factors, for instance that the party sued was peripheral to the causal chain: see for instance *Marc Rich & Co Ltd v Bishop Rock Marine* [1996] 1 AC 211, HL.

102 *Hedley Byrne v Heller & Partners* [1964] AC 465, [1963] 2 All ER 575, HL, and the line of cases applying it.

103 See for instance the comments of Lord Steyn in *Marc Rich v Bishop Rock Marine* [1996] 1 AC 211, HL, at 237. See further J Stapleton, 'Duty of Care—Peripheral Parties and Alternative Opportunities for Deterrence' (1995) 111 LQR 301.

(5) a policy against allowing parties who had adequate contractual means to protect themselves against loss from using delict to correct a failure to so protect themselves;[104]

(6) a policy against allowing delictual claims to 'subvert contractual relationships' or a contractual structure adopted by the parties, eg a chain of contracts. This is a policy of uncertain application, however, and it is not at all clear from the authorities that any consistent attitude has been adopted by the courts;

(7) in cases involving the liability in delict of public bodies for breach of a statutory duty, additional statutory considerations come into play.

The application and balancing of these policy issues is considered at appropriate junctures in the following discussion.

3.64 The policy considerations at work in a particular case may differ depending upon whether the case is a simple one involving the liability of A towards B where A and B are in a direct contractual relationship, or whether it is a more complex one involving A's liability towards a third party, C, with whom A is not in direct contractual relationship. For this reason, these two scenarios will be considered in turn.

TWO PARTY CASES

3.65 This scenario asks whether A may be liable to B in delict, where A and B are in a contractual relationship in terms of which the alleged delictual action may also be classified as a breach of the contract. In theory this scenario is easier to analyse. While in general the policy of delict law is against recovery for pure economic loss, in respect of two party cases the policy of the law favours concurrency regardless of whether the loss is physical or purely economic.[105] However, it is also important to consider further distinctions between the cases, for instance, whether the loss consists in a positive detriment or a failure to improve a party's position, or whether the loss is demonstrable actual loss or merely the loss of a chance. These matters are considered in turn.

Physical loss v Pure economic loss

3.66 Case law indicates that where a contracting party has suffered personal injury as the result of a breach of contract, that party may choose to sue in contract or in delict. So, where a doctor negligently injures a patient whilst treating the patient under a contract, an action in delict has been held to lie in Scotland[106] (as well as in

---

104 As demonstrated by the unwillingness of the English courts to permit parties in building contract chains a claim in tort against parties with whom they have no direct contractual link.

105 This is, of course, subject to any restrictions on delictual liability which have been validly imposed by the contract terms.

106 *Edgar v Lamont* 1914 SC 277, 1914 SLT 80, IH.

other jurisdictions, such as South Africa).[107] Similarly, if *B* hired a car from *A*, and the car, as a result of not having been maintained properly, crashed causing personal injury to *B*, this would provide a cause of action for *B* either for breach of contract or in delict. The same reasoning would apply to cases where the loss sustained was property damage. What of pure economic loss? It is axiomatic that the policy of the law discourages recovery for pure economic loss. A prime concern in this respect is the oft-cited 'floodgates' argument, that is, the concern that an indeterminate liability may be occasioned to the wrongdoer if liability is held to exist. This of course is much more likely to be the case where a large number of injured parties may be involved. Where the matter involves only one injured party the floodgates argument may well be inapplicable. Thus in cases where the concurrent delictual claim is sought by a direct contractual party, the courts have permitted such a claim. The following situations, among others, have given rise to liability:

Scenario 1: A professional person who provides services to his client under contract may incur concurrent delictual liability towards the client in respect of careless provision of such services:

(a) Thus, in *Kyle v P & J Stormonth Darling*,[108] a solicitor negligently failed to timeously lodge an appeal on behalf of a client, and, in consequence, the client lost the right to appeal against the judicial decision. The client was permitted to raise an action in delict against the solicitor as an alternative to any claim it may have had under its contract. The contractual duty of care will arise either as the result of an express term in the contract or, in the absence of such, by implication.

(b) A further example of professional negligence arose in *Henderson v Merrett Syndicates Ltd*,[109] where investors in the Lloyds Insurance market (so-called 'Names') incurred liability as underwriters in respect of insurance contracts. The contracts had been underwritten on their behalf by insurance agents. As a result of negligence on the part of the agents, the Names suffered heavy financial losses from the underwriting. They sued the agents in tort rather than in contract, the contract claims having prescribed. The House of Lords held that the Names were entitled to sue in tort, the agents having assumed tortious responsibility for the services provided.

Scenario 2: An employer who has caused loss to an employee through its negligence may be liable in contract if this negligence also amounts to a breach of contract. The English case *Hagen v ICI Chemicals and Polymers Ltd*[110] exemplifies this. ICI was negotiating with another company, Redpath Engineering Services (RES), for the transfer of ICI's central engineering division to RES. As part of the contract, RES were to take on several hundred of ICI's engineering employees. The employees were concerned about aspects of the transfer, including the impact it might have upon their pensions. ICI made various representations to the employees, including that the pension provision offered by RES would be broadly similar to ICI's (to within half a per cent). The transfer was effected, but the employees subsequently claimed to have suffered negative pension deviations of up to 5 per cent. The employees sued ICI for

---

107 *Van Wyk v Lewis* 1924 AD 438.
108 1994 SLT 191, IH. The same situation arose in the earlier cases of *Robertson v Bannigan* 1965 SC 20, and *Yeoman's Executrix v Ferries* 1967 SC 255, 1967 SLT 332, OH. English law has also recognised the tortious liability of a solicitor to his client: *Midland Bank Trust Co Ltd v Hett, Stubbs & Kemp* [1979] Ch 384.
109 [1995] 2 AC 145, [1994] 3 All ER 506, HL. The case also involved claims against third parties, related to the plaintiffs through a contractual chain. The claims against these third parties are discussed at **3.119**.
110 [2002] IRLR 31, QB.

these losses. The English High Court held (i) that there was both an implied duty in contract and a common law duty of care in tort upon ICI to take care in providing correct information to their employees; (ii) the existence of the contractual duty did not preclude the employees from suing in tort; and (iii) the employees were entitled to damages in tort for having relied upon the negligent misstatements made by ICI.

Scenario 3: A builder who negligently constructs a dwellinghouse which is defective, and which causes the purchaser economic and other loss, may be liable in contract or delict to the purchaser. Alternative claims in contract and delict to this effect were held relevant in the Outer House in *Black v Gibson*.[111]

3.67   An interesting feature of the *Hagen v ICI* case is comments by the judge, Elias J, on the relative damages which might have been awarded had the case been decided in contract rather than tort.[112] The tortious damages were assessed on the basis that, had the misstatements not been made, the employees would collectively have petitioned ICI to renegotiate the transfer of their contracts of employment. This would have resulted, the judge thought, in a revised deal under which no employee would have received a pension deal no more than 2 per cent less favourable than the existing pension scheme. On the other hand, the judge noted that contractual damages would have had to have been assessed on the basis that had the breach of contract not occurred, the employer would then have sought to perform the contract in the manner most favourable to it.[113] On that basis, the evidence was that ICI would have sought to lawfully terminate the contracts of employment in accordance with the notice provisions. This, said Elias J, would have meant that the employees would have been much worse off so far as any contractual damages claim would have been concerned. On such a basis, their damages claim would have been restricted to the period of notice. This approach is consistent with that taken by the Scottish courts.[114] This is a pertinent reminder of the fact that in choosing which concurrent avenue to use, contract or delict, a party should strongly consider the likely damages award from each. As *Hagen v ICI* indicates, a contractual damages claim can in practice be less valuable than a delictual one.[115]

3.68   The most influential of the concurrency cases narrated above is that discussed under scenario 1(b), the House of Lords' decision in *Henderson v Merrett Syndicates*.[116] Lord Goff delivered the leading speech. His Lordship, having noted that in the contracts between the Names and the insurance agents there was to be implied a term that the agents would exercise skill and care in the performance of

---

111   1992 SLT 1073, OH.

112   [2002] IRLR 31 at 51–52.

113   In so concluding, Elias J applied the dictum of Scrutton LJ in *Abrahams v Herbert Reach Ltd* [1922] 1 KB 477, CA, at 482 that, in assessing contractual damages for breach, the court may assume that, had the breach not occurred, the contract breaker would have, if he had several options open to him, performed the contract in the way most favourable to himself. Elias J held that this principle was not relevant to the tortious claim.

114   *Morran v Glasgow Council of Tenants* 1997 SLT 1133, IH.

115   On the other hand, in *Black v Gibson* 1992 SLT 1076 OH, an action pled on the basis of breach of contract and of negligence, the Lord Ordinary (Osborne) held it was permissible for the pursuer to include a claim for damages for worry and inconvenience, because 'the grounds of action, while including breach of contract, also include alleged fault' (at 1080D). This is a somewhat unorthodox approach, as it suggests that a pursuer is not limited to one only of contractual or delictual damages, but may 'cherry pick', so to speak, elements of both in order to maximise his claim.

116   [1995] 2 AC 145, HL.

their functions under the contract,[117] considered the arguments for and against permitting a concurrent claim in tort. The agents argued that:

(1) imposing a duty of care in tort upon them would be inconsistent with the contractual relationship between the parties. The contract regulated exclusively for the relationship between them, and therefore a tortious duty was excluded; and

(2) to allow the Names to make use of a more favourable limitation period for the tortious claim, would deprive the agents of their contractual expectation and thwart the intention of Parliament.

3.69 The first of these arguments is the so-called 'primacy of contract' argument. This argument, deriving from the notion of freedom of contract, conceives that parties to a contract have an absolute right to determine the content of their relationship in the contract and that, if they choose not to provide for a specific type of liability, it is to be assumed that they intended it not to apply. However, this doctrine, in its pure form, can be seen to be inconsistent with the understanding in Scots law of delict as a prior, imposed obligation. What did Lord Goff make of this argument? His Lordship was confronted by a judicial expression of this doctrine in the following comments of Lord Scarman, delivered in the Privy Council decision *Tai Hing Cotton Mill Ltd v Liu Chong Hing Bank*:[118]

'Their Lordships do not believe that there is anything to the advantage of the law's development in searching for a liability in tort where the parties are in a contractual relationship. This is particularly so in a commercial relationship . . . their Lordships believe it to be correct in principle and necessary for the avoidance of confusion in the law to adhere to the contractual analysis: on principle because it is a relationship in which the parties have, subject to a few exceptions, the right to determine their obligations to each other, and for the avoidance of confusion because different consequences do follow according to whether liability arises from contract or tort, eg in the limitation of action.'[119]

3.70 Whilst, as Lord Goff pointed out, that case was concerned with the issue of whether a more extensive duty in tort should be imposed, nonetheless Lord Scarman's view states a very clear opposition to concurrent liability. Lord Goff noted, however, that even before Lord Scarman's comments, English law had been moving towards an acceptance of concurrent liability. The clearest apology for concurrency was, in Lord Goff's opinion, to be found in the approach of Oliver J (as he then was) in *Midland Bank Trust Co Ltd v Hett Stubbs & Kemp*,[120] who found in favour of a client seeking to raise a concurrent tortious claim against its negligent solicitor. In Lord Goff's view, such an approach was consistent with that adopted in *Donoghue v Stevenson*[121] and *Hedley Byrne & Co Ltd v Heller & Partners Ltd*.[122] Lord Goff summed up his view thus:

---

117 [1995] 2 AC at 176G, per Lord Goff.
118 [1986] AC 80, [1985] 2 All ER 947, PC.
119 [1986] AC at 107B–D, per Lord Scarman. These views were referred to approvingly by the Lord Ordinary in *Hughes v Barratt Urban Construction (Scotland) Ltd*, 20 March 2003 (unreported).
120 [1979] Ch 384, [1978] 3 All ER 571, Ch.
121 1932 SC (HL) 31, 1932 SLT 317, HL.
122 [1964] AC 465, [1963] 2 All ER 575, HL.

'My own belief is that, in the present context, the common law is not antipathetic to concurrent liability, and that there is no sound basis for a rule which automatically restricts the claimant to either a tortious or a contractual remedy. The result may be untidy; but, given that the tortious duty is imposed by the general law, and the contractual duty is attributable to the will of the parties, I do not find it objectionable that the claimant may be entitled to take advantage of the remedy which is most advantageous to him, subject only to ascertaining whether the tortious duty is so inconsistent with the applicable contract that, in accordance with ordinary principle, the parties must be taken to have agreed that the tortious remedy is to be limited or excluded.'[123]

The words 'in the present context' are important, for, as shall be seen, the policy of the law has been antipathetic to concurrent pure economic claims in other contexts.

3.71 As to the second argument advanced by the agents (that concerning limitation periods), it may be seen from the passage just quoted that Lord Goff was not concerned that a concurrent claim would allow the plaintiffs to avoid the contractual limitation. Whilst acknowledging the argument in favour of ironing out discrepancies between causes of action such as different limitation periods, his Lordship noted that 'this is perhaps crying for the moon; and with the law in its present form, practical considerations of this kind cannot sensibly be ignored.'[124]

3.72 As to establishment of the tortious duty in the circumstances of the case before him, Lord Goff stated that the basis of the imposition of a duty of care upon the insurance agents was the principle of 'assumption of responsibility' first established in *Hedley Byrne*:

'[T]here is in my opinion plainly an assumption of responsibility in the relevant sense by the managing agents towards the Names in their syndicates. The managing agents have accepted the Names as members of a syndicate under their management. They obviously hold themselves out as possessing a special expertise to advise the Names on the suitability of risks to be underwritten; and on the circumstances in which, and the extent to which, reinsurance should be taken out and claims should be settled. The Names, as the managing agents well knew, placed implicit reliance on that expertise, in that they gave authority to the managing agents to bind them to contracts of insurance and reinsurance and to the settlement of claims. I can see no escape from the conclusion that, in these circumstances, prima facie a duty of care is owed in tort by the managing agents to such Names.'[125]

3.73 Criticism has already been made of the rationale of 'assumption of responsibility' as a reason for imposing a duty of care:[126] it borrows the terminology of voluntary obligations and improperly applies it to imposed obligations. This masks the real policy reasons underlying the decision. The House of Lords

---

123 [1995] 2 AC 193H–194B, per Lord Goff.
124 [1995] 2 AC at 186A–B, per Lord Goff.
125 [1995] 2 AC at 182D–F, per Lord Goff.
126 See **1.55–1.57**.

imposed a duty of care because it thought that one *ought to apply* in these circumstances. This conclusion is reached because it is a policy of the law that reasonable reliance by a party upon the skill and expertise of another ought to be protected. It would have been better for this policy to be expressed as the principal reason for reaching the decision, rather than adopting the unhelpful terminology of assumption of responsibility. Use of the notion of 'assumption of responsibility' additionally fails to explain adequately why an assumption of responsibility does not apply in other cases, for instance between a subcontractor in a building contract and the owner of the land. All Lord Goff says in *Henderson* of such cases is: 'there is generally no assumption of responsibility by the subcontractor or supplier direct to the building owner'[127] without explaining why.

3.74 Lord Goff made reference to comparative jurisprudence in reaching his conclusions in *Henderson*. This comparative jurisprudence is not, however, universally in favour of concurrent liability. One example of a jurisdiction which has chosen to restrict concurrent liability claims for pure economic loss between contracting parties is South Africa. The leading case on the question of a concurrent delictual action for pure economic loss caused by one contracting party to the other is *Lillicrap, Wassenaar and Partners v Pilkington Brothers (SA)(Pty) Ltd*:[128]

> Lillicrap contracted[129] with Pilkington to provide the latter with professional services in connection with the planning and construction of a glass plant. Pilkington raised an action of damages in delict against Lillicrap alleging that negligence by the latter in the performance of its services had caused Pilkington losses of R3,600,000. The question before the court was whether Lillicrap owed any duty in delict coterminous with its contractual obligation. The Appellate Division of the Supreme Court held that no delictual duty was owed by Lillicrap for the losses.

3.75 The leading judgment was given by Grosskopf AJA, with whom the majority concurred. He noted that, in principle, South African law, like Roman as well as Roman Dutch law, permitted a plaintiff a concurrent cause of action (*concursus actionum*) in delict where he already enjoyed a contractual right to sue. He cited the example of the negligent doctor, who might be sued in contract or delict. However, such delictual liability had not, to date, been recognised as arising for pure economic loss between contracting parties. South African law, he stated, took a conservative approach to the extension of liability under the *lex aquilia*.[130] Its extension to the situation before him was not justified, for the following reasons:

(1) where the contract persisted, each party had an adequate, contractual remedy for breach;[131]
(2) delictual liability did not fit comfortably into a setting where the parties were in

---

127 [1995] 2 AC 145 at 196C.
128 1985 (1) SA 475.
129 Subsequent to part-performance of Lillicrap's contractual obligations, the parties agreed to the interposition of a third party between them. Lillicrap thus became subcontractor, and the interposed party the main contractor. The case thus raised issues of concurrent liability both as it relates to direct contracting parties but also to parties indirectly linked via a contractual chain.
130 1985 (1) SA at 500C–D.
131 1985 (1) SA at 500F.

a contractual relationship because such parties in general contemplated that the contract would lay down their reciprocal rights and obligations;[132] and

(3) it would be difficult to determine what standard of duty should apply in delict, and it would be problematic to allow a standard other than the contractual one.

3.76 The first justification is often referred to as the 'economy of remedies' theory, and is a view that, where a remedy exists in law for breach of a right, the law should not seek to add further remedies for such breach if the existing remedy is adequate. While this argument recommends itself to a degree, it is clear that Scots law has not traditionally adopted it.[133] Thus, the fact that damages might be an adequate remedy for a breach of contract has never of itself been a good reason why specific implement should be refused.[134] The second justification given by Grosskopf AJA has already been encountered in the excerpt from Lord Scarman's speech in *Tai Hing Cotton Mill*—the primacy of contract. Again, it has been argued that this doctrine in its pure form does not accord with the Scots hierarchy of obligations. In addition, it is clear from South African law that some situations (such as that of the negligent doctor) do give rise to concurrent liability, so the primacy of contract clearly cannot apply in every case. The third justification, that of differing standards of duty, does raise difficult issues, but not insurmountable ones. No one would deny, for instance, that parties would be free in their contract to specify which standard of performance should apply in contract as well as delict.

3.77 While the decision in *Lillicrap* has not been universally welcomed by South African commentators, it remains the leading authority on the question. It is clear from the South African experience that the permissibility of concurrency between contracting parties in some situations but not in others is the result of policy considerations. It is also clear that the policies at work are not those listed by Grosskopf AJA, as these would equally apply to the cases where concurrency has been allowed. The South African courts, like the House of Lords in *Henderson v Merrett*, have been shy at naming the underlying policy considerations at work preventing or justifying concurrency.

3.78 What of the Scots view: is *Henderson* or *Lillicrap* favoured in our law? It has already been suggested in the foregoing comments on *Lillicrap*, that the stated reasons for denying liability in that case would be insufficient to prevent liability from arising in Scots law. No Scottish case post-*Henderson* has tackled similar facts, but *Henderson* has been referred to approvingly in the Outer House in *Strathford East Kilbride Ltd v HLM Design Ltd*.[135] It is likely and appropriate that this trend will continue and that concurrent economic loss claims in delict will be permitted between contracting parties, unless and to the extent that these are validly excluded by the terms of the contract.

132 1985 (1) SA at 500G.
133 Cf the problematic case of *Middleton v Douglass* 1991 SLT 726, OH, which suggests that no delictual claim for pure economic loss should lie where the claim is essentially a mirror of a contractual claim.
134 Cf the position in England, where if damages are deemed adequate, specific performance will not be granted.
135 1999 SLT 121, 1997 SCLR 877, OH. However, in the unreported decision of *Hughes v Barratt Urban Construction (Scotland) Ltd*, OH, 20 March 2002, a concurrent delictual pure economic case against a builder was dismissed without any reference to *Henderson*.

Positive detriment v Failure to improve

3.79   As discussed in chapter 1, contract protects (primarily) a party's perfor-mance interest, and delict only its restoration interest. For that reason, a con-current delictual action will not be able to be brought for an amount which represents a failure on the part of the wrongdoer to improve the victim's position.

3.80   Consider the following examples:

> *Example 1:* A seeks advice from B, its insurance broker, as to whether a specific type of insurance would be advisable given its circumstances. B negligently advises A that the insurance is not required. As a result, A suffers losses totalling £1,000 for which it is unable to make an insurance claim.

> *Example 2:* A instructs B, its solicitor, to conclude a contract on its behalf for the purchase of a shopping centre as a going concern for £1,000,000. The price is paid and the sale takes place. B has negligently failed to notice that several of the leases in place in the centre contain defective rent review clauses. In consequence A's expected rental income from the transaction will be £150,000 less than expected. A succeeds in selling the shopping centre to C for £900,000.

The losses of £1,000 suffered by A in example 1 may be claimed in either contract or delict. B has caused *positive detriment* to A's economic position when compared with the position before the occurrence of the delict. Restoration to that prior position permits reparation in delict for the £1,000 loss. In example 2, however, if A wishes to use its concurrent claim in delict, its damages will amount to only £100,000. This represents the price paid for the property less the price of resale. A is not, under protection of its *restoration* interest, permitted to claim the £150,000 by which it expected to *improve its position*. Clearly in this situation it will, all other things being equal, be in A's interest to use its contractual claim.

3.81   What the foregoing shows, is that it may in some cases make a difference to a concurrent delictual claim to consider whether the essence of the pursuer's claim is that the defender has failed to improve its position. Damages representing expected gains are not to be awarded in delict, though they may be in contract.

3.82   It may be useful to expand upon a point touched upon in chapter 1: failure to improve a party's position is different from failure to confer a benefit. The law of delict is not fundamentally antagonistic to a damages claim for failure to confer a benefit, so long as the benefit is designed to preserve a party's position rather than improve it. In fact, many delictual claims involve circumstances where through its negligence a party fails to confer a benefit upon another. This will be the case where the parties have had prior contact which has led one party to believe that it will be benefited by the other.[136] This will not of course be the case where the parties have had no prior contact: one cannot expect to have a positive benefit conferred upon one by a stranger. However, both the examples cited in **3.80** are situations where through the prior relationship of the parties the defender

---

136 It is in theory possible to describe every delictual situation as involving a failure to confer a benefit. Thus, it could be said that the pedestrian expects the driver of a passing car to confer upon the former the benefit of the latter's careful driving. However, this essentially describes a negative benefit—the benefit consists of not being injured, of being left alone. The usage of benefit in the main text is reserved for positive actions, rather than negative ones.

was expected to confer a benefit upon the pursuer. In the first example the benefit was the provision of competent advice concerning insurance needs, in the second the benefit was the provision of competent legal services. In both these situations a delictual claim would be admissible. The difference lies simply in that in example 1 the benefit sought (insurance) was intended to protect a party's position from being adversely affected, whereas in example 2 the benefit sought was intended to improve the party's position. As was seen, the element reflecting an expected improvement cannot be claimed in damages. Delict then is not antagonistic to every claim for failure to confer a benefit; it is, however, antagonistic to damages claims in respect of a benefit intended to improve a party's position.[137]

Actual loss v Loss of a chance

3.83 A number of reported cases involving concurrent claims in delict have been for loss of a chance rather than in respect of demonstrable actual loss.[138] A lost chance case is one where, due to some inherent uncertainty in the causal chain, a causal link cannot be made between the defender's negligence and the loss suffered by the pursuer. In such a case, the pursuer may seek to have compensated not the actual loss suffered by it (for which it cannot make out causation on the balance of probabilities), but rather the loss of the chance of avoiding the loss. Such a claim is only sustainable if there is an inherent uncertainty in the causal chain between the alleged cause and the actual loss which is due to a lack of scientific knowledge or to the inherent unpredictability of human behaviour.[139] The mere fact that the pursuer is unable to gather sufficient evidence will not suffice to permit a lost chance claim if proof of the causal link with the actual loss would otherwise be possible.

3.84 Consider the following examples:

Example 1: *A* is injured through the negligence of *B*. *A* is taken to a private hospital where he is negligently diagnosed by *C*, a doctor, who prescribes some antibiotics and sends *A* home. Three days later, *A*'s condition having worsened, *A* returns to hospital. On this occasion *A* is properly diagnosed. It is now, however, too late to prevent *A* suffering a medical condition, X, caused by the original injuries. Some people who are properly diagnosed immediately following injury can with correct treatment avoid contracting X, some, however, do not. Can *A* sue *C* in contract or delict for the injuries

137   The argument advanced here differs from the earlier position stated in Hogg, 1998 JR 1 at pp 10–11, where it was stated that delict ought not to admit claims for failure to confer a benefit.

138   For comment on this area of the law see further: A Phillips, 'Lost Chances in Delict: All or Nothing?' (1995) 5 JR 401; H Reece, 'Losses of Chance in the Law' 1996 MLR 188; M Hogg, 'Lost chances in contract and delict' 1997 SLT (News) 71; M Hogg, 'Paul v Ogilvy: A Lost Opportunity for Lost Chance Recovery' [2003] 7 ELR 86.

139   The essential criterion for a lost chance case was succinctly put by the Australian judge Deane J in *Commonwealth of Australia v Amann* (1991) 174 CLR 64 as being 'where lack of information, insufficiency of current knowledge or the unpredictability of hypothetical or future events precludes a non-speculative finding about what would have actually occurred or will actually occur but evidence (eg expert medical opinion), common sense or common experience enables an estimate of the approximate extent of the chance that a particular benefit would have been or will be actually sustained or that a particular detriment will be or would have been actually sustained' (at 146C, col 1).

sustained through having contracted X? If *A* is able to prove that, on the balance of probabilities, he would have been one of the people who would have benefited from proper treatment, then *A* will be able to sue *C* for having contracted condition X. If it can be shown on the balance of probabilities that *A* would have been one of the people who would *not* have benefited from proper treatment, *A* will not be able to sue *C*. If, however, medical science is unable to say whether *A* would or would not have benefited from proper treatment, *A* may seek to claim against *C* for loss of the chance of avoiding X, so long as *A* can show that he had a substantial chance of avoiding X. The damages *A* might receive in such a case ought to be in proportion to the percentage of the chance lost.[140]

Example 2: *A* contracts with his solicitor, *B*, for *B* to negotiate a contract on *A*'s behalf with *C*. Due to *B*'s negligence, the solicitor fails to ensure that a certain clause is put into the negotiations for inclusion in the final contract between *A* and *C*. As a result of the clause's non-inclusion, *A* incurs financial liabilities following conclusion of the contract. Can *A* sue *B* in contract or in delict for the financial losses suffered? If *A* can prove on the balance of probabilities that, had *B* included the clause in the negotiations it would have been accepted by *C* for inclusion in the contract, *A* is permitted to claim his financial losses. However, if *B* argues that looking back it is now impossible to state how it would have reacted to the inclusion of the clause in the negotiations, and that it is therefore impossible to state whether it would have accepted the clause, *A* will be unable to show that the losses would have been avoided and will thus be unable to sue for such. However, if *A* can prove on the balance of probabilities that there was a substantial chance that the clause would have been included in the contract, *A* will be permitted to sue for damages for having lost this chance. The damages awarded will be in proportion to the percentage of the chance lost.[141]

Example 3: *A* is injured when a car hits him as he is crossing the road. *A* cannot identify the driver of the car. However, *B* and *C* state that the driver was *Z*, driving a car with a particular licence plate. *D* and *E* state that it was *Y* driving a different car with a different licence plate. If the court finds the testimony of all witnesses equally credible, it will find that *A* is unable to succeed in a claim against either *Y* or *Z* for the actual injuries sustained as *A* is unable to prove on the balance of probabilities that it was either of them. Neither is *A* permitted to bring a lost chance claim against either party because *A*'s inability to prove his case for actual loss against *Y* or *Z* is not due to a lack of scientific knowledge or to the unpredictability of human behaviour, it is simply due to inconclusive evidence.

3.85   The Scottish and English courts have recognised the validity of lost chance claims, although this has not yet been extended to cases where the pursuer is alleging that the chance lost was a chance of benefiting from medical treatment.[142]

---

140   The facts are based upon those in *Hotson v East Berkshire Area Health Authority* [1987] AC 750, HL, save that the hospital was not a private one. The House of Lords decided in that case that it was possible to determine into which category the injured party fell, holding that the medical evidence indicated that he would not have benefited from prompt treatment and thus refusing his claim for damages in tort.

141   The facts are based upon *Allied Maples Group Ltd v Simmons and Simmons (a firm)* [1995] 4 All ER 907, [1995] 1 WLR 1602, CA.

142   In Scotland, the now dated decision in *Kenyon v Bell* 1953 SC 125, OH, is still referred to as authority for denying medical lost chance claims. In England, the decision in *Judge v Huntingdon* [1995] 6 Med LR 223, 27 BMLR 107, QB, was in favour of recovery for a medical lost chance. However, more recently the Court of Appeal has disapproved of recovery in medical cases: *Gregg v Scott* [2002] All ER (D) 418, [2002] EWCA Civ 1471, CA. On medical lost chances see H Stewart, 'Medical Lost Chances' (2000) SLPQ 147.

Moreover they have permitted concurrent delictual claims to be made for a lost chance. In the leading English authority, *Allied Maples v Simmons and Simmons*,[143] with facts essentially the same as in example 2 above, the plaintiff was permitted to sue for damages in tort rather than in contract in respect of the negligence of the solicitor. In Scotland, concurrent delictual claims for a lost chance have also been upheld against solicitors.[144] In the most recent Scottish case, a claim for loss of a chance of obtaining insurance cover at lower rates, stated both on contractual and delictual grounds, was allowed to proceed to proof before answer,[145] and the requirement, made in the older cases, of demonstrating that what had been lost was a 'legal right' was not insisted upon.

3.86 Difficulty has been caused by the decision of the House of Lords in *Fairchild v Glenhaven Funeral Services Ltd*:[146]

> The claimant's late husband had, during his working life, come into contact with asbestos while working for a number of different employers and at a number of sites. He went on to contract a mesothelioma of the pleura, from which he died. The precise mechanics of this disease were as yet unknown, but the medical evidence indicated that a mesothelioma could be triggered by a single fibre of asbestos. Once the disease had been triggered, further exposure to asbestos did not aggravate the symptoms of the disease. The plaintiff sued a number of parties, including a company (W) on whose premises Mr Fairchild had worked with asbestos. W admitted that Mr Fairchild had been exposed to a substantial amount of asbestos while working at its premises. The claimant was unable to prove (using either the 'but for' or 'material contribution' tests of causation) that her late husband's fatal illness had been triggered by the inhalation of asbestos on W's premises. The claim was therefore dismissed by the Court of Appeal. On appeal to the House of Lords, the House found by a majority that it was sufficient for the claimant to succeed that she demonstrate that exposure to asbestos on W's premises had materially increased the risk of her husband contracting a mesothelioma. This had been demonstrated on the facts, and damages were therefore awarded against W.

In so finding the House of Lords resuscitated the 'material increase in risk' test of causation first adopted in *McGhee v National Coal Board*,[147] a test which had lain dormant for a number of years and had been of doubtful application. Recourse to the test allows a pursuer to recover *full damages* against any defender who can be said to have materially increased the risk of injury to the pursuer, as occurred in *Fairchild*, whereas it has already been seen that a successful claimant in a lost chance case receives only a percentage of damages.

3.87 The difficulty which *Fairchild* has raised for lost chance analysis is that the House of Lords has decided that the type of case in which material increase in risk analysis is appropriate is the very same as one of the types of case (lack of scientific or medical knowledge) in which lost chance analysis has been thought to be appropriate. When Lord Rodger said in *Fairchild* that the material increase in risk test was

---

143 [1995] 4 All ER 907, [1995] 1 WLR 1602, CA.
144 *Kyle v P & J Stormonth Darling* 1994 SLT 191, 1993 SCLR 18, IH; *Paul v Ogilvy* 2001 SLT 171, OH.
145 *McCrindle v Wallace Corroon* 2002 SLT 209, OH.
146 [2003] 1 AC 32, [2002] 3 All ER 305, HL.
147 1973 SLT 14, HL.

'designed to resolve the difficulty that arises where it is inherently impossible for the claimant to prove exactly how his injury was caused. It applies, therefore, where the claimant has proved all that he possibly can, but the causal link could only ever be established by scientific investigation and the current state of the relevant science leaves it uncertain exactly how the injury was caused'[148]

he was expressing a criterion that has been used to describe the basis of a lost chance claim.[149] It is perhaps unsurprising that the criterion used under both approaches is essentially the same, as materially increasing the risk of injury is simply another way of saying that a material (or substantial) chance of avoiding the injury has been lost.[150] However, both approaches cannot be right. Either a pursuer ought, in such a case, to be able to sue for the lost chance of avoiding an illness (and receive damages corresponding to the magnitude of the chance lost), or else he ought to be entitled to damages for the loss itself, on the basis that the defender caused the loss by materially increasing the risk that it would be occasioned (in which event, the pursuer will receive full damages).

3.88 It is suggested that lost chance analysis is the more appropriate route, despite the clear line adopted by the House of Lords in *Fairchild*. The material increase in risk test seriously undermines the orthodox rules of causation, and runs the risk that a defender may be penalised for a loss which in reality he did not cause. The lost chance approach provides an equitable *via media*, which permits to a pursuer a right of limited recovery upon demonstration that the loss of a substantial chance of avoiding injury has been caused by the defender. The House of Lords should revisit its decision in *Fairchild*.

THREE PARTY CASES

3.89 It is instructive to consider whether the courts have distinguished three party cases involving physical loss from those involving pure economic loss. It will be seen that the outcome may differ in respect of a further typological division, namely between those cases where the three parties are linked by a contractual matrix (A–B–C) and those cases where although there is a contract A–B, C has no contractual link with either of these parties. These two issues are considered below. The points made above in relation to failure to improve and loss of a chance in respect of two party cases apply equally to three party cases and are not repeated below.

Physical loss

3.90 As with concurrent liability between directly contracting parties, as a general rule the policy of the law is sympathetic to delictual claims by a third party, C, for personal injury or physical damage caused by A, whether or not C is a wholly independent party or is linked through a contractual chain.

---

148 [2002] 3 All ER 305, HL, at 383f–g.
149 See above at **3.83**, especially the comment of Deane J in *Commonwealth of Australia v Amann* noted at fn 139.
150 A point made by A Phillips in 'Lost Chances in Delict: All or Nothing?' 1995 JR 401 at 411.

C as wholly independent third party

3.91 In relation to physical damage, the classic case of concurrent delictual liability to an independent third party is *Donoghue v Stevenson*, a case which has already been discussed above.[151] As with two party cases, it is in general easy to recover for physical damage using a concurrent claim, so long as the component requirements for a duty of care (foreseeability, proximity, and justice, fairness and reasonableness) can be made out. Any attempt to restrict such liability to a third party in delict in terms of the contract or by means of a non-contractual notice will be regulated by the Unfair Contract Terms Act 1977.[152]

3.92 Whilst one might have imagined that there would be no overriding policy considerations mitigating against imposition of delictual liability in such cases, the decision of the House of Lords in *Marc Rich & Co AG v Bishop Rock Marine Co Ltd*[153] (discussed at **3.99**) suggests that some such may exist in particular circumstances.

C indirectly linked to A linked through a contractual chain

3.93 The reason why a claim in delict rather than a contractual claim may be sought in such cases is that the party with whom the injured party has a contract may be insolvent or may have insufficient funds to meet the costs of the claim. Two slightly different types of case may be distinguished here. In the *first type*, there are claims where the contractual structure *A–B–C* is a single contractual framework where the nature of the contracts is related to a specific matter and the parties are aware of the structure and the existence of parties to it. The classic example is the construction contract chain:

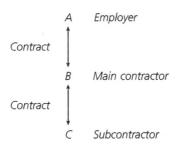

In this type of arrangement, the parties are aware of the overall nature of the project and of the existence of other parties and their function in the contractual structure. This situation may be distinguished from the *second type*, where although there are contracts *A–B* and *B–C* which affect a particular interest of

151 See **3.07**.
152 In particular, s 16.
153 [1995] 3 All ER 307, HL.

C, the contracts are not part of an overall structure and *A* and *C* are not necessarily aware of each other's existence:

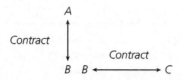

Falling within the first type of case is *British Telecommunications plc v James Thomson & Sons (Engineers) Ltd*,[154] and within the second type *Marc Rich & Co AG v Bishop Rock Marine Co Ltd*.[155]

Type 1

3.94 The facts of *BT v Thomson* were as follows:

> The defenders were subcontractors employed by the main contractor to carry out the steel work on a project to renovate a building. As a result of the defender's negligence, a fire broke out at the site causing physical damage to the premises. The owners of the building, the pursuers, sued the defenders in delict for the cost of repairing the damage. The defenders argued that they did not owe the pursuers a duty of care because it would not be fair, just and reasonable to impose such a duty upon them. This was argued on the basis that, in terms of the main contract, fire damage was to be insured against by the pursuers. The main contract also stated that the main contractor and nominated subcontractors were to have the benefit of a waiver of liability for such fire damage. The House of Lords (approving the tripartite test for a duty of care laid down in *Marc Rich*) held that the defenders were liable in delict for the damage caused. As the defenders were only domestic subcontractors, and not nominated subcontractors, the terms of the main contract reinforced rather than negated any duty of care on the part of the defenders.

3.95 As it is sometimes argued that the very nature of contractual chains such as existed in this case negatives a duty of care, it is worthwhile noting the comments of Lord Mackay, who said:

> 'In my view the contractual provisions reinforce rather than negative the existence of a duty of care toward BT by Thomson in the circumstances of the present case.'[156]

This is an important point. It is submitted that Lord Mackay was correct in his analysis. It is too simplistic to say, as has sometimes been said, that a contractual chain will always distance parties or will always prevent sufficient proximity.[157] One should have regard to the specific terms of the contracts to see whether they have any bearing upon the proximity of the parties. Where the loss suffered is physical, then unless there are clear factors distancing the parties (such as a relevant

---

154 1999 SC (HL) 9, 1999 SLT 224, HL.
155 [1996] AC 211, [1995] 3 All ER 307, HL.
156 1999 SC (HL) at 15F, per Lord Mackay.
157 This issue is discussed further below at **3.117** ff in relation to pure economic loss claims across a contractual network.

exemption of liability in the contractual arrangements), the general policy of the law favouring recovery for physical damage should permit a claim in delict by a party indirectly connected to the wrongdoer in a contractual chain such as this.

3.96 So far as Scots law is concerned, this decision is important as it clears up any uncertainty that existed as to the possibility of parties in a construction contract chain being proximate for the purposes of physical injury. English law recognises the liability of builders in tort for physical damage caused to a party with whom they are not in a direct relationship. Lord Bridge referred to this duty in *Murphy v Brentwood District Council*:[158]

'If a builder erects a structure containing a latent defect which renders it dangerous to persons or property, he will be liable in tort for injury to persons or damage to property resulting from that dangerous defect.'[159]

Such liability has been applied by the common law not just to builders,[160] but to architects also.[161]

3.97 The possibility was also considered in *Murphy* that a local authority might be liable under English law for physical damage suffered by the purchaser of a property in respect of defective plans which had been approved by the council.[162] Such a view is less likely to be taken in Scotland, if recent controversial decisions on the liability of local authorities under the Building (Scotland) Act 1959 are correct.[163]

3.98 The decision in *BT*, affirming the possibility of the delictual liability of builders for physical damage towards parties with whom they have no contract, raises the question of whether a builder will be liable to *any* party which it can reasonably foresee will be injured by its negligence. The comment of Lord Oliver in *Murphy* cited above suggests that this will be so, subject to the caveat introduced by *Marc Rich* that there must be no exceptional policy reasons mitigating against such a duty. Consider the following cases:

Example 1: *A*, a builder, constructs a house for *B*, the purchaser. *B* sells the house to *C*. *C* lets the house to *D*. One day, while *D* is sitting in his front room, the plastering on the ceiling gives way and collapses on him causing him serious injury. It is discovered that the plastering was negligently undertaken by the builder. Can *D* sue *A* in delict for his injuries, or is he forced to rely upon a contractual claim (if any)[164] against *C*, leaving *C* in turn to pursue *B*, and *B* to pursue *A*?[165]

---

158 [1991] 1 AC 398, [1990] 2 All ER 908, HL.

159 [1991] 1 AC at 475E, per Lord Bridge.

160 *Gallagher v N McDowell Ltd* [1961] NI 26, CA (NI).

161 *Clay v A J Crump & Sons Ltd* [1964] 1 QB 533, [1963] 3 All ER 687, CA; *Clayton v Woodman & Son (Builders) Ltd* [1962] 2 QB 533, [1961] 3 All ER 249, CA (decision at first instance overturned on appeal on the facts).

162 Lord Keith of Kinkel, considering obiter whether a local authority might be liable for causing personal injury or property damage, preferred to reserve his opinion on the question.

163 For instance *Forbes v City of Dundee District Council* 1997 SLT 1330, 1997 SCLR 228, OH.

164 Unless there is an express clause in the lease allowing recovery by the tenant in such a case, it is unlikely that under the common law of lease the tenant would have a valid contractual claim against the landlord in this case.

165 Tortious liability has been imposed upon a builder in such a case in England: *Sharpe v Sweeting & Son* [1963] 1 WLR 665, [1963] 2 All ER 455, QB.

Example 2: *A*, a builder, is constructing a housing development. *A* employs firm *B*, specialist electrical contractors, to install the wiring in the various units making up the development. *C* purchases one of the houses. Due to negligently installed wiring, a fire starts in *C*'s house damaging *C*'s property. Can *C* choose to sue *B* in delict for the damage to its property, rather than *C* suing *A* in contract, and *A* in turn suing *B* in contract?[166]

It is suggested that in both examples a duty of care would be imposed in Scots law. There does not appear to be any policy reason at work in either case which would trump the policy of the law in favour of compensating for physical injury.

Type 2

3.99 The second type of case is where the two contracts *A–B* and *B–C* have no inherent connection with each other, although the performance of contract *A–B* affects contract *B–C*. Will breach of the contract *A–B* entitle *C* to sue *A* in delict for physical damage sustained by it? One would expect that it would, as otherwise *C* would be in a worse position than if he were wholly unconnected by contract to any of the parties (the position of Mrs Donoghue), a conclusion which would be unjust unless there was some strong reason related to the terms of the contract *B–C* for so holding. In fact, however, the decision by the House of Lords in the English appeal *Marc Rich & Co AG v Bishop Rock Marine Co Ltd*[167] put the plaintiff in just such a disadvantaged position. The facts were as follows:

The plaintiffs' goods were being transported aboard a ship, owned by the first defendants, travelling from South America to Italy under bills of lading incorporating the Hague Rules. En route the vessel became unseaworthy and docked for repairs. It was inspected by an inspector acting for a classification society. The inspector recommended repairs in dry dock, but the owners decided to undertake temporary repairs whilst docked, which the surveyor was persuaded to agree to in order to permit the vessel to complete its voyage. One week after the ship sailed, the temporary repairs failed, and the ship sank with a total loss of cargo. The plaintiffs sued the owners of the ship, the charterers, and the classification society. The claim against the charterers was not pursued, and that against the owners was settled for the maximum applicable under the Hague Rules. The plaintiffs sought the balance from the classification society, arguing that they owed a duty of care to the plaintiffs, the physical loss suffered having been reasonably foreseeable. The House of Lords held that the classification society did not owe a duty of care to the plaintiffs. Even if it were assumed that the classification society and plaintiffs were in a proximate relationship, it would not be fair, just and reasonable to impose a duty of care because (i) it would undermine the continued operation of the system of classification societies, (ii) it would interfere with the contractual relationship between the shipowners and cargo owners, and (iii) it would introduce a new layer of insurance with attendant litigation and arbitration.

The denial of the existence of a duty of care on grounds of fairness, justice and reasonableness points to the fact that this decision is heavily policy based, the

---

166 In *Murphy v Brentwood District Council* [1990] 2 All ER 908, HL, Lord Keith (at 922c) commented on this situation that 'it might not be stretching ordinary principles too far to hold the electrical sub-contractor liable for the damage'. Lord Bridge in the same case went further, stating (at 928d) that there he saw 'no reason to doubt' that the owner of the house could recover damages in tort in such a case.

167 [1995] 3 All ER 307, HL.

stated concerns being the non-profit-making status of classification societies, the useful function which they perform, and the fear that they might cease to undertake examinations should they incur the liability contended for.

3.100 One may or may not be persuaded by the force of the stated reasons, but it is suggested that the result reached in the case is open to criticism for the following reasons:

(1) It emphasises the status of the wrongdoer as a non-profit-making organisation operating in an area free of state regulation, suggesting that this mitigates against liability, when arguably it is precisely upon parties acting outwith a clear legislative framework that a duty of care ought to be imposed.[168]

(2) There is a strong argument for saying that a party which takes upon itself the responsibility for safeguarding the seaworthiness of ships and the safety of their crew has a significant link with the damage suffered. It is not therefore in any sense 'peripheral' to the damage occasioned.[169]

3.101 Lord Lloyd gave a strongly dissenting speech. In his opinion the terms of the contract between cargo owner and charterparty (which incorporated the Hague Rules) were irrelevant to the possible liability of a third party at tort, and any such duty would not upset the balance of rights and responsibilities under the contract. The significance of the Hague Rules could thus be discounted, and the mere existence of a contract between cargo owner and shipowner could not affect the tortious liability of the third party: that had been the very fallacy exposed by *Donoghue v Stevenson*. Lord Lloyd made the following succinct point:

'I am unable to see why the existence of the contract of carriage should "militate against" a duty of care being owed by a third party in tort. The function of the law of tort is not limited to filling in gaps left by the law of contract, as this House has recently reaffirmed in *Henderson v Merrett Syndicates Ltd*. The House rejected an approach which treated the law of tort as supplementary to the law of contract, i.e. as providing for a tortious remedy only where there is no contract. On the contrary: the law of tort is the general law, out of which the parties may, if they can, contract.'[170]

This represents a very strong defence of the possibility of concurrent liability, and is, it is suggested, the preferable approach. On the facts of the case, Lord Lloyd found that there was a high degree of proximity between the parties (the surveyor knew that the lives of the crew would be at risk if he allowed the ship to sail in an unseaworthy state, which by itself created the necessary proximity) and that there was nothing unfair, unjust or unreasonable in imposing the duty.

3.102 Whilst it is suggested that Lord Lloyd's approach in *Marc Rich* was the better one, the majority view prevailed: a duty of care for physical damage was

---

168 In *Watson v British Boxing Board* [2001] QB 1134, CA, Lord Phillips MR rejected arguments that a duty of care ought not to be imposed upon the defendant because of its non-profit-making status. He referred to the same attitude to such an argument adopted by Buxton LJ in *Perrett v Collins* [1998] 2 Lloyd's Rep 255, CA.

169 Lord Steyn, with whom the majority concurred, assumed, for the purposes of the decision, that the parties were proximate, without so deciding.

170 [1995] 3 All ER at 315h–j, per Lord Lloyd.

rejected on the basis of the policy considerations of the effects in general upon parties' insurance liabilities and the operation of classification societies.

Pure economic loss

3.103 It was noted above that there is a general policy in the law of not allowing recovery for pure economic loss. The law takes the view that while we are entitled to protection from personal injury or damage to our property, protection of our economic interests would both create a risk that legitimate competition in the marketplace would be stifled and that indeterminate claims would arise. Recovery for pure economic loss is therefore exceptional, requiring a particularly strong relationship to be shown between the parties. An explanation is required of which exceptional circumstances are recognised by the law as giving rise to such liability. The discussion is focused upon situations where a concurrent contractual claim might arise, though there are many cases involving recovery for pure economic loss where this is not so.

C as independent third party

3.104 Liability in delict towards a third party for causing pure economic loss may be imposed if there has been some contact between the parties such as to found a sufficiently close relationship, for instance reasonable reliance upon a misrepresentation. The proximity of the parties is the key:

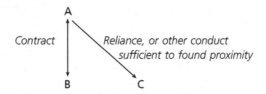

3.105 The principle of liability in pure economic loss for a directly made negligent misrepresentation was first established in English law in *Hedley Byrne & Co Ltd v Heller & Partners*.[171] The principle of liability flows from knowledge of the maker of the statement that it will reasonably be relied upon by the party to whom it is made. This brings the parties into a sufficiently proximate relationship and justifies the inference that the maker of the statement has 'assumed responsibility' for it. The principle has been followed in subsequent Scottish decisions.[172] It has been judicially suggested in England that a local authority might be liable in misrepresentation to a purchaser of defective premises if the authority in question

---

171 [1964] AC 465, [1963] 2 All ER 575, HL.
172 For instance, *John Kenway v Orcantic Ltd* 1979 SC 422, 1980 SLT 46, OH; *Eastern Marine Services (and Supplies) Ltd v Dickson Motors Ltd* 1981 SC 355, OH; *Midland Bank plc v Cameron, Thom, Peterkins & Duncans* 1988 SCLR 209, 1988 SLT 611, OH.

had given negligent information concerning the premises in response to a specific query from the purchaser,[173] thus neatly side-stepping the restriction on liability established by *Murphy v Brentwood District Council*.

3.106 If there is no evidence of a sufficiently close relationship between the parties, then there will be no possibility of the wrongdoer being under a duty of care. Consider this example:

> *A* audits the accounts of company *B*. Due to *A*'s negligence, *B*'s financial position is overstated. *C*, a shareholder in *B*, increases its shareholding in reliance on the position stated in the accounts and takes over control of the company. Following the successful acquisition of the company, *C* ascertains the correct financial position of the company. *C* sues *A* in delict for its economic loss. Is *C* entitled to recover its loss from *A*?

The facts of this example are based upon those of the English case *Caparo Industries plc v Dickman plc*.[174] The House of Lords held that there was no proximity between the parties and hence no duty of care owed by the auditors in respect of the loss. Proximity was not established because:

(1) the audited accounts had been placed into general public circulation, and might thus have been relied upon by numerous parties in relation to numerous transactions;

(2) there was no evidence to suggest that the auditors knew that the accounts would be transmitted specifically to the plaintiffs in connection with a particular transaction, in relation to which they would rely upon the accounts; and

(3) the auditor's statutory duty to prepare accounts was owed to the body of shareholders as a whole in order for that body to properly supervise the company's affairs, and not to enable individual shareholders to make a decision on whether to purchase shares.

3.107 The House of Lords, in reaching its conclusion, drew a distinction with the principles established in *Hedley Byrne* and the line of cases following it. Lord Bridge summed up the basis of liability in such cases:

> 'The salient feature of all these cases is that the defendant giving advice or information was fully aware of the nature of the transaction which the plaintiff had in contemplation, knew that the advice or information would be communicated to him directly or indirectly and knew that it was very likely that the plaintiff would rely on that advice or information in deciding whether or not to engage in the transaction in contemplation. In these circumstances the defendant could clearly be expected, subject always to the effect of any disclaimer of responsibility, specifically to anticipate that the plaintiff would rely on the advice or information given by the defendant for

---

173 The suggestion was made by Simon Brown LJ in *King v North Cornwall District Council*, 8 February 1995, CA (unreported) although on the facts of the case it was held that no actionable misrepresentation had occurred: see further, D Brodie, 'Undermining Murphy', Rep B 1996, (8) Mar, 3–5. In *Welton v North Cornwall District Council* [1997] 1 WLR 570, CA, the defendant council was held liable for the actions of one of its building inspectors who, in advising unnecessary expenditure to be undertaken on a hotel, was held to have assumed responsibility to the plaintiff for the costs of such.

174 [1990] 2 AC 605, [1990] 1 All ER 568, HL.

the very purpose for which he did in the event rely on it. So also the plaintiff, subject again to the effect of any disclaimer, would in that situation reasonably suppose that he was entitled to rely on the advice or information communicated to him for the very purpose for which he required it.'[175]

This emphasises that the *Hedley Byrne* principle requires knowledge on the part of the wrongdoer of the transaction in question and of the likely reliance of the victim upon the information conveyed in connection with that transaction. These factors demonstrate the requirement for a high degree of proximity.

3.108 Matters were not to rest there, however. Thus far, it might be assumed that reliance is a crucial element of the establishment of proximity, or at the very least, that some degree of contact between the parties is required. However, the House of Lords appeared to jettison these elements in its decision in *White v Jones*:[176]

> Mr Arthur Barratt, a widower, had two daughters. Following a row with his daughters, Mr Barratt wrote a will which excluded them from his estate. A family reconciliation occurred. Mr Barratt told his daughters of the existing will, and of his desire to alter its terms to reinstate them (they were each to receive £9,000). Mr Barratt wrote to his solicitor, Mr Jones, instructing him to prepare a new will conform to his instructions. Mr Barratt destroyed his previous will. Nothing was done for a month. Mr Jones failed to keep three appointments to see Mr Barratt. Mr Jones left instructions that the matter be progressed during his absence on holiday. Nothing was done to progress matters until Mr Jones's return from holiday. Shortly thereafter Mr Barratt died without executing a new will. The two daughters sued Mr Jones in damages for negligence, alleging that his delay in having the new will executed had caused them to lose their legacies of £9,000 each, which could not be claimed in the absence of a valid will. The House of Lords held that the solicitor had breached a duty of care owed to the two daughters, and was therefore liable in damages for their economic loss.

The decision of the House of Lords in favour of liability was based upon the notion of an 'assumption of responsibility' by the solicitor towards disappointed intended beneficiaries. Their Lordships expressed the concern that to fail to find the solicitor liable would create an injustice, because no party would have title to sue for the loss suffered. These points require further explanation.

Assumption of responsibility

3.109 The decision in *White v Jones* is clearly not analogous factually to that in *Hedley Byrne*, even though it was in the latter case that the notion of assumption of responsibility was first seriously developed. The latter case concerned a misrepresentation inducing reasonable reliance, whereas the former, whilst it involved professional negligence, did not involve a misrepresentation. The reference by the House of Lords was, however, to the notion of 'assumption of responsibility' introduced in *Hedley Byrne*. In *Hedley Byrne* the House of Lords had declared that one instance where a duty of care could be imposed was where the relationship of the parties was 'equivalent to contract', that is, where there was

175 [1990] 2 AC at 620H-621B, per Lord Bridge.
176 [1995] 2 AC 207, [1995] 1 All ER 691, HL.

an 'assumption of responsibility' which would amount to contract were it not for the absence of consideration.[177] This notion of assumption of responsibility formed the basis of the decision in *White v Jones*: the assumption of responsibility which a solicitor undertook towards his client was to be held to be extended towards the disappointed beneficiaries.

3.110 This extension of the notion of assumption of responsibility is open to criticism on at least two grounds. First, the facts of *White v Jones* disclose no contact between the plaintiffs and defendant. It would be odd therefore to describe their relationship as particularly close, and certainly odd to describe it as 'equivalent to contract'. As Lord Keith put it in his dissenting judgment:

> 'Here there was no relationship between the plaintiffs and Mr Jones, nor did Mr Jones do or say anything upon which the plaintiffs acted to their prejudice.'[178]

It might be possible to suggest that, had there been clear evidence that the solicitor was aware of reliance by the intended beneficiaries upon performance of his duties, this reliance might bring the parties into a proximate relationship. But the facts of the case disclosed in the report do not indicate any such reliance.[179]

3.111 Second, and more fundamentally, as was discussed in chapter 1,[180] the notion of assumption of responsibility, based upon 'equivalence to contract', fundamentally disguises the nature of the obligation in question. If the obligation is genuinely delictual (or tortious) in nature, it has nothing to do with voluntary assumption. To describe the basis of liability in tort as *voluntary* in nature does damage to the proper understanding of the nature of the obligation. Delictual duties are imposed in circumstances where the law thinks that they *ought* to apply. They have no relationship with voluntarily assumed responsibilities. In a case such as this, the law might well consider that a delictual duty ought to apply, but that will be so for specific policy reasons. A more honest approach to have adopted here would have been for their Lordships to have said: 'We believe that where a solicitor performs his professional services negligently, in circumstances where he can reasonably foresee that that negligence may cause specific economic harm to a defined class of person, the law should impose upon him a duty to make reparation for the losses caused by such negligence.' One might not agree with so widely formulated a proposition, but it would have been more transparent than a rationale clothed in the language of assumption of responsibility.

Need to do justice in circumstances of the case

3.112 This second point discloses the real basis of the decision in *White v Jones*. Their Lordships were concerned that, no other form of liability being suitable to sustain a claim, the negligent solicitor would avoid liability for the consequences

---

177 See the speech of Lord Devlin in *Hedley Byrne* [1965] AC 465 at 528–529.
178 [1995] 2 AC at 251F-G, per Lord Keith.
179 As Lord Browne-Wilkinson put it in *White v Jones* ([1995] 2 AC at 275F): 'It is true that the intended beneficiary (being ignorant of the instructions) may not rely on the particular solicitor's actions'.
180 See **1.55–1.57**.

of his negligence. The testator's estate, having suffered a breach of contract by the solicitor, had suffered no loss, as the estate fell to be distributed under the rules of intestacy in any event; on the other hand, the beneficiaries, having suffered a 'loss', appeared to have no cause of action, unless tort could be brought to avail. The loss would therefore fall into a black hole and, in these circumstances, their Lordships concluded that the tortious route was the only way to do 'practical justice' in the case.

3.113 Such a desire, whilst no doubt laudable, should not be allowed to pass without a note of caution being sounded. The concern raised in the minority judgments is that in the haste to do 'practical justice' the principles underlying the law may have been trampled upon. As Lord Mustill said in his dissent of the solution proposed by the majority:

'This is undoubtedly a possible result, but I would wish to guard against assuming too readily that it so reflects the moral imperatives of the situation that the law of delict should be strained to bring it about'.[181]

Is failure to receive a legacy a valid loss?

3.114 A final point arising from *White v Jones* needs to be addressed, and that is the nature of the loss for which damages were awarded. The essence of the plaintiffs' claim was not that they were worse off financially as a result of the defendant's negligence, but that their financial position had not been improved by the amount of the legacy which they were expecting. This is an unusual damages claim for a tort (or delict) action, as it reflects the performance interest which is normally associated with contract claims, and not the restoration interest associated with tort/delict claims. It was suggested in chapter 1 that the law of delict should not compensate in the measure of the performance interest. This argument was put by counsel for the defendant, and was summed up by Lord Goff as follows:

'[N]o claim will lie in tort for damages in respect of a mere loss of an expectation, as opposed to damages in respect of damage to an existing right or interest of the plaintiff. Such a claim falls within the exclusive zone of contractual liability; and it is contrary to principle that the law of tort should be allowed to invade that zone.'[182]

3.115 It was suggested in chapter 1 that the language of 'expectation' does not adequately describe the contractual interest: the victim of a delict may have 'expected' not to be harmed, or even expected in some cases that his position would be preserved by the wrongdoer. It is preferable to use the language of *performance* to describe the contractual interest. Lord Goff, in talking of expectation, may have confused matters. He opined that the disappointed beneficiaries were entitled to have their expectations protected:

'[A]n expectation loss may well occur in cases where a professional man, such as a solicitor, has assumed responsibility for the affairs of another; and I

---

181 [1995] 2 AC at 278H-279A, per Lord Mustill.
182 [1995] 2 AC at 257B, per Lord Goff.

for my part can see no reason in principle why the professional man should not, in an appropriate case, be liable for such loss under the *Hedley Byrne* principle.'[183]

Whilst a victim of a delict may be entitled to claim protection for his interest in not being harmed, or even, in some cases, his interest in having his position preserved, Lord Goff goes too far in claiming protection in delict for an expectation of improvement.[184] The result in *White v Jones* is, it is suggested, an aberration which ought not to be encouraged.

3.116 Nonetheless, *White v Jones* has been approved by the Inner House in the unreported case of *Robertson v Watt & Co*,[185] and in the Outer House in *Holmes v Bank of Scotland*,[186] despite its inconsistency with a prior Scottish House of Lords authority *Robertson v Fleming*,[187] which now appears de facto to have been departed from. Its approval by the Inner House was given without much consideration, however, and the implications for Scots law of the decision require to be worked out. The underlying principle of *White v Jones* seems to be little more than that a duty of care is to be implied on the basis of assumption of responsibility when a court feels that the needs of justice are served. Even given that the delimitation of delictual liability using the concept of duty of care has always been heavily policy based, this seems somewhat vague as a basis for future development of the law and has the potential for a reawakening of the expansionist attitude of the courts in the 1970s and early 1980s.

C indirectly linked to A through a contractual structure

3.117 We turn now to pure economic loss cases where the third party is linked via means of a contractual chain. As with physical loss cases, it is possible to distinguish two types of case: (1) cases where the contractual structure A–B–C is a single contractual framework where the nature of the contracts are related to a specific matter and the parties are aware of the structure and the existence of the parties to it, and (2) cases where although there are contracts A–B and B–C which affect a particular interest of C, the contracts are not part of an overall structure, and A and C are not necessarily aware of each other's existence. These two types of case are discussed in turn.

Type 1 cases: where contractual structure A–B–C is a single contractual framework

3.118 Several issues have been thought relevant in relation to the possibility of delictual liability in these cases. It has in some cases been suggested that the very existence of a contractual chain mitigates against delictual liability arising. There

---

183 [1995] 2 AC at 269B–C.
184 See further discussion of this point at **3.82**.
185 IH, Second Division, 4 July 1995.
186 2002 SLT 544, OH.
187 (1861) 4 Macq 167, HL.

has also been a trend of treating cases involving defective performance in construction contracts differently from the provision of other professional services.

Provision of services under building contract v provision of other services

3.119   It may be instructive to illustrate the differences in approach by considering a few of the major cases. The first two concern the construction industry, the latter two the surveyors' profession and the financial services industry respectively

Case 1: In *Junior Books Ltd v Veitchi Co Ltd*,[188] the pursuers were the owners of a factory. They contracted with a builder for the provision of certain construction work to be undertaken at the factory. The pursuer's architect nominated the defenders, a specialist flooring company, as subcontractors with responsibility for laying a new floor. The floor was defective and required to be replaced by the pursuers. The pursuers sued the defenders in delict for the costs of the replacement of the floor. The House of Lords held that the defenders had breached a duty of care owed by them to the pursuers and awarded damages against them.

Case 2: In *Scott Lithgow Ltd v GEC Electrical Projects Ltd*[189] the Ministry of Defence had commissioned a new submarine, HMS Challenger. Scott Lithgow were employed as the main contractor. They subcontracted electrical work to GEC, who in turn sub-subcontracted various work to four businesses. Certain defects in the electrical wiring came to light, and the MOD and Scott Lithgow sought damages from GEC and the sub-subcontractors in delict.[190] The pursuers relied in their arguments upon *Junior Books* arguing that it had laid down a general principle of liability for pure economic loss where someone does something specially for another party without due care. Lord Clyde, sitting in the Outer House, held that as the averments had not disclosed who owned the submarine a claim for damages in delict could not be maintained. In any event, he was of the opinion that the contractual structure in place between the parties mitigated against a duty of care.

Case 3: In *Martin v Bell-Ingram*[191] the pursuers were prospective purchasers of a property who approached their building society for a loan to finance the purchase. In connection with this transaction the building society instructed the defenders, a firm of chartered surveyors, to survey the property. The surveyor reported that there were no major problems with the property. The manager of the building society reported the contents of the survey by telephone to the pursuers, something which the defenders were aware would happen. Following purchase of the property by the pursuers, a serious sag in the property's roof was discovered. The pursuers subsequently sold the property for a reduced price. The pursuers sued the defenders in delict for the economic loss suffered by them. The defenders attempted to rely upon an exclusion of liability on their part in the loan offer sent to the pursuers. This exclusion was not communicated to the pursuers until after missives for the purchase of the property had been concluded. The Inner House held that the defenders owed a duty of care to the pursuers in respect of the losses suffered by them, a duty which was not negatived by the pursuers eventually being informed of the exclusion clause.

---

188   1982 SC (HL) 244, 1982 SLT 492, HL.
189   1989 SC 412, 1992 SLT 244, OH.
190   A contractual claim was also mounted against GEC.
191   1986 SC 208, 1986 SLT 575, IH. A duty of care upon a surveyor in such circumstances has also been recognised by the English courts: *Smith v Eric S Bush* [1990] 1 AC 831, [1989] 2 WLR 790, [1989] 2 All ER 514, HL.

Case 4: Some of the plaintiffs in *Henderson v Merrett Syndicates*, discussed above in relation to two party cases,[192] were not in a direct contractual relationship with the defendants, but were linked indirectly through a contractual chain. The House of Lords also permitted those defendants a concurrent remedy in tort for the economic loss suffered by them.

3.120 One may begin by asking whether the nature of the subject matter of the contracts is important, and whether, in particular, there is, or ought to be, any difference between cases involving the provision of construction services, as opposed to the provision of other services, for instance financial services.

3.121 Cases 1 and 2 may on the face of it appear contradictory, *Junior Books* allowing liability, *Scott Lithgow* taking the opposite view. The House of Lords in *Junior Books* took the view that, on the facts before it, the subcontractor employed in relation to construction work was in a proximate relationship with the employer and owed the owner of the building a duty of care in respect of the economic loss caused to it. The facts highlighted by the House of Lords as establishing this proximity included: (i) the defenders were nominated subcontractors, ie they had been specifically chosen by the pursuers; (ii) the defenders were specialists; (iii) the pursuers relied upon the defenders' skill and experience; (iv) the defenders must have known that their skill and expertise was being relied upon; (v) the relationship of the parties was as close as it could be short of contract; (vi) the defenders must have been able to foresee that their negligence would cause economic loss to the pursuers. Point (v) is an application of the 'equivalence to contract' doctrine developed in *Hedley Byrne*. In the eyes of the House of Lords, the relationship of the parties in *Junior Books* was, as in *Hedley Byrne*, as close as it might be without being contractual.

3.122 A criticism often levied at the decision in *Junior Books* is that it falls foul of the general rule of delict that liability does not sound in economic loss for the mere supply of defective goods or premises. Attempts to justify it on the basis of reliance are insufficient, as many consumers of products no doubt rely upon the product being in sound condition, but such reliance will not found a duty of care for the pure economic loss caused by damage to the product itself. There are two principal approaches one might take in justifying the decision:[193]

(1)   One approach is to say that it is a radical decision which lays down a new general principle for the recovery of economic loss where there is a *very high degree of proximity* between the parties. This general principle ought conceivably to apply in other types of case apart from construction chain cases.[194] To put it another way, for such general principle to apply, one would need to be able to point to clear aspects of the relationship which

---

192 See **3.68–3.74**.

193 Additionally, Professor Thomson has argued that the decision may be viewed as an example of the delict of interference with contract: see *Delictual Liability*, at p 92.

194 This was conceded as much by Lord Clyde in *Scott Lithgow* who said 'If a duty of care can exist in circumstances of the *Junior Books* case there seems to be no reason why in other circumstances where a correspondingly close proximity of relationship can be found a duty of care should not also be affirmed' (1989 SC at 420).

indicated an 'assumption of responsibility' by the defender[195]. Such aspects could include, but would not be restricted to, reliance by the pursuer, and knowledge by the defender of such reliance and the likelihood of economic loss being caused to the pursuer.

(2) The second approach is more restrictive. It says that the case does not lay down a general principle for recovery of economic loss based upon a high degree of proximity of the parties, but rather represents a specific factual exception to the non-recoverability of economic loss in a contractual matrix (or even a construction matrix, if one was to be even more restrictive). The criteria for the exception to apply would be the negligent performance of a contract A–B by A, where A can foresee that such negligent performance will result in B being unable to fulfil a related contract it has with C, thus causing C economic loss.[196] In order for future cases to fall within this ambit therefore one would require to show (i) a contractual matrix (ii) in which the contract B–C would have to be in existence at the time of A's breach under its contract, in order that (iii) A could foresee the economic loss suffered by C under its contract. Such a restricted interpretation would exclude other cases involving defective buildings (such as *D & F Estates Ltd v Church Commissioners for England*,[197] discussed below[198]) from its ambit, where no such loss could have been anticipated by the defendant builder.

3.123 The English courts have not simply chosen to adopt a restrictive attitude to *Junior Books*, describing the case as an 'exceptional case',[199] but have gone further and suggested that indirectly linked parties in a construction matrix are not to be considered in a proximate relationship for the purposes of pure economic loss claims in tort.[200] In other words, without an appropriate opportunity having yet arisen for the case to be overruled, they have effectively chosen to ignore the case by saying that it is a one-off, which could never be repeated. With respect to the English bench, the facts do not seem to be particularly exceptional. It is surely relatively commonplace for a specialised subcontractor to be nominated by an employer or their architect or engineer.[201] The explanation that, in relation to other construction cases involving the liability of a subcontractor, *Junior Books* is somehow 'special' does not convince.

3.124 *Junior Books* has been applied by the Outer House in Scotland.[202] It was referred to as an authority in *Scott Lithgow v GEC*[203] in which it was discussed at

---

195 Lord Roskill refers, a number of times, in his speech in *Junior Books* to the speech of Lord Devlin in *Hedley Byrne* in which the notion of assumption of responsibility was first developed.
196 This is the explanation suggested in the *Stair Memorial Encyclopaedia*, vol 15, para 279.
197 [1989] 1 AC 177, [1988] 2 All ER 992, HL.
198 At **3.138**.
199 Lord Bridge in *D & F Estates v Church Commissioners* described *Junior Books* as involving a 'unique, albeit non-contractual, relationship' between the pursuer and defender ([1989] 1 AC at 202A).
200 Lord Goff, commenting in *Henderson v Merrett*, said of parties indirectly linked through construction contracts: 'there is generally no assumption of responsibility by the sub-contractor or supplier direct to the building owner' ([1995] 2 AC at 196C).
201 A point acknowledged by Lord Clyde in *Scott Lithgow*: see **3.124**.
202 See for instance *Kelly v Meldrum*, 7 May 1986, OH (Lord McCluskey) (unreported); *Lamont v North East Fife District Council*, 10 November 1987, OH (Lord Clyde) (unreported).
203 1989 SC 412, OH. For the facts of the case, see **3.119**.

length by Lord Clyde, sitting in the Outer House. The attitude adopted by his Lordship to the case was, on the whole, a positive one. He began his discussion of the case by asserting its authoritative status in Scots law, and doubting that its facts were as unique as suggested by some English judges: 'it is not easy to see that the circumstances of it were necessarily unusual or unique. A building contract involving a nominated subcontractor who is a specialist in his particular trade is by no means unusual'.[204] He rejected, however, an appeal to the case as establishing the novel general principle argued for by counsel for the pursuers, namely that someone doing something special for someone else without due care should be liable to that other in damages for pure economic loss.[205] The essence of *Junior Books* for Lord Clyde lay critically in its requirement for a 'close proximity which was there found to exist between the parties.'[206] In applying *Junior Books* to the case before him, he tended to the conclusion that the contractual matrix adopted by the parties seemed 'to point away from any conclusion of a duty of care being placed on the defenders'[207] although he was not prepared to dismiss the possibility of a delictual claim without reference to the terms of the contracts. One particular concern with the contractual matrix in the case was in relation to a contractual limitation in the contract of the subcontractors, the suggestion being that this might negative a delictual duty. Overall, although the opposite result was reached in *Scott Lithgow*, this can be explained as an application of the *Junior Books* requirement of close proximity, something which Lord Clyde felt was not present given the particular contractual matrix.

3.125 Since *Scott Lithgow*, however, there has in Scotland too been a developing judicial trend of treating the case as 'special' and thus as restricted in its scope.[208] The trend of marginalising *Junior Books* has culminated in the recent comment of Lord Gill in *Landcatch Ltd v International Oil Pollution Compensation Fund*[209] that it 'seems now to be generally accepted that *Junior Books* does not lay down any principle of general application in the law of tort or delict'.[210] The current judicial approach to the case is thus certainly away from its potential as the basis of any general principle of recovery for pure economic loss based upon a high degree of proximity, and probably even to reject it as a precedent likely to be of use in any future case, even though it still remains as an authoritative decision of the House of Lords. Following an uncertain start, *Junior Books* is being frozen out in its own jurisdiction.

3.126 Following the approach of English law, the Scottish judicial approach is now likely to be that parties in a construction contract matrix are not proximate to each other as regards pure economic loss. This requires examination. The argument that subcontractors are not to be considered proximate to the owner of premises in respect of pure economic loss *in any circumstances* is an unconvincing

---

204 1989 SC at 420, per Lord Clyde.
205 1989 SC at 419, per Lord Clyde.
206 1989 SC at 420, per Lord Clyde.
207 1989 SC at 426, per Lord Clyde.
208 This appears to have been the attitude adopted by Lord Maclean in *Strathford East Kilbride Ltd v HLM Design Ltd* 1999 SLT 121, 1997 SCLR 877, OH.
209 11 November 1997, OH (unreported).
210 Per Lord Gill at section (c)(iii) of his opinion.

one. There seems to be nothing inherent in the nature of the construction industry which could explain why those involved in it should always be considered to be distanced from parties further up the contractual chain. An employer in a construction project may as equally rely upon the skill of a subcontractor, as did the house purchaser upon the skill of the surveyor in *Martin v Bell-Ingram* and its English counterpart *Smith v Bush*, or the underwriter upon the skill of the insurance agent in *Henderson v Merrett*. True, in a very large construction project in which there are numerous layers of subcontracts, the parties may be more distanced from each other, but this, as the facts of *Junior Books* indicate, will not always be so. It must surely be a question of fact whether the high degree of proximity which *Junior Books* asserts is necessary exists in any given situation.

3.127 The reasons stated by the courts for treating building cases differently from other cases do not convince. If there are other reasons at work, then they are undisclosed. What these might be is considered below.[211]

Does the contractual matrix necessarily distance the parties or bring them closer?

3.128 The question of whether parties across a contractual matrix may be proximate or not is not simply an issue affecting construction cases, but arises in any setting. One encounters varying views in relation to this issue: (1) the view that parties linked through such a chain will always be proximate; (2) the view that such parties will never be proximate; or (3) the view that it depends upon the facts of the case, including where the parties lie in the chain, and what the terms of the various contracts are. It is suggested that the third view is the correct one.

3.129 In some cases, especially construction cases, the assertion has baldly been made that a contractual matrix will necessarily distance parties. The rationale is that if parties choose a contractual matrix, they intend only to undertake duties to the party with whom they have a direct contractual link. They thus impliedly intend to be distanced from other persons with whom they have no direct link. In *Simaan Contracting v Pilkington Glass*,[212] Bingham LJ said of the alleged tortious duty between indirectly linked parties: 'such a responsibility is, I think, inconsistent with the structure of the contract the parties have chosen to make.'[213] The difficulty with this view is that it is never judicially explained exactly why a contractual matrix does *not* distance parties in relation to physical damage or, following recent decisions, in relation to pure economic loss in other settings (such as that in *Henderson v Merrett*). It is suggested that to infer that a contractual structure will *always* have been adopted with the express intention of distancing parties is to superimpose onto business people a sophistication of intention which may hardly, if ever, be present. A contractual matrix is likely to be adopted for the most part because it is convenient for the parties, and also in many cases because it is the method recommended for doing business by professional bodies in their model forms of contract.

3.130 A further reason sometimes advanced by those taking the view that a contractual matrix necessarily precludes delictual liability, is that a defender

---

211 See **3.133–3.140**.
212 [1988] 1 QB 758, CA.
213 [1988] 1 QB at 781G.

might be sued twice, first by his direct contracting party, and second by the party having the right to sue in delict. By extension, such an argument could be maintained against the permissibility of concurrent liability in general (indeed if successful it would have denied Mrs Donoghue her claim). It is, however, a spurious argument. If, for instance, *A*, a subcontractor, is sued by *C*, the employer, in respect of defective performance, it will not in addition be liable to *B*, the main contractor, in contract. The reason for this is that if *C* successfully sues *A* in delict, it will thereby recover its loss, and therefore be unable to sue *B* in contract, thus precluding *B* from suing *C* in turn in contract as *B* will not have suffered any loss.

3.131 On the other hand, a contractual matrix will not always guarantee that indirectly linked parties will be in a proximate relationship. A subcontractor may have had very little if any contact with an employer, and to suggest in such a case that the parties are in a close relationship would be fanciful.

3.132 The better view is that of Lord Clyde in *Scott Lithgow* who stated that the existence of a contractual matrix is a 'relevant consideration in deciding whether the possibility of a direct liability for negligence was intended'.[214] The matrix is to be seen as a 'relevant consideration' without pre-determining the result which that consideration will produce. It will be necessary to consider the specific details of the contractual arrangements before one can take a view on the proximity of the parties.[215] One needs to have regard, among other considerations, to the following: (i) whether the subcontractor has specifically disclaimed delictual liability in its contract with the main contractor,[216] (ii) whether such a disclaimer is valid,[217] (iii) whether the subcontractor has given any contractual warranty to the employer,[218] (iv) the particular location in the chain of the parties in question; (v) whether the pursuer knew of any disclaimers; (vi) the contact between the parties, if any, and the expectations engendered by it; and (vii) whether the contracts were all concluded as part of a single process, or whether some parties came into the picture at a later stage. The existence or otherwise of any alleged delictual duty must surely be considered in relation to questions such as these as well as to the terms of the relevant contracts in general. But to dismiss such a duty out of hand because of the presence of a contractual matrix is to deny delict its legitimate role.

Underlying policy considerations at work in the cases

3.133 It was suggested earlier that bald assertions that parties in a construction chain are never proximate to each other, or that contractual chains in general

---

214 1992 SLT 244 at 252L.
215 As Lord Clyde noted in *Scott Lithgow v GEC*.
216 This was suggested as a relevant consideration by Lord Clyde in *Scott Lithgow v GEC*.
217 It may conceivably be struck down by UCTA.
218 This was a crucial factor in the decision of the English Court of Appeal in *Greater Nottingham Co-operative Society Ltd v Cementation Piling* [1989] 1 QB 71, CA, where the presence of a contractual warranty made by the subcontractor to the employer was held to exclude a duty in tort for causing pure economic loss. The actual decision may be open to question however. None of the contractual warranties touched upon the matter of liability for pure economic loss in tort; however, it was held that silence on this matter excluded a duty in tort. This view might be said to sit ill at ease with the approach to concurrent liability of the House of Lords in *Henderson v Merrett*.

necessarily distance parties, will not do as sufficient explanations for the attitude of the courts in pure economic loss claims across contractual matrices. Are there therefore wider considerations at work which explain why the courts are antagonistic to claims in some circumstances?

3.134 At this point some of the policies referred to in the list given at **3.63**, which it was suggested are at work in concurrent claims, may usefully be considered. The following policies might explain differences in attitude in different cases: (1) the policy of protecting parties who reasonably rely upon another party's expertise; (2) the policy against finding peripheral parties liable where there is another party who may be considered more directly to have caused the loss; and (3) the policy against allowing parties who had adequate contractual means of protecting themselves against loss from suing in delict (this is essentially a policy of consumer protection). On the other hand, any policy against allowing contract to subvert delict (if such exists as a coherent policy in the law) cannot explain matters, as delictual claims are entertained against the background of some contractual matrices but not others.

3.135 The policy of protecting reliance certainly underpins some of the decisions. In *Junior Books; Martin v Bell-Ingram*, and *Henderson v Merrett*, there was demonstrable reliance by the injured party upon proper performance by the wrongdoer. Reliance may certainly be present in construction cases, and the unwillingness of English law (and increasingly perhaps Scots law too) to allow delictual claims in such cases needs another explanation. The policy against not finding peripheral parties liable is more relevant to cases such as *Murphy v Brentwood District Council*; it is less evidently applicable to cases such as the negligence of a subcontractor, where the subcontractor's fault cannot be considered peripheral to the loss. The answer lies perhaps in the law's policy against allowing parties who had adequate means of contractual protection from using delict where they have failed to take up the contractual option.[219] Thus, it can be argued that an employer in a construction contract has the ability to obtain adequate protection of its financial interests either through its contract with the main contractor (who can be made liable for any damage caused by the subcontractor) or by requiring direct contractual warranties to be given to it by all subcontractors. On the other hand, the purchaser of a modest house, such as the pursuer in *Martin v Bell-Ingram*, or the Names in *Henderson v Merrett*, is unable to obtain sufficient protection for his financial interests via contract, because he is in a weak bargaining position and must accept the terms presented to him. This is a policy which essentially protects consumers but not commercial parties. Conceivably, an employer under a construction contract might be a 'consumer' if he was a private individual who was unable to influence the terms of the contract.

3.136 If this policy does explain the cases, then it would suggest that, for instance, the purchaser of a large commercial property, rather than a modest private house, might not be able to avail itself of the delictual claim permitted in

---

219 This argument is advanced by Jane Stapleton in 'Duty of Care—Peripheral Parties and Alternative opportunities for Deterrence' (1995) 111 LQR 301.

Martin v Bell-Ingram.[220] It would also seem to suggest that *Junior Books* was incorrectly decided, thus reinforcing the attitude adopted by the English, and latterly Scots, courts. What is clear, however, is that any such policy, if it is in operation, is not being enunciated by the courts. This is regrettable, for it ensures that the law cannot sufficiently be explained except by reference to guesswork, and it prevents adequate predictions of likely outcomes in areas where there is a dearth of precedent. The courts require to be more explicit in their recourse to policy considerations. The explanations currently advanced by the judiciary for the decisions reached fail to explain the divergent approaches at work in the case law.

Type 2 cases: where contracts A–B and B–C not part of overall structure

3.137 This type of third party contractual case was defined, it will be recalled, as cases where although there are contracts *A–B* and *B–C* affecting a particular interest of *C*, the contracts are not part of an overall structure and *A* and *C* are not necessarily aware of each other's existence. Because of the unrelated nature of the contracts, there is less likely to be proximity between *A* and *C*.

3.138 An example of such a case is the English case *D & F Estates Ltd v Church Commissioners for England and others*:[221]

> The first defendants were owners of land on which a block of flats was to be constructed by main contractors. The main contractor engaged a subcontractor to carry out plastering work at the block. The subcontractor carried out the plastering work negligently. The plaintiffs were long lessees of a flat in the block. The plaintiffs brought an action in tort for the costs of remedial work to rectify the defective plastering against several parties, including the main contractor. The House of Lords held that the main contractor, having hired what it believed to be a competent plasterer, owed no further tortious duty to the lessees.

As may be appreciated, the contract *A–B* (between developer and main contractor) had no inherent connection with the contract *B–C* (between lessees and owner), thus differentiating this kind of case from the type 1 contractual chain cases. Indeed, the lease was not entered into until construction work on the building had been completed. The reason for the House of Lords finding that no duty of care was owed by the builders in respect of the defective plastering lay principally in the fact that it was not the main contractor which had directly caused the loss, but the subcontractor. The main contractor's duty was held to be

---

220 For suggestions that this may indeed be the case, see the comments of Lord Griffiths in *Smith v Bush* [1990] 1 AC at 859. An interesting contrast to the decisions in *Smith v Bush* and *Martin v Bell-Ingram* is *Bank of Scotland v Fuller Peiser* 2002 SLT 574, OH. In this case, the bank had relied upon a survey report provided by the purchaser's surveyor in making a decision as to whether to offer a loan facility in connection with the purchase of a commercial property. When the bank sought to recover from the surveyor financial losses flowing from alleged undervaluation of the property, the surveyor sought to rely upon a disclaimer of liability contained in the survey report. The Lord Ordinary (Eassie) held that the disclaimer was not struck down by UCTA, and that accordingly it negatived any assumption of responsibility towards the bank.

221 [1989] 1 AC 177, [1988] 2 All ER 992, HL.

exhausted by having employed what it considered to be a competent plasterer. In addition the House doubted the approach of *Junior Books*, preferring the traditional view of English law that no tortious liability should be imposed upon a builder for pure economic loss caused by inherent defects in his workmanship.[222]

3.139 While the House of Lords clearly felt the need to express its opinion on the approach taken in *Junior* Books, it would have sufficed simply to point to clear differences with the facts of that case. The facts of *D & F Estates* can clearly be distinguished on the following grounds: (1) the lessee and contractor did not even know of each other's identity; (2) there was no evidence of reliance by the lessee upon the contractor's skill; (3) the contractor did not have economic loss to the plaintiff within its reasonable contemplation at the time when it was performing its duties; and (4) the lessee's lease was not concluded until after the building had been completed. It is evident that such a case discloses little if any proximity between the parties.

3.140 There was a similar failure to recover in the Scottish case of *Strathford East Kilbride Ltd v HLM Design Ltd*,[223] where lessees of a building were not permitted to recover against the architects in respect of pure economic loss stemming from design defects in the building. Lord Maclean, referring approvingly to the recent authorities including *Henderson v Merrett* and *White v Jones*, said of the pursuer's claim:

> '[I]n the absence of any averments by the pursuers that the defenders assumed responsibility towards them, the defenders owed them, as tenants of the property, no duty in the particular circumstances to take reasonable care to avoid causing them financial loss in the architectural and other services which the defenders were obliged to provide under a contract with the pursuers' landlords, the building owners.'[224]

Lord Maclean was at pains to point out that this case was not similar to a contractual matrix situation such as *Junior Books*:

> '[T]he pursuers in this case never were within the contractual chain. The pursuers were strangers to the contract, and were in a similar position legally to a derivative acquirer, successor or possessor. Such a person is owed no duty of care by those involved in the erection of the structure, except in relation to the avoidance of physical injury or physical damage to the property.'

A comment which re-emphasises the crucial difference so far as proximity is concerned between type 2 and type 1 three party pure economic loss cases.

Claims by a party other than the owner of defective property or premises

3.141 In *Junior Books* the action for damages was brought by the owner of the factory, in *Martin v Bell-Ingram* by the owner of the house. Where a claim in delict

---

222 See, for instance, the speech of Lord Bridge [1989] 1 AC at 206D. It is worth noting that, in Lord Bridge's opinion, had the plasterer been sued, his Lordship would have held the plasterer to owe no duty of care either.

223 1999 SLT 121, 1997 SCLR 877, OH. The case is discussed further below at **3.159** as it relates to an alternative claim by the pursuers of *jus quaesitum tertio*.

224 1999 SLT at 126L, per Lord Maclean.

for pure economic loss stemming from damage to property or premises is brought by a party other than the owner[225], it will not be entertained by the courts.[226] Thus, if the main contractor in a building contract chain seeks to sue the sub-subcontractor for the latter's negligent work, claiming that this negligence has made performance of its contractual obligations with the employer more expensive, this claim will be rejected by the courts. The failure in *Scott Lithgow* of the pursuers to state who owned the submarine (or more particularly, the faulty wiring in the submarine), was held to preclude an action for pure economic loss. A similar approach was taken in the English case *Candlewood Navigation v Mitsui OSK Lines Ltd.*[227]

3.142 In fact the Scottish courts have gone further and have even refused to allow a pursuer who has suffered consequential *physical* damage to its property as the result of damage to another's property from claiming for such loss in delict. In *Coleridge v Miller Construction Ltd,*[228] damage caused by the defenders to a power cable caused a power failure, which in turn caused physical damage to glass being manufactured in the pursuer's factory. The Lord Ordinary held that no duty of care was owed by the defenders to the pursuers in respect of the damage suffered. The damage suffered was not reasonably foreseeable, nor would it be fair, just and equitable to impose a duty of care, as the pursuer ought to have had insurance in place to cover these losses. This last point is somewhat surprising. Would it imply that, for instance, a party whose house was burned down by another's negligence would be prohibited from suing for such loss if there was no insurance in place over the house? If that is the implication, it would be startling indeed.

3.143 In such cases therefore, the party wishing to claim in respect of loss suffered will have to have regard to any contractual remedy it may have, including any possible claim based upon *jus quaesitum tertio* or via assignation.[229] In a case such as *Coleridge* there is likely to be no available contractual remedy, as unless a continuous electricity supply is specifically contracted for, the terms of a contract for the supply of electricity will usually exempt a power cut from being a breach of contract.[230]

3.144 The foregoing must, however, be read subject to this caveat. Where a party owns particular property and this is damaged by another party, the fact that the former transfers the property to a third party will not prevent a relevant action in delict being pled by the former against the wrongdoer.[231]

---

225 Or a person in an equivalent position to the owner, eg a long lessee having the obligation of repair of the property: see *North Scottish Helicopters v United Technologies Corporation Inc (No 1)* 1988 SLT 77.

226 *Dynamco Ltd v Holland and Hannen and Cubitts (Scotland) Ltd* 1971 SC 257, 1972 SLT 38, IH.

227 [1986] 1 AC 1, HL.

228 1997 SLT 485, OH.

229 A ground argued as an alternative to the delictual claim in *Scott Lithgow.*

230 Even where there is a contract for a continuous supply of electricity, any losses caused would have to be reasonably foreseeable before the provider of electricity could be liable in damages for breach of contract: *Balfour Beatty Construction (Scotland) Ltd v Scottish Power plc* 1994 SC (HL) 20, 1994 SLT 807, HL.

231 This topic is discussed further at **3.178** ff.

Critique of underlying policies in cases of both independent third parties or those related via contractual chains

3.145   One might legitimately ask whether a policy of 'consumer protection', in the sense outlined above at **3.135**, if it is being applied by the courts, is a legitimate one. For, while consumer protection is no doubt a laudable aim for legislatures to pursue, its pursuit by the judiciary might be thought to be illegitimate.[232] It might respectably be argued that the policy of the law of delict ought to be to protect *any* party who has been harmed by wrongful conduct. Of course one must take into account a concern such as the floodgates argument, when deciding whether this general principle should be constrained in any way. But to restrict the class of persons who may claim pure economic loss purely on the basis that they failed to seek contractual protection against loss is arguably an undue restriction upon the right to claim reparation for injury caused. In essence, such a consumer protection policy punishes the careless or inadvertent party who had a chance to protect himself. This might be an acceptable position for contract law to adopt, where one's rights are determined essentially by what one has bargained for, but is it a legitimate principle of delict? Whilst delict does penalise those who are contributorily negligent, it has not been the tradition of our law to state that failure to obtain protection of one's interests by contract is such a reprehensible act that it should deprive one of a remedy in delict.

3.146   If these concerns were to lead one to challenge the operation of a tacit judicial policy based upon allowing recovery in pure economic loss only for those in a weak bargaining position, would there exist any alternative policy which might be adopted to prevent the boundaries of pure economic loss recovery being extended too far? Whilst suggesting so may seem blatantly obvious, it is suggested that a solution based upon a proper regard for the contractual framework, coupled with an emphasis upon a high degree of proximity between the parties would provide the starting point for an equitable approach. One might flesh out a suggested approach in more detail as follows.

(1) Policy in contractual chain cases

3.147   Where a court is faced with a claim for recovery of pure economic loss in delict by a pursuer indirectly linked to the defender via a contractual chain it should begin with an examination of the details of the contractual matrix in place between the parties.[233] If this is not inconsistent with delictual liability, then the court should have regard to the interaction (if any) of the parties and the expectations engendered by such. If the behaviour of the defender has led the pursuer reasonably to rely upon the performance of the defender, and if the defender could foresee that such reliance might result in economic loss to the pursuer, then this will strongly suggest that a duty of care to avoid causing economic loss should arise. It is conceived that reliance need not be a necessary

---

232   As Lord Bridge put it in *D & F Estates* ([1989] 1 AC at 208A): 'I cannot help feeling that consumer protection is an area of law where legislation is much better left to the legislators'.

233   Some particular matters for consideration were noted above at **3.132**.

element in every case, though it would strongly assist a pursuer.[234] Such cases will not raise any floodgates concerns, as the potential claimants will be restricted by the contractual matrix. Such an approach, if adopted, might question the correctness of the actual decision in *Junior Books*, although not the general approach. The concern with the actual decision in this case is that there was no examination by the court of the terms of the relevant contracts. Indeed, Lord Roskill said in his speech:

'Your Lordships were not told whether that contract included as between the main contractors and the respondents any relevant exceptions clause, nor whether if there were such an exceptions clause it might be available for the benefit of the appellants. Nor were your Lordships told why the respondents had chosen to proceed in delict against the appellants rather than against the main contractors in contract, nor indeed why the main contractors had not been joined as parties to these proceedings.'[235]

These deficiencies did not appear to trouble the House of Lords, a remarkably lax attitude to the importance of the contractual arrangements. However, on the approach suggested, there might well be construction cases where, following a review of the contractual matrix and the contact between the parties, delictual liability could be found to lie in respect of pure economic loss.[236] The same decision in both *Henderson v Merrett* and *Martin v Bell-Ingram* would be reached under this suggested approach, as in both cases delictual liability was compatible with the contractual matrix, and reasonable reliance had occurred.

(2) Policy in independent third party cases

3.148   Where the pursuer is an independent third party, then the basis of liability should again lie in the interaction of the pursuer and defender with each other. The requisite high degree of proximity could be created by the pursuer's reasonable reliance upon the defender's actions or representations, and the defender's reasonable foreseeability that economic loss might be suffered by the pursuer as a result of its negligence, but should not be found in any vague notion of 'assumption of responsibility'. If the defender is a party peripheral to the damage caused, then the requisite proximity will be lacking and any reliance on the part of the pursuer will be unreasonable.[237] Where there are numerous potential third parties, then proximity will certainly not be made out, and the floodgates concern will prevent a duty of care from arising. On the approach suggested, the same result would have been reached in *Caparo Industries v Dickman*.[238] There would,

---

234   This point was made by Lord Clyde in *Scott Lithgow*, 1989 SC at 423–424.

235   1982 SC (HL) 244 at 270.

236   This would not be so if the courts were to reassert the traditional view that the provision of defective premises ought never to give rise to liability for pure economic loss. This seems an arbitrary view however.

237   Alternatively, it would be possible to explain such cases by reference to the requirement of causation, stating that the actions of a peripheral party could not be considered the *causa causans* of the damage suffered.

238   Discussed at **3.106–3.107**.

however, have been no liability in delict in *White v Jones*,[239] any evidence of actual closeness of relationship being wholly absent from that case.

3.149 In essence, the approach suggested above is anchored firmly in the relevant contracts and on specific evidence of a high degree of proximity between the parties. The approach adopted by the House of Lords in *White v Jones*, an approach based upon the vague concept of assumption of responsibility, is fraught with danger and is liable to produce a blossoming of litigation attaching itself to this vague concept.

3.150 For those cases where delict does not provide a remedy for the pursuer, a creative approach based upon alternative avenues for recovery is to be commended. It is proposed now to discuss some of the alternatives open to a party for whom the delictual route is unavailable.

Solutions to problems 1: contractual warranties[240]

3.151 It has become commonplace in the construction industry for subcontractors to be required to give contractual warranties to the owner of the property guaranteeing the quality of the workmanship undertaken by them. Such undertakings may also be given by a main contractor to the owner of the property, if the main contractor is in a direct contractual relationship not with the owner but with a developer.[241] The rationale for such undertakings is to grant to a party who would not otherwise have it a direct contractual right to sue where the quality of workmanship of the party giving the undertaking is not conform to the standard stipulated in the warranty.

3.152 A warranty is usually viewed as contractual in nature, even though it is unlike other contractual obligations in that it is not an undertaking to do or to refrain from doing something. A warranty is a statement as to a state of affairs which the maker of the statement vouches (warrants) to be true. The remedy of the party to whom the warranty is addressed in the event that the warranty is shown to be untrue is to seek damages for any attendant losses, or termination of the contract (if, in the circumstances of the case, breach of the warranty founds a right to rescind). As a warranty is contractual in nature, some behaviour indicating consent to the contract must be demonstrated by the party to whom the warranty is addressed. A warranty is not a cautionary obligation, as there is no undertaking to stand as a substitute performer for a primary obligant.

3.153 A warranty is not usually conceived of as being promissory in nature, but if the concept of contract can be used to accommodate the notion of warranty, there seems little objection to considering promise as a possible alternative. The promissor would not be promising to do or to refrain from doing anything, but

239 Discussed at **3.108–3.116**.
240 The term 'duty of care deed' is now also encountered where the nature of the warranty is as to the careful performance of undertakings.
241 Such a structure may have been chosen for a number of reasons, for example VAT or other tax considerations: see *Alfred McAlpine Construction Ltd v Panatown Ltd* [2001] 1 AC 518, [2000] 3 WLR 946, [2000] 4 All ER 97, HL.

would be promising that a state of affairs was the case (eg that a building had a certain floor space, or that construction work had been carried out with due skill and care). On the other hand, if the warranty is part of the consideration given by the contractor in respect of payment from the employer, the traditional contractual analysis may be preferable.

3.154 The great benefit of a contractual warranty is that it may obviate the need to seek redress for losses through delict, a route which as has been seen will not always be available for pure economic loss. Caution should be exercised however. The party to whom the warranty is to be made should ensure that it is drafted as widely as is likely to be necessary. Case law indicates that where an inadequate contractual warranty is in place, the courts may deem that to be exhaustive of a party's rights, thus precluding any recourse to delict[242] or to transferred loss claims.[243]

Solutions to problems 2: jus quaesitum tertio[244]

3.155 Another alternative to a delictual damages claim may be for the injured party to assert that it has a *jus quaesitum tertio* in terms of a contract in the chain to which it is not a direct party, and that it is thereby entitled to damages for defective performance. The situation may be represented thus:

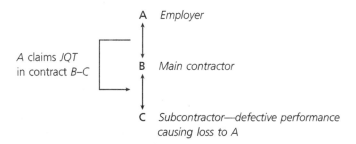

A   *Employer*

A claims JQT in contract B–C

B   *Main contractor*

C   *Subcontractor—defective performance causing loss to A*

Whilst this argument has not been made before our courts very often, for the reasons explained below, it has at least this attractive quality which commends it: whilst a delictual claim may be thought by the courts to be subversive of the contractual arrangements, especially where the loss claimed is pure economic loss, the claim based upon a *jus quaesitum tertio* cannot be so stigmatised, as by its very nature it depends upon the contractual intention of the parties to establish the right in the third party. A claimed *jus quaesitum tertio* therefore will only ever be held to exist where this is deemed to be consistent with the contractual arrangements between *B* and *C* and the overall contractual matrix.

---

242   This at least is the ratio of *D & F Estates v Church Commissioners* [1989] 1 AC 177, [1988] 2 All ER 992, HL. In the light of more recent decisions on concurrent liability, the correctness of the decision is open to question.

243   As to which, see **3.169** ff below.

244   For a general discussion of *jus quaesitum tertio* see McBryde, chapter 10; *Stair Memorial Encyclopaedia*, vol 15, 'Obligations', paras 824–852.

The attractiveness of this argument has not been overlooked by litigators in recent years, as the increase in reported cases in which this argument has been pled demonstrates.[245]

3.156 The two principal hurdles to bringing such a claim are the requirement to show an intention to benefit the *tertius* (or third party), and the requirement to show an intention to confer a right to damages upon the *tertius* should the performance expected by the *tertius* be defective. These two hurdles are considered in turn.

3.157 Before a *jus quaesitum tertio* can exist in Scots law, there must be demonstrated a clear intention of the contracting parties to confer an enforceable right upon the *tertius*. The intention may be express, or it may be implied, but it must be present. If the contract *B–C* can be shown expressly to demonstrate such an intention to confer a right upon *A*, then *A* will have overcome this hurdle. However, the mere fact that *C* is carrying out work under a contract *B–C* which will have the effect of benefiting *A* is not the same as an intention by *B* and *C* that *A* should receive a direct right to sue.[246] Thus, mere mention of *A* in the subcontract, which is very likely, is unlikely to constitute sufficient evidence of an intention to confer a direct right upon *A*.[247] Furthermore, a contractual warranty given by *C* to *A* is likely to suggest that no *jus quaesitum tertio* exists in *A*'s favour, as the natural inference is that *C* intended to benefit *A* by means of the warranty and not via a *jus quaesitum tertio*. This inference could be countered by the express conferral of a *jus quaesitum tertio* in the subcontract. In the absence of any express or inferred intention to confer such a title to sue, the contracting party retains the right to sue for losses.[248]

3.158 The second hurdle is the requirement to demonstrate an intention by the contracting parties that the *tertius* should have the right to claim damages should the performance rendered to it be defective. An important authority in this respect, albeit only an Outer House authority, is a case already referred to above[249] in the context of delictual claims for pure economic loss, namely *Scott Lithgow Ltd v GEC Electrical Projects Ltd*.[250] In addition to the delictual claims in the case, the Ministry of Defence claimed a *jus quaesitum tertio* in the contract between the shipbuilder (Scott Lithgow) and the subcontractor (GEC Electrical) which it argued entitled it to claim damages for pure economic loss in respect of the defective work of the subcontractor. Lord Clyde was of the opinion that a *tertius*

---

245 See further on the attractiveness of the argument and on relevant cases: H L MacQueen, 'Concrete Solutions to Liability: Changing Perspectives in Contract and Delict' (1998) 64 Arbitration 285; also MacQueen, 'Third Party Rights in Contract: *Jus Quaesitum Tertio*', in *A History of Private Law in Scotland*, at p 248, fn 156.
246 See Lord Clyde's discussion of this point in *Scott Lithgow*, 1989 SC at 441–442.
247 A point made by Lord Clyde in *Scott Lithgow* (1989 SC at 439–440), who said (at 440) of the bare averment by the pursuers of the reference by name to the MOD in the subcontract: 'The averment is remarkably unspecific in failing to explain the context in which the reference is made . . . while absence of the reference may exclude the *jus quaesitum tertio* it does not follow that the presence of a reference necessarily creates it.'
248 See in this respect the recent decision in *Scottish Enterprise v Archibald Russel of Denny Ltd* 2002 SLT 519, IH.
249 See **3.124**.
250 1989 SC 412, 1992 SLT 244, OH.

may in appropriate cases be entitled to sue for damages. Again, it is a question of the intention of the parties:

> 'In general I can see no reason why a third party should not be entitled to sue for damage for negligent performance of a contract under the principle of *jus quaesitum tertio*, but whether he is so entitled must be a matter of the intention of the contracting parties. That has to be ascertained from the terms of their contract.'[251]

Such an intention might arise by express provision, or, as with the intention to confer the benefit, by implication, although Lord Clyde accepted that 'it may well be difficult'[252] to infer such an intention. His Lordship also made the important point that the mere fact that the *tertius* might not be the only party to receive a benefit under the contract would not of itself prevent the *jus* from arising. So, in the circumstances of a construction chain, the fact that a main contractor will receive a benefit from the subcontractor's performance will not of itself prevent a *jus quaesitum tertio* from arising in favour of the employer. On the facts of the case before him, although the written pleadings required further specification of the claim, Lord Clyde thought that a right on the part of the MOD to claim damages under a *jus quaesitum tertio* might be capable of arising.

3.159 A more recent case, in which both the delictual and *jus quaesitum tertio* arguments failed is *Strathford East Kilbride Ltd v HLM Design Ltd*.[253]

> The pursuers were tenants of premises from which they operated a car dealership business. The pursuers were controlled by the Ford Motor Company, which was also their landlord. Defects were discovered in the premises which it was alleged were due to the negligence of the defenders, who were architects who had designed the premises. The pursuers sued the defenders for their pure economic loss in contract and delict. The contractual claim was pled on the basis that the pursuers had a *jus quaesitum tertio* in the contract between Ford and the defenders. That contract contained an indemnity clause in terms of which the defenders agreed to indemnify the owner of the premises against all 'costs charges and expenses' arising from the actions of the defenders. The pursuers argued that, in terms of the definition given in the contract, they fell within the definition of 'owner'. The pursuer's claim as to *jus quaesitum tertio* was rejected on the basis that the indemnity clause expressed the extent of any contractual liability which the defenders had intended to undertake, and that clause was not to be interpreted as including the pursuers within the ambit of the term 'owner'.

The *jus quaesitum tertio* argument failed here for the very simple reason that the court found there to be no intention to confer any contractual right to claim for losses, beyond the indemnity clause. As the court held that the pursuers did not fall within the definition of persons entitled to claim under that clause, that was the end of the matter.

---

251 1989 SC at 438, per Lord Clyde.
252 1989 SC at 438, per Lord Clyde.
253 1999 SLT 121 (*jus quaesitum tertio* point not reported), 1997 SCLR 877, OH.

'Negative benefits'

3.160   The situations thus far examined in relation to *jus quaesitum tertio* involve cases where the pursuer has sought to claim damages in respect of a negligently conferred benefit which the pursuer hoped would improve its position. However, that is not the only context in which a *jus quaesitum tertio* claim may be of benefit in a contractual chain case. A further situation in which a party may wish to claim a *jus quaesitum tertio* is where the right claimed is a right to be indemnified in a damages claim made against the party claiming to be the *tertius*. In other words, the pursuer seeks to claim the <u>benefit of an indemnity which will protect its position from being diminished</u>. This can be conceived of as a 'negative benefit', in contrast to the 'positive benefit' of having one's position improved. In addition to the indemnity cases, there are some 'negative benefit' cases where the clause that the *tertius* was seeking to rely on was an <u>exclusion clause</u> conceived in its favour.

3.161   There is nothing inimical to the concept of negative benefits within the doctrine of *jus quaesitum tertio*, and there are several reported cases where such a negative benefit has been pled as being the subject of a *jus quaesitum tertio*. An important authority in this respect is the decision of the Inner House in *Aberdeen Harbour Board v Heating Enterprises Aberdeen Ltd.*[254]

> The pursuers owned an office block which had been leased and in turn subleased to the third party in the case, Ferranti. The building was damaged by a fire started through the negligence of the defenders, who were carrying out works at the building as subcontractors. The pursuers sued the defenders in delict for the losses caused. The defenders pled in their defence that they were entitled to be indemnified in respect of any such claim by Ferranti. The basis of the indemnity claim was a *jus quaesitum tertio* claimed by the defenders in terms of a clause in the contract between Ferranti and the main contractors.

The relationship between the various parties may be represented in the following diagram:

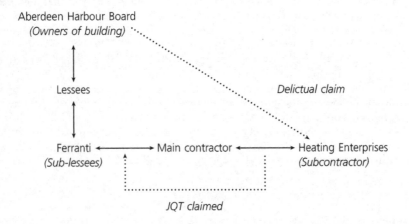

____

254   1990 SLT 416, 1989 SCLR 716, IH.

3.162 The defenders pointed to a clause (20C) in the main construction contract which stated that 'The existing structures together with the contents thereof owned by him or for which he is responsible and the works and all unfixed materials and goods, delivered to, placed on or adjacent to the works and intended therefor shall be at the sole risk of the employer as regards loss or damage by fire and the employer shall maintain adequate insurance against those risks.'[255] The defenders had been informed of, inter alia, this provision in the main contract. The defenders argued that, by taking upon itself the risk of damage to the building caused by fire, Ferranti had impliedly intended to confer the benefit of an indemnity upon the defenders for any fire damage which the defenders might cause to the building. The Inner House, however, disagreed with this argument, holding that the correct interpretation of the effect of clause 20C in the circumstances of the case was that it was not intended to deal with claims by parties other than those to the main contract, and, if that had been the intention, then one would have found in it the explicit language of indemnity. As Lord Cullen put it: 'the subject-matter of the clause related to what was at risk only so far as the contracting parties were concerned'.[256] To put it another way, the court could not find in the language of the clause any intention of the parties to confer a benefit upon a third party.

3.163 The failure of the *jus quaesitum tertio* argument in *Aberdeen Harbour Board* may explain its absence from the approach of counsel in *BT v Thomson*.[257] It will be recalled from earlier discussion,[258] that the case concerned a delictual claim by the pursuers, owners of a building, in respect of physical damage done to the building by the defenders, subcontractors working at the building. The thrust of the defenders' argument was that no duty of care should be imposed upon them because the terms of the main contract imposed upon the pursuers a duty to insure the building against loss caused by, inter alia, fire,[259] and such clause negatived any duty of care upon the defenders. An alternative to such argument would have been to adopt the approach taken in *Aberdeen Harbour Board*, and to argue that the terms of the main contract conferred a contractually enforceable indemnity upon the defenders. This was not pled, however, and there is no indication of how the House of Lords in *BT* would have responded to such an argument. It is likely, however, that they would have taken the same approach as the Inner House in *Aberdeen Harbour Board* and found that the main contract disclosed no intention to benefit the defenders. This is highly likely given that the terms of the main contract only provided for a right of insurance (or a waiver of the right of subrogation by the insurance company) in favour of a nominated subcontractor, and not a domestic subcontractor such as the defenders.

---

255 It should be added that the terms of the subcontract obliged the defenders to have in place insurance against fire damage caused by its negligence.
256 1990 SLT at 425A, per Lord Cullen.
257 1999 SC (HL) 9, 1999 SLT 224, 1999 SCLR 126, HL.
258 At **3.94–3.97**.
259 The relevant clause, whilst from the same standard form contract as was at issue in prior cases such as *Scottish Special Housing Association v Wimpey* 1986 SC (HL) 57, 1986 SLT 559, had been subject to modification since the date of the earlier cases.

3.164 On the other hand, the negative *jus quaesitum tertio* argument was successful in *Melrose v Davidson and Robertson*.[260] In that case, the defenders, who were surveyors from whom damages were sought in delict by a house purchaser in respect of a negligent survey, successfully argued that they were entitled to rely upon an exclusion clause in the contract between the house purchaser and the building society. Lord President Hope stated that they were entitled so to do 'on the principle of *jus quaesitum tertio*'.[261] In fact, however, this did not assist the surveyors' position greatly, as it was held that the exclusion clause was struck down by the Unfair Contract Terms Act 1977, s 16.

Claims by beneficiaries

3.165 A final scenario worthy of discussion in relation to the possibilities of a *jus quaesitum tertio* argument is that of the *White v Jones*[262] disappointed beneficiary. Could such a disappointed beneficiary claim to have a *jus quaesitum tertio* in the contract between the deceased and the solicitor? Any claim would have to be for damages in respect of the solicitor's negligent performance of his duties, as the executors of the deceased could not be compelled to transfer a legacy to the disappointed beneficiaries which was not supported by a valid testamentary provision. In this respect the same points arise in relation to the right of a *tertius* to claim damages as arose in the *Scott Lithgow* case.[263]

3.166 There are, however, more fundamental conceptual difficulties relating to whether this sort of case may be analysed as giving rise to a *jus quaesitum tertio*. In *Scott Lithgow* Lord Clyde was referred by counsel to a discussion in Gloag on the earlier Scottish authority of *Robertson v Fleming*,[264] also on the question of a possible remedy of a third party disappointed by a solicitor's negligence. Referring to comments of the late T B Smith on Gloag's discussion of this case, Lord Clyde noted:

> 'As Professor Smith points out that case, and indeed others referred to by Gloag, are cases of persons disappointed by the negligence of a law agent who was acting for another trying themselves to claim damages against the law agent. They were not claims truly based upon a *jus quaesitum tertio*.'[265]

These comments were echoed by comments of Lord Goff in *White v Jones*. Having discussed the notion of a *jus quaesitum tertio*, which in any event English law did not recognise at that point, his Lordship said of the facts of *White v Jones*:

> '[T]he ordinary law could not provide a simple answer to the problems which arise in the present case, which appear at first sight to require the imposition of something like a contractual liability which is beyond the scope of the ordinary *jus quaesitum tertio*.'[266]

---

260 1993 SC 288, 1993 SLT 611, IH.
261 1993 SLT at 614.
262 [1995] 2 AC 207, [1995] 1 All ER 691, HL.
263 Discussed at **3.158**.
264 (1861) 4 Macq 167, HL.
265 1989 SC at 437, per Lord Clyde.
266 [1995] 2 AC at 263A, per Lord Goff.

3.167 What makes the position of the disappointed beneficiary inapt for analysis as that of a *tertius*? It cannot be that the difficulty lies in the fact that the disappointed party is attempting to claim damages, for as Lord Clyde noted in *Scott Lithgow* such a claim is not inimical to the doctrine of *jus quaesitum tertio*. The answer may lie in the nature of the contract. The traditionally conceived contract giving rise to a third party right is one where one party (the stipulator) requests the other party (the debtor) to confer a benefit upon the *tertius*. This model does not seem to fit the facts of *White v Jones*. In such a case, the testator appears to be both stipulator and debtor. It is the testator who stipulates for the benefit to be conferred upon the beneficiaries, but it is upon the testator's estate that the debt rests. All that the solicitor does is to enable the transaction to have proper legal effect. A further answer may be that *jus quaesitum tertio* is concerned with the irrevocable grant of a right upon a party. However, any right which an expectant beneficiary may have under a will before the testator's death can only ever be an imperfect right, as the testator may change his mind at any point prior to death. A third answer may be that the solicitor may argue that he has no intention of directly benefiting anyone other than his client by his actions. It is to the client alone that the services are performed. Any incidental benefit to the beneficiary is just that, an incidental benefit.

3.168 It may be possible to counter the first argument by pointing out that it will not be in every contract that one party will be the sole debtor and one the sole stipulator. It is conceivable that under a contract benefits might be conferred upon the *tertius* by both parties to the contract. It may be an answer to the second argument to point out that the case law demonstrates that while an irrevocable grant of the right is a pre-requisite to the formation of a *jus quaesitum tertio*, the case law also demonstrates that it is possible to grant a right over which the parties to the contract retain the power to vary or revoke.[267] An answer to the third argument may be that the whole purpose of executry work is to benefit the client's beneficiaries after the client's death, and that to argue that no benefit is intended to be conferred upon the beneficiary is simply disingenuous. Despite these counter arguments, the judicial comments cited above indicate a reluctance to construe the disappointed beneficiary as a *tertius*. The opportunity will no doubt arise to challenge such judicial reluctance at a future date.

Solutions to problems 3: transferred loss analysis

3.169 The term 'transferred loss' is not a term of art,[268] and can be used in a number of ways. Essentially, however, it encapsulates the idea of a party with title to sue for losses seeking to include within its claim losses suffered by another party. These losses are, if claimable, treated as if they were the losses of the party claiming even though they are not strictly its own losses.

---

267 *Love v Amalgamated Society of Lithographic Printers* 1912 SC 1078, 1912 2 SLT 50, IH.

268 Lord Goff said (in *Alfred McAlpine v Panatown* [2001] 1 AC at 557C) of his own use of the term: 'an expression which I have myself adopted from time to time, though not I fear with any great accuracy'. On transferred loss, see further H Unberath, *Transferred Loss: Claiming Third Party Loss in Contract Law* (Hart Publishing, 2003).

3.170 Two variations of such claims may be drawn. The first variation concerns cases where rights which *A* has to claim for losses caused by *B* are validly assigned to a third party *C*. *C* seeks to have losses suffered by it deemed to be part of *A*'s losses. As shall be seen, such a claim for increased losses cannot be permitted without undermining the rule regarding the nature of an assignee's rights. The second variation concerns cases where a party, *A*, has not validly assigned its claim for losses caused by party *B* to party *C*. *A* therefore seeks to have losses suffered by *C* deemed to be part of *A*'s losses.

3.171 *Variation 1*: The type of case arising under this variation may be portrayed as follows:

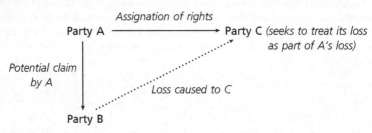

3.172 A case which appears at first glance to fit this scenario is the decision of the House of Lords in *GUS Property Management Ltd v Littlewoods Mail Order Stores Ltd*.[269]

> Rest Property Ltd ('Rest') owned a building which was damaged by contractors working on a neighbouring building owned by the defenders, Littlewoods. Rest sold its building to the pursuers, GUS, a related company, for its book value (£259,000, a figure which ignored any repair costs required to rectify the damage done to the building). GUS thereupon undertook repairs to the building. Thereafter, Rest assigned any claims it might have in respect of the building to GUS. GUS sued Littlewoods in delict for the difference between the value of the building undamaged (£650,000) and its value as damaged (£300,000) or, alternatively, for the cost of repairs (£100,000). The defender argued that because at the time of the assignation the repairs had already been carried out by GUS, Rest would have had no claim to sue for such costs, not having undertaken them. Therefore, they could not assign any such claim to GUS. The House of Lords disagreed, holding that the pursuers were entitled to a proof before answer to determine the measure of the damages to which they were entitled.

3.173 It is well-settled law that an assignee gets no better right and title than its cedent. The question therefore was whether the cedent, Rest, would have been entitled to sue for the damage done to the building at the time of the assignation. Lord Keith affirmed that where specific property had been damaged as the result of a delict, it was a general rule that the owner of the property did not, by parting with it to another, lose his title and interest to pursue a claim for damages against the wrongdoer.[270] Where the transfer price for the property (if any) was ascertained without reference to its real value, as had been the case here, such price was irrelevant in determining the *true loss* which the transferor may have suffered as a

269 1982 SC (HL) 157, 1982 SLT 533, HL.
270 See Lord Keith, 1982 SC (HL) at 179.

result of the delict. Such loss, whether it might be depreciation in value or cost of repair, fell to be determined by proof.[271]

3.174   In fact, therefore, the explanation given by the House of Lords is that this was not a case of transferred loss. The House of Lords was saying that the *actual* loss of the cedent fell to be properly assessed as including the value of the claim against the negligent contractor, even although it had not undertaken the repairs. It was not therefore a case of treating *another party's* losses as if they were the losses arising under the claim.

3.175   It is suggested that the analysis of the House of Lords is correct. If that were not so, then whenever, for instance, as happens on a daily basis, A's property was damaged by B, and repaired by A's insurers at no cost to A, A would be barred from raising an action in delict on the basis that A had suffered no loss, the costs of repairs having been met by the insurer. This of course is not the case.[272]

3.176   The decision reached in *GUS* might suggest that a pursuer would never seek to have its costs included in a claim assigned to it by another party. However, there may be cases where costs incurred by C are much greater than the losses held to be suffered by A. Consider the following example:

> A's antique car, worth £50,000, is damaged by B. The car in its damaged state is worth £45,000. A lives in Glasgow near a specialist mechanic who could have repaired the damages for £2,000. A decides not to have repairs undertaken himself but sells the car to C, his cousin, for £45,000. Prior to conclusion of the sale, C, who lives in the north of Scotland has the repair carried out locally at his expense at a cost of £4,000. At the conclusion of the sale, A assigns his rights against B to C. Is C's claim against B restricted to £2,000, or may he claim £4,000?

3.177   In such a case C might wish to be able to have its extra costs treated as if they were the losses of A. The ratio of *GUS* does not extend to such a claim, although on principle it should be the case that C cannot claim its increased costs. To do so would subvert the well-established rule *assignatus utitur jure auctoris* (an assignee enjoys his author's rights). It is doubtful that the rationale of variation 2 cases would apply to permit a transferred loss claim in such a case. After all, the rationale at work in variation 2 cases is, as shall be seen, an equitable one operating in favour of a party who has *no* claim at all. That is not the position of a party who has had a valid claim assigned to it, albeit one which does not extend to the full extent of its own expenditure.

3.178   *Variation 2:* English law has exceptionally permitted a claim for contractual damages to be made by A on behalf of C for losses suffered by C. The situation may be depicted thus:

---

271   Lord Keith kept an open mind as to whether the correct measure of loss might be found to be diminution in value or costs of repairs: 'It may well be that at the end of the day the proper measure of Rest's loss will turn out to be the estimated cost of making good the damage to the building, rather than the diminution in its market value. It may also be that there will not be found to be any substantial difference between the two measures. But these are considerations which will properly arise after evidence has been led' (Lord Keith, 1982 SC at 178–179).

272   See in support of this view, the comments of Lord Drummond Young in *McLaren Murdoch & Hamilton Ltd v The Abercromby Motor Group Ltd* 2003 SCLR 323, OH, at para 34 of His Lordship's opinion.

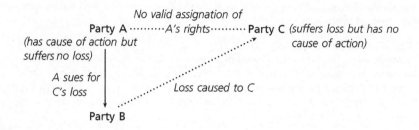

This is an exception to the normal rule that damages in contract are only awarded to a party in respect of losses suffered by it.[273] This claim can provide a useful alternative to a tortious (or delictual) claim by C, where such a claim may not be permitted by the law.

3.179 Such a type 2 situation has arisen in the construction industry. Consider the following example. B constructs a building for A. A transfers ownership of the building to C for full value but A does not validly assign its rights under its contract with B to C. Defects are discovered in the building which cause the new owner, C, to suffer economic loss. A is, on the face of it, unable to sue B for these losses as they are suffered by C not A, A having received full value for the price of the building upon its sale. C on the face of it is unable to sue for its losses as C is not a party to the contract.

3.180 In this situation, the courts are highly unlikely to allow C to sue in delict for its purely economic losses. C may be able to sue A in contract if, for instance, A had purported validly to transfer its rights under the contract A–B to C but had in fact failed to do so. However, A is unlikely to have an onward contractual claim against B for losses amounting to the damages paid by it to C, because such damages are likely to be unforeseeable and thus too remote so far as B is concerned.[274]

3.181 In circumstances such as these, the English courts have allowed A to raise an action against B and claim the losses suffered by C. This result was reached in *St Martin's Property Corporation Ltd and another v Sir Robert McAlpine & Sons Ltd*:[275]

> The first plaintiff entered into a standard form building contract with the defendant for the construction of a building. While the construction was underway the first plaintiff sold the property for full value to the second plaintiff, a related company. The first plaintiff also purported to assign its rights under the contract to the second plaintiff, however it failed to obtain the consent of the defendant to this assignment as required in terms of the contract. After completion of the construction works, the building was discovered to be defective. The second plaintiff carried out remedial works costing £800,000. The first plaintiff reimbursed the second plaintiff for the cost of these repairs. The first and second plaintiffs sued the defendants for the costs of

273   The correctness of this 'normal rule' being of general application has been questioned. In *Alfred McAlpine v Panatown*, Lord Goff, referring to doubts of Professor Treitel concerning the rule, said in reference to such doubts: 'I share his scepticism about the existence of this "rule" ' ([2001] 1 AC at 544D).

274   This was the view taken in the *St Martin's Property* case, discussed at **3.181**.

275   [1994] 1 AC 85, [1993] 3 WLR 408, [1993] 3 All ER 417, HL.

such remedial works. The defendant argued that the second plaintiffs had no title to sue, the purported assignment being invalid, and that the first defendant had suffered no loss, having sold the property for full value,[276] and was not permitted to claim for the second plaintiff's loss. The House of Lords held (1) that the second plaintiff could not recover for the cost of the repairs under the contract, as the purported assignment was of no effect; and (2) that the first plaintiff was entitled to claim for the cost of the repairs undertaken by the second plaintiff.

3.182   The first plaintiff had tried to argue that it had suffered substantial losses, because it had been liable under its contractual arrangements with the second plaintiff to pay for the cost of the repairs undertaken by the second defendant. However, as Lord Browne-Wilkinson noted, this loss was considered too remote to sound in a contractual damages action against the builder.[277] However, His Lordship was prepared to treat the facts of the *St Martin's* case as an extension of the principle established by *The Albazero*.[278] That decision had established, as an exception to the rule that a contracting party may only recover damages for its own loss, the principle that:

> '[I]n a commercial contract concerning goods where it is in the contemplation of the parties that the proprietary interests in the goods may be transferred from one owner to another after the contract has been entered into and before the breach which causes loss or damage to the goods, an original party to the contract, if such be the intention of them both, is to be treated in law as having entered into the contract for the benefit of all persons who have or may acquire an interest in the goods before they are lost or damaged, and is entitled to recover by way of damages for breach of contract the actual loss sustained by those for whose benefit the contract is entered into'[279]

That principle was extended to the *St Martin's* facts: the parties to the construction contract were to be taken as having entered into the contract on the basis that the first plaintiff would be entitled to enforce a contractual claim for the benefit of a party who had suffered loss as a result of defective performance of the contract but who, in terms of the contract, could 'not acquire any right' to enforce the claim.[280]

Difficulties with the transferred loss approach

3.183   This was an attractive approach, as it prevented the loss from falling into a black hole. But a number of difficulties may be identified with it:

(1)   The rationale is based upon the presumed intention of the parties. However, might it not be said that the *express* intention of the parties as to how a third

---

276   In similar circumstances in *McLaren Murdoch & Hamilton Ltd v The Abercromby Motor Group Ltd* 2003 SCLR 323, OH, Lord Drummond Young expressly rejected the view that a sale at full value by the contracting party negated loss: 'Nor does it matter that the defenders may have transferred the property to [the third party] at full value; the loss resulting from the breach of contract was still sustained by the defenders, and the involvement of [the third party] is *res inter alios acta*' (para 34).

277   See the comments of Lord Browne-Wilkinson [1994] 1 AC at 110B–D.

278   [1977] AC 774, [1976] 3 All ER 129, HL.

279   *The Albazero* [1977] AC at 847, per Lord Diplock.

280   [1994] 1 AC at 115B, per Lord Browne-Wilkinson.

party might acquire an interest in performance was clearly set out in the clause detailing how an assignment might be effected? Arguably such a clause should have been taken to be exhaustive of the parties' intentions as to the interest of any third party. This difficulty flies off if one bases the rationale of the decision not upon the presumed intention of the parties, but upon legal policy, an approach which has subsequently been adopted in the Scottish courts.[281]

(2) It is factually incorrect to state, as Lord Browne-Wilkinson did, that the second plaintiff could 'not acquire any right' under the contract. A clear mechanism for acquiring rights was set out in the assignment clause.

(3) It is not stated in *St Martin's* how the second plaintiff might compel recovery from the first plaintiff of damages claimed for the former's losses.[282] In fact, it was later asserted in the *Alfred McAlpine* case, discussed below at **3.190–3.192**, that there is a clear duty upon the first plaintiff in such a case to account.[283] The approach of English law would be to view the funds as held in trust. In Scots law, a preferable answer to creating a constructive trust would be that, if the party suing for the damages refused to transfer these to the party who had suffered the loss, restitution of the damages could be sought on the principle of unjustified enrichment.

3.184 More fundamentally, it is possible to question whether the *St Martin's* facts ought properly be seen as involving 'transferred loss' at all. This was indeed the approach of the majority of the court, who extended the transferred loss rationale of *The Albazero* to a building case, an approach subsequently dubbed the 'narrow approach'.[284] However, a more radical approach was suggested by Lord Griffiths in his speech, an approach subsequently dubbed the 'broader approach'. This broader approach treats the innocent party's recovery of substantial damages as losses properly seen as *its own losses*. The losses are to be seen as its own because, it is said, the loss is not constituted by the cost of any repairs, but is constituted by the mere fact that the contracting party did not receive the performance it expected. Lord Griffiths suggested that, for instance, the husband who contracts to have his wife's property repaired is entitled to substantial damages if the contract is breached, because his loss lies in the failure to receive the performance expected. If Lord Griffiths' more radical approach is correct, then the *St Martin's* case is not really about transferred loss at all. It represents a restatement of the legal basis upon which a party's own entitlement to damages for breach of contract is to be viewed. It will be argued below[285] that this more radical approach is inconsistent with established principles for assessing damages, and should not be adopted.

---

281 In this respect one may note the comment of Lord Drummond Young in *McLaren Murdoch & Hamilton Ltd v The Abercromby Motor Group Ltd*: 'It should not in my view be based on the intention of the parties; the right is rather conferred as a matter of general legal policy, to ensure that if a loss results from a breach of contract damages can be recovered from the party responsible for the breach' (2003 SCLR 323, OH, at para 42).

282 Although in the *St Martin's* case itself, the first plaintiff had reimbursed voluntarily the second plaintiff before the action was raised.

283 See the comments of Lord Browne-Wilkinson ([2001] 1 AC at 575F), who refers to a recognition of this duty to account in *The Albazero*.

284 See the discussion of the narrow versus broad approaches in the speeches of the House of Lords in *Alfred McAlpine*, discussed below at **3.190–3.192**.

285 See **3.228–3.331**.

Need to show proprietary interest before loss may be claimed?

3.185 Whilst Lord Griffiths' broader approach to damages may be doubted, it can still be argued that the first plaintiff in *St Martin's* suffered losses of its own. The argument may be stated as follows. It is to be recognised that neither of the two principal measures for calculating contractual damages, cost of cure or difference in value, is tied to the requirement that the pursuer have a proprietary interest in the thing damaged (whether moveable or heritable property) at the time the action is raised. In this respect one may note the comments of Lord Lloyd in *Ruxley Electronics v Forsyth*,[286] who, commenting on the assessment of loss in construction matters, said 'it is not the diminution of the value of the freehold which provides the correct comparison, but the diminution in the value of the works.'[287]

3.186 Applying this approach to the *St Martin's* facts, the first plaintiff could be argued to have suffered actual loss based upon the cost of cure of the defects (for which it had indemnified the second plaintiff) or by reference to the difference in value of the services received (the defective building works) from those con-tracted for.[288] So viewed, the case could be argued to be one involving actual loss to the first plaintiff, without the need to resort to the more radical approach of Lord Griffiths. The approach outlined may be dubbed the 'non-proprietorial approach', lacking as it does any requirement that the claimant show a proprie-tary interest in the thing constructed or repaired before loss may be considered the claimant's own. However, even adopting a non-proprietorial approach to loss, the position of the first plaintiff in *St Martin's* might not have been greatly advanced. It might well have been held that, using either method of calculating loss, cost of cure or difference in value, its losses were unforeseeable from the point of view of the defendant.[289] In which case, recourse to a transferred loss approach might still have been necessary in order to provide an equitable solution. Of course, if in another case it could be shown that losses suffered were foreseeable, the non-proprietorial approach might provide a means of avoiding recourse to *The Albazero* exception, so long as an actual financial impact upon the party suffering breach could be shown. This might be so where, for instance, the party which had suffered the breach was obliged to make good defects to the third party, although this would not be so where no such obligation existed.[290]

---

286 [1996] AC 344.

287 [1996] AC at 371G.

288 It might be argued that difference in value would be inappropriate, as it had received full value for the works upon transfer of the land to the third party. However, given that it had later indemnified the third party in respect of the defects, thus effectively reducing the value of what it had received, it might still be argued that the value of what it had received was less than the value contracted for. Moreover, it has been subsequently commented judicially that the fact that a transfer for full value takes place is irrelevant: see the comments of Lord Drummond Young noted at fn 276 above.

289 The House of Lords did hold that the costs of indemnifying the second plaintiffs were unforesee-able from the point of view of the defendant. However, in opposition to this view, it might be argued that it is foreseeable that a commercial party which receives defective building services will undertake remedial works to cure them or, if it has sold the building at a time when the defects were latent, may incur liability to the buyer when the defects become patent.

290 For instance, where a husband contracted for repairs to his wife's property, the husband would not be considered to have suffered loss unless he was obliged to make good the defects in the services provided.

3.187 This non-proprietorial approach is well established in claims by main contractors against subcontractors. Where *A* (a main contractor) enters into a contract with *B* (a subcontractor) for the performance by *B* of work on *C*'s property, *A* will itself be able to recover substantial losses on its own behalf if it is obliged to remedy defective workmanship by *B*. The costs of so doing, so long as they are foreseeable losses, will constitute losses for which *A* can sue in its own name, and there will be no need to show that *A* has any proprietorial interest in *C*'s property, or to resort to the doctrine of transferred loss.[291]

3.188 The question of the proper method for calculating contractual damages is discussed in more detail below.[292]

Transferred loss claims by disappointed beneficiaries

3.189 The possibility of a transferred loss claim was considered by the House of Lords in *White v Jones*.[293] The possibility was considered of the executors of the deceased's estate claiming as contractual damages the losses suffered by the disappointed beneficiaries. In his speech Lord Goff made the following points in relation to such a claim:

(1) The application of transferred loss analysis to the *White v Jones* situation was not wholly apposite, as the testator could never have suffered the loss suffered by the beneficiaries. This distinguished it from, for instance, the case of the owner of a defective building, where the injury caused by a negligent builder would have been suffered by the original owner of the building had ownership in it not been transferred. Is it important, as Lord Goff suggests, to make such a distinction? If he is correct, then the following situation would also not be strictly classifiable as a transferred loss scenario: a man purchases tickets for his wife and children to go on a roller-coaster ride, although himself does not join them as he is not fond of that particular form of entertainment. The terms of the contract require the consent of the roller-coaster operator before rights under the contract may be assigned. An accident occurs during the course of the ride, injuring the man's family. If the family do not wish to claim in delict, but request him to sue on their behalf in contract, is he permitted to use transferred loss analysis to claim for their injuries? They are injuries which he himself would never have suffered, not having gone on the ride, and thus on Lord Goff's analysis this would not strictly amount to a transferred loss claim.[294] It seems, however, that English

---

291 Somewhat surprisingly, this well-established rule was challenged by the defender in *Scottish Enterprise v Archibald Russel of Denny Ltd* 2002 SLT 519, IH. The defender argued that as Scottish Enterprise (the main contractor) had voluntarily assumed the cost of the repairs, they had suffered no loss. Before the Sheriff Principal, it was held that in the absence of any inference that the parties had intended to confer a title to sue upon the owner of the land, Scottish Enterprise, as the contracting party, retained title and interest to seek damages for the costs of the repairs. On appeal to the Inner House, the Sheriff Principal's decision was upheld.

292 See **3.226** ff.

293 [1995] 2 AC 207, HL.

294 Although it is true to say that, in relation to the example given, the husband could in theory have gone on the roller-coaster, and could therefore have been injured, whereas the solicitor's negligence in *White v Jones* could not have caused any loss to the estate, given that it had in any event to be distributed.

law would have no difficulty in allowing a claim to be raised by the husband in such a case. In the *St Martin's* case, Lord Griffiths cites a similar example concerning a husband who enters a contract for the repair of property owned by his wife.[295] Lord Griffiths states that it would be absurd to conclude that the husband could not sue for the losses suffered by the wife if the repairs were defective.[296] If that is correct, which it is suggested that it is, then the distinction made by Lord Goff in *White v Jones* may not be significant.

(2) A transferred loss claim might well be unsuitable in testamentary cases as 'the family relationship may be such that the executors may be unwilling to assist the disappointed beneficiary by pursuing a claim of this kind for his benefit.'[297] With respect, the same practical problem might have arisen in the *St Martin's* case had the governing bodies of the two plaintiff companies been antagonistic to each other. In any event, however, the transferred loss approach was not attempted by the plaintiffs in *White v Jones* and we therefore lack any definitive ruling on whether a claim by executors for losses suffered by disappointed beneficiaries could be sought.

Transferred loss revisited by House of Lords: Alfred McAlpine v Panatown

3.190 The House of Lords had occasion to review its approach in the *St Martin's* case in its subsequent decision in *Alfred McAlpine Construction Ltd v Panatown Ltd:*[298]

The appellants, Alfred McAlpine Ltd, were contractors under a contract for the construction of an office and car park for the respondents, Panatown Ltd. The site was owned by a sister company of Panatown, UIPL, in whose favour the appellants were required to issue a so-called 'duty of care deed' by which the appellants undertook to exercise due skill, care and attention in the performance of their contractual duties. The respondents raised proceedings under the contract alleging defective workmanship and delay, and sued for substantial damages. The appellants contested the proceedings, inter alia, on the ground that the respondents, having no proprietary interest in the site, had suffered no loss. The House of Lords held (by 3–2)

---

295 [1994] 1 AC at 96–97, per Lord Griffiths.
296 Such a case might more naturally be seen in Scots law as one where the wife had a *jus quaesitum tertio*. Lord Griffiths took the view that the husband has suffered loss 'because he did not receive the bargain for which he had contracted' ([1994] 1 AC at 97A). However, Lord Clyde in his majority speech in *Alfred McAlpine* expressed dissatisfaction with this approach, stating: 'A breach of contract may cause a loss, but is not in itself a loss in any meaningful sense. When one refers to a loss in the context of a breach of contract, one is in my view referring to the incidence of some personal or patrimonial damage' ([2001] 1 AC at 534D). Per contra, Lord Griffiths' approach was praised by Lord Goff in his dissenting speech in *Alfred McAlpine*: 'I find persuasive the reasoning and conclusion expressed by Lord Griffiths in his opinion in the *St Martin's* case that the employer under a building contract may in principle recover substantial damages from the building contractor, because he has not received the performance which he was entitled to receive from the contractor under the contract, notwithstanding that the property in the building site was vested in a third party' ([2001] 1 AC at 547A–B).
297 [1995] 2 AC at 267G, per Lord Goff.
298 [2001] 1 AC 518, [2000] 4 All ER 97, [2000] 3 WLR 946, HL.

that as the owner was entitled to exercise a direct remedy against the appellants under the duty of care deed, the respondents were not entitled to anything other than nominal damages.

So far as the majority of the House of Lords were concerned, the crucial distinction between these facts and those of the *St Martin's* case was the existence in *Alfred McAlpine* of the direct contractual claim available to the owner under its duty of care deed (a contractual warranty). The majority viewed the existence of this contractual right to claim for losses as fatal to the possibility of a transferred loss claim being raised by the respondents.[299] The exception established by *The Albazero* and extended in the *St Martin's* case was just that, an exception, and should not be available where another avenue could be used.[300] A concern was also expressed, that to give the respondents a claim for substantial damages, would have opened up the danger of the appellants being held liable twice in respect of the same loss.[301]

3.191 Lord Goff gave a lengthy dissenting speech, in which he called for a radical re-assessment of the theoretical basis of damages for breach of contract.[302] He threw his weight behind the broad approach of Lord Griffiths in *St Martin's* suggesting that this should form the basis of an assessment of contractual damages based upon protection of the performance interest, rather than loss suffered. This matter is considered further below under a general discussion of the assessment of contractual damages.[303]

3.192 It was suggested above that a 'non-proprietorial' approach to damages in *St Martin's* could have allowed the first plaintiff in that case to be viewed as suffering actual loss (although the problem of the foreseeability of the loss might have remained). Could the same have been said of *Alfred McAlpine*? Cost of cure would not seem to be appropriate, as it does not appear that the respondents incurred any liability for cure towards the third party. However, it could still be maintained that the value of the services contracted for was less than those provided under the contract. This would not be conclusive as to the appropriateness of such a direct claim by the respondent however. Importantly, it does not seem from the facts of the case that Alfred McAlpine suffered any actual detriment to its financial position by the breach, irregardless of the method of valuation adopted. In particular, it was under no obligation to the owner of the building to make reparation for the defects. Furthermore, as already noted above, to have allowed a direct claim by Alfred McAlpine would have opened up the possibility of double recovery against the defendant. In the light of these factors, it appears more consistent with the intention of the parties to give precedence to any direct claim available to the third party, rather than to have recourse to transferred loss analysis.

---

299   See, for instance, [2001] 1 AC at 567H-577A, per Lord Browne-Wilkinson.
300   See Lord Clyde's comments, [2001] 1 AC at 532B, and those of Lord Jauncey at 568E–F.
301   See Lord Jauncey [2001] 1 AC at 574F.
302   In this he was supported by Lord Millett, who also spoke at length of the merits of a broad approach to assessment of contractual damages.
303   See **3.226** ff.

Attitude of the Scottish courts

3.193   The approach of the House of Lords in *St Martin's* and *Alfred McAlpine* has been considered in a number of Scottish cases.[304] The Scottish courts have accepted with little dispute that where *A* contracts with *B* for services to be provided by *B* for the benefit of *C*, the measure of damages in the event of breach by *B* is properly seen as the actual loss suffered by *C*. In *Blyth & Blyth Ltd v Carillion Construction Ltd*,[305] Lord Eassie referred to the same sorts of case which had troubled Lord Griffiths in *St Martin's*, commenting:

> 'If a husband contract with a surgeon for the treatment of his wife, the liability of the surgeon for negligently treating the wife will be the loss sustained by her. If a father engage a garage to repair his son's small, elderly car by a particular date and the garage fails timeously to repair it, the liability of the garage would be measured by the cost of hiring a replacement small car and not, say, the cost of the father's hiring a large limousine because the son has borrowed the family saloon.'[306]

The use of transferred loss analysis to solve the problem of the damages 'black hole' was approved in the Outer House in *McLaren Murdoch & Hamilton Ltd v The Abercromby Motor Group Ltd*,[307] in which Lord Drummond Young considered the relevant English authorities in detail.

> The pursuers, a firm of chartered architects, were appointed in connection with a project for the construction of four car showrooms for the defenders. The workshops were constructed to the design of the pursuers. The pursuers raised an action in respect of unpaid fees, and the defenders counterclaimed for damages in respect of alleged negligence in the design of a heating system for the showrooms. The pursuers argued, inter alia, that any losses suffered in respect of the heating system had not been suffered by the defenders, but by related companies in whose names title to the showrooms was taken. The Lord Ordinary, Lord Drummond Young, applying the transferred loss analysis developed by the House of Lords in *Alfred McAlpine*, held that the defenders were entitled to include the losses sustained by its related companies within its counterclaim.

Lord Drummond Young, having reviewed the English authorities on transferred loss which culminated in the *St Martin's* decision, commented: 'Although the approach of the majority of the House of Lords in the latter case was based on a series of English authorities ..., the result is in my opinion wholly consistent with the principles of Scots law.'[308] His Lordship summarised the rule on transferred loss as being that

---

304   *Adams v Young*, 19 January 2001, OH (unreported); *Clark Contracts v The Burrell Company* 2003 SLT (Sh Ct) 73; *McLaren Murdoch v The Abercromby Motor Group* 2003 SCLR 323. Although *Alfred McAlpine* was not cited in the judgment of the Lord Ordinary, similar issues were also raised in *Blyth & Blyth v Carillion Construction Ltd*, 18 April 2001, OH (unreported).

305   18 April 2001, OH (unreported).

306   Per Lord Eassie, at para 36. What this means, of course, is that *A*, the contracting party, cannot claim its own losses if they are greater than the third party's, a position applied by the court in *Blyth & Blyth*.

307   2003 SCLR 323, OH.

308   Per Lord Drummond Young at para 42.

'[I]f a breach of contract occurs, causing loss that can be measured in financial terms, the party who is not in breach may recover substantial damages even if that loss has been sustained by another person; if a loss has been sustained by a person other than the contracting party, however, the contracting party must sue on behalf of that other, and must accordingly account to that other for the damages recovered.'[309]

3.194   Approval was also given in *McLaren Murdoch* to their Lordships' approach in *Alfred McAlpine* to cases where the third party has a free-standing right to claim damages on its own behalf:

'[I]f the third party who suffers loss has a direct right of action against the party in breach of contract, for example under a duty of care warranty, there is no need for the contracting party to have a right of action on the third party's behalf, and the law will not deem such a right to exist.'[310]

Transferred loss and jus quaesitum tertio

3.195   To the Scots lawyer, an alternative approach to the *St Martin's* type problem might be found in the doctrine of *jus quaesitum tertio*. One could argue that the third party *C* is a *tertius* under a *jus quaesitum tertio* conferred by the building contract *A–B*. However, the success of such an argument will depend upon a close reading of the terms of the contract.[311] If the contract contains a clause permitting assignation of *A*'s rights to a third party according to a specified procedure (such as the prior written consent of the other party), a court might conclude that this procedure represented the full extent of *B*'s intention to confer rights upon a third party. The possibility of assignation of the employer's rights might thus be held to exclude any intention to confer a *jus quaesitum tertio* upon a singular successor as owner of the property. On the other hand, it might be argued that the very presence of an assignation clause should not necessarily be seen as exclusive of any rights a third party might have. There are after all reported cases of *jus quaesitum tertio* where the parties to the contract have provided for the possibility of assignation of contractual rights in addition to the rights conferred upon a *tertius*.

3.196   The fact that the contracting parties might have chosen to confer a *jus quaesitum tertio* upon a third party, but did not do so, does not necessarily prevent the operation of transferred loss analysis. This view would seem to follow from the willingness of a Scottish court to apply transferred loss analysis in *McLaren Murdoch*, in circumstances where the contracting parties might have chosen to confer a *jus quaesitum tertio* had they so wished.[312]

---

309   Per Lord Drummond Young at para 42.
310   Per Lord Drummond Young at para 42.
311   As Lord Drummond Young noted in *McLaren Murdoch*: 'The *jus quaesitum tertio* is of limited utility, however, owing to certain of the restrictions that have been built in to its application. In the first place, the parties must intend to benefit the third party ... [this restriction] would exclude from the application of the *jus quaesitum tertio* any case in which one party to a contract was unaware that the other intended to benefit a third party, such as a member of his family or a company in the same group' (para 39).
312   Lord Drummond Young discusses the possibility of a *jus quaesitum tertio* in the case at para 39 of his opinion.

3.197   Where, however, a third party has been given an express warranty under a duty of care deed, the existence of such a deed may give rise to the inference that it was through that medium that the third party was to be given enforceable rights, rather than via the doctrine of *jus quaesitum tertio*.[313] Parties using the route of contractual warranties should therefore be aware that by so doing they are likely to be taken to have excluded the conferral of a *jus quaesitum tertio*. This should not be problematic for the third party, so long as the terms of the contractual warranty are sufficiently robust to meet any likely claims of the party in whose favour the warranty is made.

Conclusion on the three solutions to problems

3.198   The purpose in considering the three foregoing 'solutions to problems' was to evaluate alternative solutions which might be preferable to an uncertain delictual claim for loss caused by a contracting party to a third party. Solution 1, the contractual warranty, is the simplest, but by its nature requires forward planning to be effective. It will also, if *Alfred McAlpine* is correct, exclude the possibility of solution 3, transferred loss analysis. Solution 2, *jus quaesitum tertio*, is also to be commended. It shares the merit with solution 1 of being a contractual solution, and thus likely to be favoured by the courts over delict. If solution 2 is to be adopted, it will require a clear indication of intent by the contracting parties. It is more likely to be argued as a fall-back position should a delictual claim fail, and is also more likely to be argued in the absence of an express contractual warranty. Indeed, if such an express contractual warranty exists, then this is likely to mitigate against any inference that a *jus quaesitum tertio* was intended. Solution 3, transferred loss analysis, has now received approval in the Outer House. The House of Lords has chosen not to apply it where an alternative contractual route exists, such as solution 1 (the contractual warranty), an approach which emphasises the majority view in *Alfred McAlpine* that it is an exception to the ordinary rules for the assessment of contractual damages. While it has been suggested that, using a non-proprietorial approach to assessing damages, in some cases it may be possible to view damages sustained as those of the pursuer, rather than a transferred loss, there remain cases where reference to transferred loss analysis will be necessary, and its approval by the Scottish courts is welcome.

IMPACT OF CONTRACTUAL EXCLUSIONS ON DELICTUAL LIABILITY

3.199   The availability in the circumstances outlined above of a concurrent delictual remedy as an alternative to a contractual remedy raises the question of the extent to which a party's liability in delict may be restricted or excluded by terms in the contract. This question arises in cases where the attempted exclusion or restriction is in respect of the other contracting party, in cases where it is in

---

313   A third party, C, enforcing rights conferred under a duty of care deed, is strictly not enforcing rights under the contract A–B, and cannot be considered as exercising a *jus quaesitum tertio*.

respect of a third party, and in cases where it is in relation to any party. Consideration needs to be given both to the common law but also to legislative considerations stemming from the Unfair Contract Terms Act 1977 as well as the Unfair Terms in Consumer Contracts Regulations 1999 (SI 1999/2083).

First, the common law position is discussed, then statutory limitations upon it.

Exclusion/restriction in respect of another contracting party

3.200   The generally accepted position at common law is that parties to a contract are free to exclude or restrict their liabilities towards each other howsoever arising, whether such liabilities are common law, contractual or delictual liabilities, or liabilities imposed by statute.[314] This is subject to any legislative limitations on such power of exclusion or restriction, some of which are discussed below. Thus, parties to a contract may seek to exclude or restrict delictual liability between themselves either by specific reference to such delictual liabilities within the terms of the contract, or, it is thought, by a general exclusion or restriction of any other liabilities other than those arising under the contract.[315] Such contractual power to exclude or restrict delictual liability between the parties was affirmed by Lord Goff in *Henderson v Merrett*.[316]

Exclusion/restriction as regards third parties

3.201   Ought an exclusion or restriction of delictual liability towards the other contracting party be held to constitute a similar exclusion or restriction towards a third party, even if such third party is not explicitly mentioned within the terms of the exclusion? For instance, if a solicitor were to limit his liability in contract or delict towards his client to the sum of £5,000, should such a restriction be deemed to apply in relation to a third party also, even although liability towards third parties was not expressly addressed in the limitation clause? Lord Goff touched upon this matter in his speech in *White v Jones*, where he said of any potential assumption of responsibility by a solicitor towards someone other than his client:

> 'Such assumption of responsibility will of course be subject to any term of the contract between the solicitor and the testator which may exclude or restrict

---

314   Proposition 2, stated at **3.20** above.

315   It has been said that the older, pre-UCTA authorities suggesting that general exclusions might be ineffective in restricting liability for negligence may have adopted strained interpretation (see for instance the comments of Lord Wilberforce in *Photo Production Ltd v Securicor Transport Ltd* [1980] AC 827 at 851). On the other hand, there are post-UCTA cases denying effect to exclusions or restrictions in relation to a negligence claim on the basis that the clause was wide enough to cover liability other than negligence: see for instance *Twins Transport Ltd v Patrick & Brocklehurst* (1984) 25 BLR 65, QB, and *Golden Sea Produce v Scottish Nuclear plc* 1992 SLT 942, OH.

316   Lord Goff cited with approval the comments of the Canadian judge Le Dain J in *Central Trust Co v Rafuse* (1986) 31 DLR (4th) 481 who said (at 522): 'A concurrent or alternative liability in tort will not be admitted if its effect would be to permit the plaintiff to circumvent or escape a contractual exclusion or limitation of liability for the act or omission that would constitute the tort.'

the solicitor's liability to the testator under the principle in *Hedley Byrne*. It is true that such a term would be most unlikely to exist in practice; but as a matter of principle it is right that this largely theoretical question should be addressed.'[317]

If this remark may be taken to have broader application beyond the specific case of the solicitor-client relationship, then Lord Goff may be taken as suggesting that, at least so far as cases based upon the notion of assumption of responsibility are concerned, a contracting party may not even require to state expressly that exclusions or restrictions of liability are to extend to a third person, they may be deemed so to extend.[318]

3.202 Can such a view be considered as correct? The discussion ought to be broadened out to include those cases where an exclusion or restriction is specifically intended to affect liability towards third parties (such as the disclaimer of the surveyor in *Smith v Bush*[319]). It has been seen already that in theory it is possible for A to claim the benefit of an exclusion clause in contract B–C via the doctrine of *jus quaesitum tertio* in order to limit or negative A's delictual liability to C, although in practice this has seldom been pled successfully before the courts.[320] Ought, however, A to be entitled in contract A–B to disclaim delictual liability to C?

3.203 A satisfactory justification for the operation of exclusions or limitations of liability towards third parties in some cases may be found in one of the following two reasons:

(1)   The third party may have consented to the exclusion or limitation. Where the third party is a subcontractor, for instance, it may have undertaken with the main contractor not to pursue any delictual claims against the main contractor and/or employer, although the employer might have some difficulty in enforcing this undertaking directly.

(2)   In other cases, even although the third party has not consented, it may have been explicitly informed that no duty of care was undertaken in respect of it. In such a case, the third party, having been forewarned, has no reasonable expectation of careful behaviour on the part of the wrongdoer.[321]

3.204 However, for cases where the parties have had no contact prior to the commission of the delict, neither of these two justifications can operate.[322] One justification for the operation of disclaimers in such cases might be that, where a contracting party has undertaken to perform services or deliver goods to another,

---

317   [1995] 2 AC at 268G, per Lord Goff.
318   This must be read subject to: (i) questions of interpretation of the exclusion; and (ii) legislative restrictions concerning fairness of the exclusion. It might be that in a particular case a specific restriction which was fair and reasonable in relation to the client, would not be so in relation to a third party (especially where the work was undertaken for the benefit of the third party).
319   [1990] 1 AC 831, [1989] 2 WLR 790, [1989] 2 All ER 514, HL.
320   See the discussion at **3.161–3.164** of *Aberdeen Harbour Board v Heating Enterprises Aberdeen Ltd* and *Melrose v Davidson & Robertson*.
321   Which was essentially the position in *Hedley Byrne v Heller*.
322   *White v Jones* being just such a case, where Mr Jones had had no prior contact with the testator's daughters.

it will have chosen to perform at a price which takes into account an allocation of risk for losses caused. This risk allocation will relate to any exclusion or limitation clause between the parties. It might be argued that to prevent such a clause operating against third parties would be to the detriment of the economic balance between the contracting parties. However, this argument does not seem strong enough to override the protectionist policy of the law of delict.

3.205 Judicial pronouncement on the subject has not been uniformly of one view:

> In *Muirhead v Industrial Tank Specialities Ltd*,[323] pumps for use in a refrigerated tank had been supplied through a chain of contracts and installed in the plaintiff's tank. The pumps failed, causing the complete destruction of livestock contained in the tank. As well as raising a contractual claim, the plaintiffs sued a number of parties in tort, including the manufacturer of the motors comprised in the pumps. The Court of Appeal dismissed the claim against the manufacturer on the basis that it had not owed the plaintiff a duty of care, but it considered the question of whether, had such a duty of care existed, the manufacturer could have sought to avoid liability by reference to an exclusion clause[324] in the contract under which it had supplied the pumps. Robert Goff LJ opined that the manufacturer would have been entitled to rely upon the exclusion clause.[325]

3.206 On the other hand, the decision of the Queen's Bench in *Twins Transport Ltd v Patrick & Brocklehurst*[326] is against the effectiveness of contractual restrictions on liability without the consent of the third party. The case concerned liability for a defective roof, the various parties in the action being linked by a contractual chain. In relation to the effect upon a claim in tort by the owner of an exclusion clause in the contract between the property developer and the contractor, the judge commented: 'There was no suggestion that [the owner] knew of, or consented to, the exclusion clause.'[327] More recently, in seeming contrast to his comments in *White v Jones* noted above, Lord Goff in *Henderson v Merrett*, talking of the potential liability of a subcontractor for causing physical damage to a building, remarked that the subcontractor might take advantage of a 'contractual exemption clause authorised by the building owner',[328] the inclusion of the word 'authorised' suggesting a preference on his Lordship's part for a specific consent to a restriction on liability.[329]

3.207 Judicial opinion on the effect at common law of contractual disclaimers of delictual liability towards non-contracting parties is thus mixed. It is suggested

---

323 [1986] 1 QB 507, CA.
324 The relevant clause stated 'Our liability is in all cases limited as provided in these conditions and does not extend to consequential damages, either direct or indirect, nor to expenses for repairs or replacements or otherwise paid or incurred without authority' (quoted [1986] 1 QB at 530).
325 See his discussion of the question, [1986] 1 QB at 529–530.
326 (1983) 25 BLR 65, QB. The case was decided shortly after the *Junior Books* decision, and is outdated in holding a building contractor liable in tort for pure economic loss to a party with whom it had no direct contractual link.
327 Per His Hon Judge Lewis Hawser QC, at 86.
328 [1995] 2 AC 145, HL, at 196B.
329 It is unclear why, in Lord Goff's opinion, a solicitor should be able to restrict his liability to a testator without the testator's consent, but a subcontractor should not be allowed to rely upon a restriction unless consented to by the owner.

that that strain of opinion which is against the effectiveness at common law of a contractual restriction or exclusion in relation to a delictual claim by a party who has not consented to, or who was unaware of, the restriction or exclusion is to be preferred. The alternative would undermine the protection which the law of delict is designed to provide to the public.

Legislative control on exclusions/restrictions of delictual liability

3.208 The Unfair Contract Terms Act 1977 ('UCTA') and the Unfair Terms in Consumer Contracts Regulations 1999 (SI 1999/2083) ('UTCCR') have established legislative controls on the use of some types of unfair terms in certain types of contract.[330] The types of term covered by these two regimes extend to attempts by contracting parties to exclude or restrict delictual liability towards third parties.

3.209 A good example of the operation of the provisions is seen in *Smith v Bush*,[331] the leading English authority on the duty of care owed by a surveyor towards the private purchaser of a house in respect of economic loss caused by misstatements in the surveyor's report. This case, like its Scottish counterpart *Martin v Bell-Ingram*,[332] established that a surveyor does owe a duty of care to a purchaser who reasonably relies upon the survey. In *Smith v Bush*, the House of Lords had to consider whether the surveyor could competently exclude its liability towards the house purchaser by means of an exclusion clause. The exclusion of the surveyor's liability was intimated to the purchaser both on the mortgage application form and also on the report itself. Applying the relevant provisions of UCTA, the House of Lords held that it was not fair and reasonable for the surveyor to rely upon its disclaimer of liability. Attention was drawn to the fact that the parties were not of equal bargaining power, the task which the surveyor was undertaking was not a difficult one, and that the modest cost to the surveyor of it being held liable in such a case would not be unduly burdensome.[333]

3.210 Consider the following examples from the perspective of UCTA and UTCCR:

Example 1: A wealthy entrepreneur owns an office block which he wishes to have renovated. He contracts the work to a main contractor. The main contractor sub-contracts the plumbing work (the value of which is £5,000) to a subcontractor. Due to negligent workmanship by the subcontractor, the existing pipework bursts, flooding the premises and causing £2,000 of damage to fittings and £3,000 damage to the structure. The subcontractor points to a limitation clause in the subcontract restricting its liability for any damage caused negligently to £2,000. Can the subcontractor rely upon the limitation clause to restrict its liability in negligence to the owner?

In this case, the entrepreneur is acting in the course of a business, and thus the UTCCR are not relevant, being applicable only to consumer contracts. The

---

330 And, in the case of UCTA, non-contractual notices also.
331 [1990] 1 AC 831, [1989] 2 WLR 790, [1989] 2 All ER 514, HL.
332 1986 SC 208, 1986 SLT 575, IH.
333 See, on these points, the speech of Lord Griffiths [1990] 1 AC at 858–859.

damage caused by the subcontractor is physical damage to the building, for which (on the authority of *BT v Thomson*) it may prima facie be liable. Assuming that the restriction on liability would otherwise be effective, it is possible that it might be struck down by UCTA, s 16, which controls attempts (either by contract clause or extra-contractual notice) to exclude or limit liability for loss caused as a result of a breach of duty. For loss other than death or personal injury, the exclusion or restriction will be of no effect if it would not be fair and reasonable to allow reliance upon the provision. In relation to this example, therefore, one needs to consider whether it would be fair and reasonable to allow the subcontractor to rely upon this limitation. Various matters might be brought to the attention of the court in considering this matter, including the relative bargaining and financial positions of the parties, the value of the work being undertaken, the difficulty of the task, and the ease with which the subcontractor might have obtained insurance without substantially increasing the cost of its services. The limitation in this case may be fair and reasonable, but a final determination would require further factual examination by a court.

3.211   *Example 2*: An owner of land wishes a house built on the land. The owner instructs various parties in connection with the project, including an architect. The architect negligently advises the building contractor's foreman that an old wall on the property can be safely left standing while ground next to it is excavated. During the excavation works the wall collapses injuring two employees of the building contractors. The architect points to a clause in its contract excluding liability for any loss caused by its negligence. Can it rely upon the clause?

This example has a simple answer. The architect's attempt to exclude its liability for the personal injuries caused as a result of its negligence will be ineffective as a result of UCTA, s 16. An attempt to exclude liability for death or personal duty caused by a breach of a duty undertaken in the course of business is void by virtue of that section of the Act.

3.212   *Example 3*: A prospective house purchaser writes to a local authority enquiring whether a recently constructed property was constructed in accordance with building regulations. The local authority's planning department replies that to the best of its knowledge the property was so constructed. The enquirer purchases the property which is then discovered to have defective foundations. The repairs to the foundations will cost £10,000. The purchaser sues the local authority for having made a negligent misrepresentation. The local authority points to a statement on the letter sent to the purchaser stating 'While the council undertakes to answer all queries promptly and to the best of its ability, no liability can be accepted for any inaccuracies contained in our reply. You may wish to seek professional advice in relation to any matter forming the substance of your enquiry.' The local authority claims that this statement exempts it from liability. Does it?

The UTCCR are not relevant here, as there is no contract between the parties. The local authority might potentially be liable in delict for the economic loss caused by its misrepresentation (on the authority of *King v North Cornwall District Council*[334]). Its attempt to exclude liability for its breach of duty is controlled

---

334   8 February 1995, CA (unreported).

by UCTA, s 16.[335] The disclaimer of liability must again meet the fairness and reasonableness test. It is likely that this will be so here. The local authority is not obliged to answer such queries as part of its statutory functions. In addition, the information which it has available to answer such queries will be limited. It is almost universal practice for purchasers to have a survey undertaken before purchasing property, and such survey would be expected to show up structural defects. In such circumstances, a court is likely to find it fair and reasonable for the local authority to rely upon the exclusion of liability.

3.213   *Example 4*: A development company enters into a contract with a builder for the erection of a warehouse on land owned by a company in the same group of companies as the development company. The contract specifically designates the sister company as a third party entitled to enforce performance of the builder's obligations. The value of the contract is £100,000. The contract specifically states that the value of any claim for economic loss which the third party may have as a result of the builder's negligence shall be limited to £20,000. Serious defects are discovered in the warehouse as a result of the builder's negligent workmanship. These defects will cost £30,000 to remedy. May the restriction on liability be enforced by the builder?

This is a tricky example. As was seen earlier, a *tertius* does not have an automatic right to claim damages for defective performance, and it is necessary to demonstrate an intention on the contracting parties to confer such a right.[336] However, the stipulation of a limit upon the third party's claim might well be held to demonstrate such an intention. Assuming that this right was established, the question would then arise of whether it was permissible to restrict the damages payable to the third party. Again, UCTA, s 16 would be relevant here, and consideration of issues of fairness and reasonableness would have to be had.

It should be added in relation to this last example that, should the limitation be deemed to be fair and reasonable, it would not be possible for the third party to seek to evade its application by asking the development company to raise a transferred loss claim on its behalf for, as has been seen,[337] such a claim will only be available where the third party has no other right to sue, which in this case, as a *tertius*, it does.

3.214   Apart from UCTA and UTCCR, there are other legislative provisions which control attempts to exclude or restrict delictual liability. One should note, for instance, the prohibition against limitations or restrictions on the strict liability of manufacturers of products under the Consumer Protection Act 1987.[338]

DIFFERING STANDARDS OF DUTY BETWEEN CONTRACTUAL AND DELICTUAL CLAIMS

3.215   Concern has been expressed over the years by some members of the judiciary that the availability of concurrent delictual claims against parties who

---

335   The local authority comes within the definition of a 'business' as this term is defined in s 25(1) of the Act as including the activities of a local authority.

336   *Scott Lithgow v GEC Electrical Projects*, discussed above at **3.155–3.158**.

337   See **3.190**.

338   Consumer Protection Act 1987, s 7.

also incur contractual liability may potentially give rise to the problem of differing standards of skill and care being applied in contract and delict.[339] If this were to be the case, it is said, a party might conceivably come under a more onerous duty in delict than it had agreed to be bound to in contract, something which would 'subvert' the contractual intention of the parties.

3.216 It may be worth noting that in practice many cases are likely to involve a strict contractual liability, a standard which will be likely to be much more onerous than any corresponding delictual standard. Thus, if a builder fails to use a contractually agreed material in the contract works, this will give rise to contractual liability on a strict basis. The builder is liable for breach of contract simply by his failure to use the material specified. If there is an alternate delictual liability, it will have to be based upon the alleged negligence of the builder in not using the specified material. This is fault-based liability, and thus of a less onerous nature than the strict contractual liability.

3.217 However, where the breach of contract consists of failure to meet a specific standard of care imposed by the contract's terms, then it is possible that a pursuer might seek to hold the contract breaker liable by reference to a more onerous delictual standard. Should this be a cause for concern? To the extent that any concern is based upon the view that placing a contracting party under an alternate delictual duty (of whatever standard) necessarily subverts the intention of the contracting parties, it may be questioned for the reason that has already been advanced earlier in relation to the availability of concurrent remedies at all, namely that delictual obligations are prior obligations which ought to apply unless they are specifically excluded. The more specific question then becomes: by specifying a particular contractual standard of performance, is a party to be deemed to have intended the same standard to apply to any delictual liability? One may wish to give a different response to this question depending upon whether the injured party is the other contracting party or a third party. The issues at play here might arguably be said to be the same or similar as those in relation to whether contractual exclusions or limitations of liability should affect delictual duties.

3.218 Consider the following two examples:

Example 1: An accountant undertakes a transaction for a client relating to the client's taxation liability. In terms of the contract, the accountant undertakes to achieve a specific result (in financial terms) for the client. If the accountant fails to do so, and if the client chooses to sue the accountant in delict, is the delictual standard of performance that of the ordinarily competent accountant (the *Hunter v Hanley* standard for professionals), or is it the stricter contractual standard of guaranteeing a particular result?

Example 2: A central heating engineer undertakes to install a new central heating boiler in a second floor office. Because the engineer has agreed to install the boiler at cost price, it restricts its liability for any resultant damages to losses caused by its gross negligence. Due to ordinary negligence in the engineer's workmanship, the boiler leaks causing water damage to property of the owner of the first floor office beneath the boiler. Is the owner of the damaged property entitled to sue the engineer for the

---

339 See, for instance, the dissent of Lord Brandon in *Junior Books v Veitchi* 1982 SC (HL) 244, HL, at 282.

losses caused arguing that the engineer broke its duty to take reasonable care, or is the engineer entitled to plead that it was only bound to avoid losses caused by its gross negligence?

No clear answer to problems such as these emerges from the cases, although where it is a third party which has been injured, it would seem in principle unacceptable to allow a duty of care owed to that third party to be restricted by reference to a lower standard of care in a contract. Of some relevance may be the decision of the English Court of Appeal in *Holt v Payne Skillington*.[340] In an action of damages for alleged breach of contract and tort committed by a firm of solicitors, Hirst LJ commented:

> '[T]here is no reason in principle why a *Hedley Byrne* type duty of care cannot arise in an overall set of circumstances where, by reference to certain limited aspects of those circumstances, the same parties enter into a contractual relationship involving more limited obligations than those imposed by the duty of care in tort. In such circumstances, the duty of care in tort and the duties imposed by the contract will be concurrent but not coextensive.'[341]

It might be observed of this comment, however, that if the duties breached relate to different factual circumstances, then the liability is concurrent only in the sense that it arises at the same time, and not in the sense in which concurrent liability has been primarily discussed in this text, namely liability stemming from the same facts. A further problem with the comment of Hirst LJ is that in cases such as *Holt*, which proceed upon a *Hedley Byrne* assumption of responsibility basis, it is difficult to see why, if a defender has voluntarily assumed a duty in delict, the duty voluntarily assumed in contract should be any less.

CONTRACTUAL DAMAGES

3.219   To conclude this chapter on the relationship between the obligations of contract and delict, two issues concerning the nature of contractual damages are considered. These issues challenge the oft held view that the purpose of an award of contractual damages is, by compensating the pursuer for losses suffered by him, to put the pursuer into the position he would have been in had the contract been performed properly.

Protection of performance or restoration interest in contractual damages

3.220   In chapter 1 consideration was given to the different interests protected by the law of obligations, these being the performance interest, the restoration (or *'status quo ante'*) interest, and the restitutionary (or 'disgorgement') interest.[342] It was noted that with contract and promise it may in some circumstances be

---

340   49 Con LR 99, 77 Build LR 51, CA.
341   77 Build LR at 73F–G.
342   See **1.34**.

possible to seek protection of the restoration or restitutionary interests rather than the performance interest. Possible protection of the restitutionary interest is discussed in chapter 4.[343] At this point, the possibility of protection of the restoration interest is discussed.

3.221 There are a variety of losses which might be claimed by reference to the restoration interest. These include: trading overheads, such as running costs or salary costs, undertaken in preparing to perform or in performing the contract; losses made through turning down alternative work; and location costs and travel expenditure (eg where an individual moves to take up new employment).

3.222 A classic example of loss which equates to the restoration interest is expenditure undertaken in preparation for performance of the contract. This is not normally claimed for as an explicit head of loss. Where the innocent party has agreed to perform for a fixed price, it will simply claim the price due under the contract:

> *Example:* A enters a contract to perform services for B. A agrees to provide the services for a fee of £2,000. B incurs £1,000 costs in making preparations for A's performance, but expects to make £4,000 from the arrangement. On the due date for A's performance, A fails to perform. B's expenditure is wholly wasted, no adequate substitute for A's performance being available.

In a case such as this, B will normally sue for its expected gross profit of £4,000. However, an alternative way of analysing B's loss is to say that it has lost £3,000 net profit plus £1,000 in wasted expenditure. Looked at in this way, it is possible to see many damages claims for protection of the performance interest as including an element protecting the restoration interest. It is, however, less usual to see such expenditure claimed as a separate head, and a pursuer will normally frame its claim by reference to the expected gross profits, simply choosing to absorb the wasted expenditure.[344] While it is possible to claim for both expected lost *net* profits and for wasted expenditure,[345] one cannot claim for *gross* profits as well as wasted expenditure. To award both such elements would be to over-compensate the pursuer, because the pursuer would have had to outlay the expenditure to make the gross profit.

3.223 Whilst it is more common to see a gross profit figure being claimed as damages, a pursuer will not wish to frame its claim in such a fashion where, due to unforeseen circumstances, expected profits have by the time the action is raised fallen to such an extent that they are cancelled out by expenditure undertaken. In such a case a pursuer will wish to abandon any gross profit claim and simply claim for wasted expenditure. Take the following example:

---

343 See **4.56–4.60**.

344 One reported example of a claim for wasted expenditure as part of a larger claim for lost profits is seen in *R & J Dempster Ltd v Motherwell Bridge and Engineering Co Ltd* 1964 SLT 353, IH. In the case, the award of damages made by the court included, in addition to the element of lost profits, an element for loss of recovery of overheads. This case is discussed by L Macgregor, 'The expectation, reliance and restitution interests in contract damages', 1996 JR 227 at 239.

345 See for instance the comments of Lord Gill in *Shetlands Seafarms v Braer Corporation* 1999 SLT 1189, OH, at 1194L: 'In an appropriate case a claim for damages may be presented for outlays wasted on an asset and for the loss of the net profits that the asset would have earned.'

Example: A contracts with B for B to perform services to A. At the time of the contract A expects to make £5,000 gross profit from the contract, and to incur £1,000 in costs. However, on the eve of the stipulated date for B's performance, A's expected profits have dropped to £500. B fails to perform on the agreed day. A does not seek to claim its lost expected profits of £500, but instead wishes to recoup its wasted expenditure of £1,000.

Such a claim is not, however, permitted save in exceptional circumstances. A pursuer is not permitted to avoid the consequences of a bad bargain by claiming for wasted contractual expenditure.[346]

3.224 English and Commonwealth courts have exceptionally permitted wasted expenditure to be recovered as contractual damages in one principal circumstance, namely where it is not feasible to calculate likely profits from a contract. Such a situation might prevail where the contractual venture is highly speculative, or where it is difficult or impossible to allot a pecuniary value to contractual performance. In *Anglia Television Ltd v Reed*,[347] the plaintiff was permitted to recoup its wasted expenditure when an actor failed to perform the services for which he was engaged. The profit likely from the making of the television programme in which the actor was to appear was too speculative to found the basis for an award of damages based upon lost profit. In a similar vein, in its decision in *McRae v Commonwealth Disposals Commission*,[348] the High Court of Australia permitted wasted expenditure to be claimed by the plaintiff. The plaintiff was a salvor which expended considerable sums in preparing to salvage an oil tanker which turned out to be non-existent. An award based upon expected profit in relation to a non-existent vessel was deemed too speculative.

3.225 While there is very little authority on this point in Scotland, the decision in *Daejan Developments v Armia*[349] follows the same approach as *Anglia* and *McRae*.

The pursuers concluded missives with the defenders for the purchase of heritable property. Thereafter the pursuers carried out various works at the site prior to the date of entry. Due to a defect in title, the defenders were unable to convey the property at the date of entry. The pursuers sued the defenders in contract for damages in the amount of their wasted expenditure. In the Outer House, Lord McDonald, applying the rule in *Hadley v Baxendale* [(1854) 9 Exch 341], held that the pursuers were entitled to recover such wasted expenditure as might reasonably be supposed to have been in the contemplation of the parties at the time the contract was made as the probable result of the breach, and ordered a proof before answer.

In a case such as this, there may be very little in the way of expected loss of profits, if alternative premises can be located from which to trade, so it will be important for a pursuer to be permitted to claim lost expenditure. The pursuer in the case was not, however, permitted to claim any expenditure arising after the date of

346 The comments of Lord Prosser in *Dawson International plc v Coats Paton plc* 1993 SLT 80, OH, at 100, may be noted: 'It was competent to claim abortive expenditure, without a claim for profit, but it would be necessary to show not merely that the expense had been incurred, but that it would have been recovered if the breach of contract had not occurred.' See also, for English law, *C & P Haulage v Middleton* [1983] 1 WLR 1461, CA.
347 [1972] 1 QB 60, [1971] 3 All ER 690, CA.
348 (1950) 84 CLR 377, [1951] 25 ALJ 425.
349 1981 SC 48, OH. See also *Fielding v Newell* 1987 SLT (Notes) 530, OH.

entry had passed, as it could have mitigated its loss by halting any such expenditure at that point. In respect of the losses which were claimable, there was not any concern that the pursuer might be attempting in claiming wasted expenditure to avoid a bad bargain.

Assessing contractual damages: loss to pursuer or failure to receive expected performance?

3.226 The important decision of the House of Lords in *Alfred McAlpine Construction Ltd v Panatown Ltd* [350] was discussed above[351] in relation to the issue of transferred loss claims. In his dissenting judgment in the case, Lord Goff propounded a more radical restatement of the purpose of contractual damages. Whilst the majority of the House of Lords affirmed the decision in *The Albazero*, as applied in *St Martin's Property Corporation*, as being exceptional, Lord Goff sought to develop opinions expressed in these cases as laying the foundation for a restated general rule for the assessment of damages. Lord Goff was sceptical as to the existence of a general rule that a contracting party can only recover for losses suffered by it alone.[352] His Lordship preferred recent academic re-emphasis on protection of the 'performance interest' as lying at the heart of the assessment of damages.[353] His Lordship, echoing earlier observations of Lord Griffiths in the *St Martin's* case, took the view that a party is entitled to contractual damages where it has not received the performance for which it bargained, even if the only loss was suffered by a third party to whom contractual performance had been tendered. Lord Goff asserted that his restatement of these principles was in accordance with existing principle, but that, even were it not, 'it is surely within the scope of the type of development of the common law which, especially in the law of obligations, is habitually undertaken by appellate judges as part of their ordinary judicial function.'[354] His Lordship did not feel constrained by the impending development of English law at the time of the decision through the Contracts (Rights of Third Parties) Act 1999, for he took the view that the facts before him would not have given rise to a *jus quaesitum tertio* even if the Act had been in force, the owner of the building having deliberately contracted so as not to be the employer under the contract, and the third party having received direct rights to sue via a duty of care document (a contractual warranty).[355]

3.227 Lord Goff's opinion raises two important questions: (1) is he right to restate the principles underlying the assessment of damages in the way he does, divorcing such assessment from loss suffered by the claimant?; and (2) how would the principles enunciated by Lord Goff be affected in a case in which there was a valid *jus quaesitum tertio* in favour of a third party?

---

350 [2001] 1 AC 518, [2000] 4 All ER 97, [2000] 3 WLR 946, HL.
351 See **3.190–3.192**.
352 See [2001] 1 AC at 539A, per Lord Goff.
353 See [2001] 1 AC at 546C, per Lord Goff.
354 [2001] 1 AC at 553C, per Lord Goff.
355 [2001] 1 AC at 552B–E, per Lord Goff.

Assessment of damages

3.228 First consider Lord Goff's general restatement of the principles under-lying contractual damages. In support of his view that damages should not be tied to losses suffered by the contracting party, Lord Goff cited an example used by Lord Griffiths in the *St Martin's* case, and gave a further example of his own. Lord Griffiths had cited the case of a husband who had contracted for the replacement of the roof on the matrimonial home, title to the home being in the name of the wife. Lord Griffiths had opined that it would be absurd to believe that the husband could not sue for damages resulting from defective perfor-mance of the roofer.[356] Lord Goff added a further, similar, example of a wealthy philanthropist who contracts for work to be done to a village hall. Again, Lord Goff did not doubt that the philanthropist can sue for damages caused by defective workmanship, even though personally he suffers no financial loss. Both of these examples evoke sympathy, for one would expect the principles of contractual damages to accommodate a claim in such circum-stances,[357] but do such cases justify the radical restatement of the law proposed by Lord Goff?

3.229 It is suggested that Lord Goff's approach is too radical a departure. Among the reasons for disapproving his approach are the following:

(1) Lord Goff's approach is tantamount to compensating a claimant for having lost the rights bargained for in the contract. However, this ignores the fundamental point that contractual rights are *not* lost by breach: the innocent party can still insist upon performance. This point can be more strongly made in Scotland than in England, where our contractual theory, with its emphasis upon performance, sees specific implement as a primary remedy. In a jurisdiction which sees damages as the primary remedy, it is perhaps unsurprising that a tendency has arisen to seek to permit damages to be available whenever a breach occurs.[358]

(2) If the general principles for assessment of damages were to be divorced from loss to the pursuer, there would be nothing to prevent damages claims being extended to disgorgement of gains made by the defender, something which our law has consistently rejected, or to prevent the development of punitive damages, a concept likewise alien to our law.

---

356 See *St Martin's Property* [1994] 1 AC at 97A, per Lord Griffiths. Where *A*, having a right to sue under the contract, will suffer substantial loss by being required to remedy the defect to *C*'s property, then this will itself constitute substantial loss so far as *A* is concerned, and will be recoverable against *B*, the party in default, so long as such loss was foreseeable by *B* (which it was held not to be in the *St Martin's* case). A recent Scottish case which supports this view is *Scottish Enterprise v Archibald Russel of Denny Ltd* 2002 SLT 519, IH. Although *Panatown* was not cited in the judgment of the Lord Ordinary, similar issues were also raised in *Blyth & Blyth v Carillion Construction Ltd*, 18 April 2001, OH (unreported).

357 Although a possible approach in Scots law might be to view them as cases of *jus quaesitum tertio*.

358 A point made by the Lord Ordinary in *McLaren Murdoch*: 'It seems to me that the difficulty that confronts English law is that damages is regarded as the primary remedy for breach of contract. Consequently the minority of the House of Lords in *Alfred McAlpine Ltd v Panatown Ltd* took the view that that primary remedy should be available whenever there is a breach of contract' (per Lord Drummond Young at para 41).

(3)   It was suggested earlier[359] that the adoption of a non-proprietorial approach to damages would permit a number of cases to be dealt with under existing principles without the need to redefine the principles underlying contractual damages. There is therefore no proven need to embark upon a fundamental restatement of such principles.

3.230   Lord Goff's approach of divorcing damages from loss was explicitly rejected in *McLaren Murdoch & Hamilton Ltd v The Abercromby Motor Group Ltd*.[360] Lord Drummond Young said of it:

> 'The purpose of damages is to provide financial redress for the loss caused by a breach of contract. That result is achieved by ordering the party in breach to pay a sum sufficient to place the other party in the same position as he would have been in had the contract been performed. Thus the notions of loss and financial redress for that loss are central to the remedy. That indicates that loss itself must be substantial, capable of being measured in financial terms. The mere existence of a breach of contract does not of itself create a loss of that nature .'[361]

As to the proper party to sue for such losses, Lord Drummond Young was clearly of the view in *McLaren Murdoch* that the party suing must be able to show actual financial detriment to itself if it wishes to claim the losses as its own:

> 'In a case, for example, where a husband has contracted for repairs to a house that belongs to his wife, or a company has contracted for building works on land belonging to another company in the same group, it cannot be said that the person who is a party to the contract is the person who has suffered loss ... The person who suffers loss is rather the person who owns the property on which the work is performed. '[362]

It was suggested at **3.185** that, while rejecting the broad approach favoured by Lord Goff, it may nonetheless be possible to see certain parties as suffering loss, even where they do not own the thing damaged, using what was dubbed a 'non-proprietorial' approach to the assessment of damages. This approach would not seem to find favour with Lord Drummond Young, who prefers instead to give a contracting party who is not the owner a transferred loss claim in respect of losses suffered by the non-contracting owner.[363]

3.231   In response to the first question posed, therefore, whether Lord Goff was right to suggest that the assessment of damages ought to be divorced from loss suffered by the plaintiff, the clear view from subsequent reported Scottish decisions is that he is not.

---

359   See **3.185–3.187**.
360   2003 SCLR 323, OH.
361   2003 SCLR 323, per Lord Drummond Young, at para 41.
362   2003 SCLR 323, per Lord Drummond Young, at para 41.
363   As to such transferred loss claims, see above at **3.178–3.197**.

Interaction of broad approach with doctrine of jus quaesitum tertio

3.232 Although Lord Goff's approach to the assessment of damages has been rejected, one ought for completeness to pose the second question. This question was as to how the broader approach to damages would operate if a valid *jus quaesitum tertio* had been conferred upon a third party. It should first be remarked that the majority of the House of Lords saw the right of the owner of the building in *Alfred McAlpine* to enforce a damages claim through the duty of care deed as effectively a third party right by any other name.[364] In this light, they saw no need to permit the contracting party to enforce the contract on behalf of the third party. While the majority were no doubt right to state that the third party was entitled to sue under the duty of care deed, this was not strictly a *jus quaesitum tertio*. Lord Goff correctly noted that any rights which the owner might enforce derived from a separate contractual warranty, and not from the contract itself.

3.233 The question may still therefore be put as to how Lord Goff's approach to contractual damages would interact with a genuine *jus quaesitum tertio*. Lord Goff did not consider the issue, but it would seem reasonable to conclude from his approach that under his theory of contractual damages a contracting party would *not* be permitted to sue for substantial losses suffered by a third party where the third party itself had a free-standing third party right to sue for damages. Under the English Contract (Rights of Third Parties) Act 1999, a third party might indeed now acquire such a right. It ought, however, to be recalled that under Scots law a *tertius* will not automatically acquire a right to sue for damages.[365] In specific circumstances, however, a *tertius* might acquire such a right. If the dangers of double recovery are to be avoided, then Lord Goff's theory ought not to permit a contracting party to claim damages where the third party had acquired a genuine contractual third party right to sue for damages in its own name.

3.234 Given the view expressed above, that cases such as the *St Martin's* case are exceptional instances of transferred loss where no other claim for damages would lie, then the logical view must be that in Scotland, where a *tertius* itself acquires a right to claim damages, the contracting party is not to be permitted to do so on behalf of the *tertius*. However, there would seem to be nothing objectionable to a contracting party suing on behalf of a *tertius* where a right to claim damages for defective performance had not been extended by the parties to the *tertius*. There are, however, no reported decisions considering this question.[366]

---

364 See for instance Lord Browne-Wilkinson [2001] 1 AC at 578.
365 See earlier discussion of this point at **3.158**.
366 McBryde comments on the *Alfred McAlpine* case that it 'may help to remove any doubt about the ability of a third party to recover damages for breach of the contract which confers on that party a *jus quaesitum tertio* (para 22-06, fn 18). This comment must be seen as based upon the view that in *Alfred McAlpine* the owner of the building had effectively received a *jus quaesitum tertio* through its duty of care deed. However, a distinction ought surely to be made between the enforcement of a free-standing duty of care deed (essentially a contractual warranty) on the one hand, and the enforcement of a *jus quaesitum tertio* on the other.

Chapter 4

Unjustified Enrichment and Contract

PART I: A SUMMARY OF UNJUSTIFIED ENRICHMENT LAW

CURRENT STATE OF LAW OF UNJUSTIFIED ENRICHMENT

4.01 The Scots law of unjustified enrichment is in a state of flux. Following a long period when this obligation was neglected by academic writers and the courts, the period since the mid-1980s has seen an explosion in writing and decisions.[1] The outcome of this has been a general sense of dissatisfaction with the traditional categorisation and analysis of the law, but as yet no universally agreed approach to law reform has emerged. There is at least, however, an emerging judicial consensus that underlying the various actions recognised by Scots law is a general principle for the redress of unjustifiably retained enrichment. Before considering possible routes to reform of the law, it is important to consider thoroughly the current state of the law.

4.02 The obligation of unjustified enrichment imposes upon a party (the enriched party) who has made a gain at the expense of another party (the impoverished party), the retention of which cannot be justified, the duty to relinquish this gain in favour of the impoverished party. This general principle underlies the three actions traditionally recognised by Scots law as operating in this field, namely repetition, restitution and recompense, or the '3 Rs' as they have been referred to collectively. These actions were recognised and discussed by Stair in his *Institutes*, although he did not expressly link all three by reference to the principle of unjustified enrichment. Indeed, in former times it was more common to see these actions analysed by reference to the notion of 'quasi-contract'.[2] It was said that relinquishment of unjustifiably retained benefits occurred as if there was a contract between the parties requiring such relinquishment. This notion of implied contract was wholly fictional, and recourse to such a fiction has now been recognised to be unhelpful.

---

1 For a history of the recent debate, and a comparison of the differing views in relation to reform, see *Stair Memorial Encyclopaedia*, vol 15, paras 73–86; also R Evans-Jones, 'Unjustified Enrichment', in *A History of Private Law in Scotland*, vol II, at pp 382–395. For a general summary of the current law together with cases and materials see Hogg and Sellar, 'Scots Law', in *Cases, Materials and Texts on Unjustified Enrichment* (eds Beatson and Schrage (2003)).

2 The term 'quasi-contract' was still being used in the 9th edition of Gloag and Henderson (1987), although by the time of the 10th edition (1995) this had been replaced by 'unjustified enrichment'.

Role of equity

4.03 It has long been asserted that the actions available to a pursuer to remedy an unjustified enrichment in the hands of the defender are equitable in nature.[3] However, in a recent pronouncement of the Inner House on the role of equity in repetition, it was stated that it is not for the pursuer to demonstrate that it would be equitable for the remedy to be awarded to him, but that it is rather for the defender to demonstrate that it would be inequitable to grant the remedy. This point was clearly made by Lord President Hope in *Morgan Guaranty Trust Co of New York v Lothian Regional Council*:[4]

> '[O]nce the pursuer has averred the necessary ingredients to show that *prima facie* he is entitled to the remedy, it is for the defender to raise the issues which may lead to a decision that the remedy should be refused on grounds of equity.'[5]

This approach treats equity, or a 'balancing of the equities' as the exercise may be called, as a defence to an action of repetition, rather than as a necessary component of the action to be met by the pursuer. It is not yet clearly established that this approach is also the case for restitution and recompense, but it would be consistent were this to be so.

4.04 One difficulty with treating the balancing of the equities as a defence is that such an approach has the potential to swallow up all other defences. For instance, the general availability of a balancing of the equities defence would seem to obviate the need for a specific defence of change of position.[6] All, for instance, that a defender would need to assert in a repetition claim would be that, having spent the money in good faith, the equities lay in favour of his retention of the sum transferred.

4.05 If an over-arching defence of balancing the equities were indeed to swallow up all other defences, this might hinder the development of clear principles in the area of defences. On the other hand, the only guaranteed way of preventing this would be to remove balancing the equities as a recognised defence. If that were to happen, it would leave the role of equity in unjustified enrichment in limbo. A dilemma thus presents itself for the future development of the law of unjustified enrichment.

---

3 See for instance, on repetition, the comments of Lord Cowan, in *Bell v Thomson* (1867) 6 M 64 at 69 ('The remedy afforded by the *condictio indebiti* is essentially equitable in its origin and character') or more recently of Lord Sorn in *Haggarty v Scottish TGWU* 1955 SC 109 at 114 ('The *condictio indebiti* is an equitable remedy'); on recompense, see the comments of Lord President Emslie in *Lawrence Building Co v Lanarkshire County Council* 1978 SC 30 at 41–42 ('It must be shown that in all the circumstances it would be equitable for the pursuers to be reimbursed') or of Lord Justice-Clerk Wheatley in *Varney (Scotland) Ltd v Burgh of Lanark* 1974 SC 245 at 252 ('Since recompense is an equitable doctrine, all facts and figures should be looked at in any particular case').
4 1995 SC 151, 1995 SLT 299, IH.
5 1995 SC at 166A–B, 1995 SLT at 316F.
6 Change of position is discussed further below at **4.16**.

Repetition, restitution and recompense

4.06 The nature of the actions of repetition, restitution and recompense was described by Lord President Hope in the leading case of *Morgan Guaranty Trust Co of New York v Lothian Regional Council*[7] thus:

> 'As a general rule it would appear that restitution is appropriate where the demand is for the return of corporeal property, repetition where the demand is for the repayment of money and recompense where the defender has been enriched at the pursuers' expense in the implement of a supposed obligation under a contract other than by the delivery of property or the payment of money. Recompense will be available as a more broadly based remedy, in cases where the benefit was received by the defender in circumstances other than under a contract or a supposed contract.'[8]

As Lord Hope himself acknowledged in his opinion, this summary ignores a number of difficulties with the classification, or taxonomy, of the law. Nonetheless, his comment is significant in two respects. First, it restates the generally held view that the basis of repetition and restitution lies in the nature of the benefit sought to be recovered, in the case of repetition, money, and in the case of restitution, corporeal property. Second, while the boundaries of recompense are harder to delineate, his Lordship's comments indicate both that many cases concern claimed payments under a void or otherwise invalid contract, but also that recompense has come to be viewed, by many at least, as a residual enrichment remedy, applicable in cases which are not otherwise redressed by repetition or recompense. Whether or not historically this was the case, such a view is now gaining ground, a development which is noted below.[9]

4.07 The following are classic examples of fact situations giving rise to the actions of repetition, restitution and recompense:

Repetition: A pays his annual income tax bill to the Inland Revenue. A erroneously pays too much money. A is entitled to raise an action of repetition to claim back the amount of the overpayment.

Restitution: A wrongly delivers goods to B. A is entitled to raise an action of restitution against B to recover the goods.[10]

Recompense: A is negotiating a contract for the provision of services to B. Whilst negotiations are ongoing for the conclusion of the contract, B persuades A to perform. The negotiations break down and no contract is concluded. A is entitled to raise an action of recompense to recover the value of the services rendered to B.

---

7 1995 SC 151, 1995 SLT 299 (IH).
8 Lord President Hope, 1995 SC at 155.
9 See **4.44**, **4.47**.
10 A classic example is the case of the 'salted ox': *Findlay v Monro* (1698) Mor 1707.

Meaning of 'restitution'

4.08 It should be noted that the term 'restitution' is not used in Scotland as a synonym for the law of unjustified enrichment as a whole. English law by contrast has opted to use the term restitution to describe the whole body of the law containing various personal actions for the redress of unjustified enrichment as well as certain proprietary actions for the disgorgement of gains. Caution must be shown here. The Scots law of unjustified enrichment does not equate exactly to the English law of restitution, as in Scots law unjustified enrichment contains only personal actions, and never proprietary ones. Although many of the general principles underlying the Scots law of unjustified enrichment and the English law of restitution are comparable, cross-citation of authorities is in general unhelpful, as the specific classifications adopted in each system are quite different.

4.09 It is worth noting further that in Scotland the term 'restitution' has at least three further meanings to that described above (a remedy for the repayment of money), viz: (1) it can be used as an umbrella term to describe both repetition and restitution in the narrow sense; (2) it is a remedy in property law for the return of property belonging to the pursuer which is in the hands of another party;[11] (3) it appears in contract law in the requirement of *restitutio in integrum*, namely the requirement that parties must be capable of being restored to their pre-contractual position before a voidable contract may be reduced. Care should be taken when use of the term is encountered to ascertain which meaning is intended.

Role of the *condictiones* in unjustified enrichment

4.10 In addition to the threefold classification of the law of unjustified enrichment in terms of the actions of repetition, restitution, and recompense, there is also a tradition in Scots law of utilising the Roman law's *condictiones* to classify enrichment actions. Those *condictiones* of which there has been a clear reception into Scots law are the *condictio indebiti*, the *condictio causa data causa non secuta*, and the *condictio ob turpem vel injustam causam*. It is possible that the *condictio sine causa specialis* was also received into Scots law, although it is hard to point to any clear example of it in the reported cases. The terminology of the *condictiones* has been used alongside that of the native actions of repetition and restitution, although not in conjunction with the action of recompense, as the *condictiones* did not lie in Roman law in respect of a *factum*,[12] with which the remedy of recompense is largely concerned. Thus, it has been common to see in Scottish pleadings usage of the Scots terms of repetition or restitution alongside the appropriate Roman *condictio*.

---

11 In his *Institutes*, Stair makes no clear distinction in his treatment of restitution between those cases flowing from what would today be called unjustified enrichment and those cases flowing from a vindication of ownership.

12 A *factum* being the provision of services.

ure of each *condictio* of which there is clear recognition in the law is as follows:

...debiti: this is an action for the return of money or a thing which was ... in fulfilment of a supposed but non-existent debt:

Example: A pays B £500 believing that this amount is due as a debt. In fact A only owes B £300. B is entitled to bring the *condictio indebiti* for return of the £200 which was not due.[13]

Condictio causa data causa non secuta: this is an action for the return of money or a thing which was given in respect of a contemplated cause or reason which did not then transpire. Lord President Rodger put it thus:

'The term *condictio causa data causa non secuta* covers situations where A is enriched because B has paid him money or transferred property to him in the expectation of receiving a consideration from A but A has not provided that consideration. The relevant situations in this group also include cases where B paid the money or transferred the property to A on a particular basis which fails to materialise'.[14]

Example 1: A makes B a gift of £500 towards B's air fare for a round-the-world journey. B decides not to travel around the world after all. A is entitled to bring the *condictio causa data causa non secuta* for the return of the money, as the reason for which the gift was given has not transpired.

Example 2: A makes an advance payment of £1,000 in respect of goods which have been ordered under a contract with B. Subsequent to this advance payment the contract is frustrated and the goods are never delivered. A is entitled to recover the advance payment under the *condictio causa data causa non secuta*.[15]

Condictio ob turpem vel injustam causam: this is an action for the return of money or a thing which was given in respect of an immoral or illegal cause. It will lie only where the pursuer is considered morally blameless, but the defender is morally blameworthy, as public policy precludes recovery by a culpable pursuer. Since the time of the institutional writers, there has been a tendency to treat those circumstances which in the past would have given rise to this *condictio* as part of the law relating to *pacta illicita*. This is not wholly satisfactory, however, as it

---

13 For a recent example in which an overpayment was alleged, see *Semple Cochrane plc v Hughes*, 25 July 2001, OH (unreported).

14 A variation of this *condictio* is the *condictio ob causam finitam*. This lies for the return of money or a thing given in respect of the continuation of a contemplated state of affairs, where the state of affairs ceases. An example would be payment of a sum of money on the understanding that an individual continue to attend an institution, eg a university or church. If the individual ceases to attend the institution during a period for which the payment was made then the *condictio ob causam finitam* will lie. The *condictio ob causam finitam* is often viewed as subsumed within the *condictio causa data causa non secuta*, although it strictly describes a present state of affairs which ceases, rather than a contemplated future state of affairs which fails to occur.

15 *Cantiere San Rocco v Clyde Shipbuilding and Engineering Co* 1923 SC (HL) 105, 1923 SLT 624, revsg 1922 SC 723, 1922 SLT 477. There has been much subsequent debate as to whether an enrichment action is appropriate in these circumstances. It has been strongly argued by some commentators that the solution to the problem should be found through contractual means: see R Evans-Jones, 'Unjust Enrichment, Contract and the Third Reception of Roman Law in Scotland' (1993) 109 LQR 663. See also MacQueen and Thomson, para 4.110.

ignores types of case which would not arise for consideration under the doctrine of *pacta illicita*:

> *Example: A* is blackmailed by *B*, who extorts money from *A* by threatening to expose *A*'s extra-marital affair. *A* is entitled to seek return of the funds extorted from him by the *condictio ob turpem vel injustam causam*.

ANALYSIS OF TRADITIONAL ACTIONS

Pleading a case of repetition

Elements of the action

4.12   For the action of repetition to lie, *A* must have transferred a monetary sum to *B*. If the transfer is justified by a valid debt due by *A* to *B* then the action of repetition will not lie. If the transfer was made in exchange for a counter-stipulation which has been received, then the action will not lie.[16]

4.13   Where the action of repetition discloses facts falling within the *condictio indebiti*, the pursuer must allege that there was no intention of donation and that the transfer was made erroneously, although he need not prove that his error was excusable.[17] Where the action discloses facts falling within the *condictio causa data causa non secuta* the pursuer must allege that the transfer was made in consideration of an expected event or a state of affairs that has not transpired. Where the action discloses facts falling within the *condictio ob turpem vel injustam causam* the pursuer must allege that the transfer was made for an illegal or immoral purpose, in relation to which the pursuer is not culpable. Further specification of the circumstances will in all cases of repetition be given, for instance, specification that the transfer occurred under compulsion, thus constituting it as an immoral transfer for the purposes of the *condictio ob turpem vel injustam causam*. There may certainly also be circumstances outwith the three *condictiones* that could give rise to an action of repetition. Not only does the reception (albeit an underdeveloped reception) of the *condictio sine causa specialis* justify this response, but, in any event, the *condictiones* are not to be used as an artificial straightjacket to limit the circumstances in which repetition of money or things may be claimed. So long as retention would be unjustified, recovery will be allowed, whatever the precise circumstances of the case.

4.14   The necessity of proving error as an element of a repetition action based upon the *condictio indebiti* has been doubted.[18] On this view, it is argued that all that is necessary is to demonstrate that the payment made was not due. However, whatever the merits of this alternative view might be, it is not the law, and the accepted view remains that error is a necessary element in proving

---

16   *Connelly v Simpson* 1994 SLT 1096.
17   See Lord President Hope in *Morgan Guaranty* 1995 SC at 166A.
18   See, for example, R. Evans-Jones, 'Some Reflections on the Condictio Indebiti in a Mixed Legal System' (1994) 111 SALJ 759.

that there was no intention of donation.[19] Since the important decision in *Morgan Guaranty Trust Co of New York v Lothian Regional Council*[20] the erroneous position that an error of law could not found the *condictio indebiti* has been overturned, and the prior view[21] that either an error of fact or of law is relevant has been re-established.

Measure of recovery

4.15 The pursuer is entitled to recover the amount received by the defender, together with interest.[22] What if the defender has profited from receipt of the money beyond the amount received—is the pursuer entitled to claim further gains from the defender? Such a further gain might have occurred in a number of ways, for instance through interest earned whilst the money was in a bank account, or through use of the money to speculate for a profit. The pursuer is entitled to claim interest;[23] however, where profit has been made from the sum retained through the industry and ingenuity of the defender, such gains will not be recoverable.[24] To award this to the pursuer would be contrary to considerations of equity.

Defences

4.16 It has been asserted that it is a defence to an action to demonstrate that the defender has a legal entitlement to retain the money. In fact, it is probably better to state that, if the defender is able to demonstrate such entitlement, the pursuer will have failed to make out the necessary elements of the action. The principal genuine defences recognised are:

(a) *Change of position.* Where the defender can demonstrate that he has consumed or otherwise alienated the sum received in bona fides, repetition will not be ordered. This is increasingly referred to as the defence of 'change of position'.[25] The principal authority in relation to this defence in Scots law is *Credit Lyonnais v George Stevenson & Co Ltd.*[26] The elements of the defence were described in that case by Lord Kyllachy as follows:

---

19 See the comments in *Morgan Guaranty* of Lord President Hope, 1995 SC at 165D: 'the essentials of the condictio indebiti are that the sum which the pursuer paid is not due and that he made the payment in error' as well as Lord Cullen's comments, at 176A, that the pursuer 'has to set out averments as to the nature of that error, how it arose and how it accounted for his making the payments'.
20 1995 SC 151, 1995 SLT 299, IH.
21 As laid down in *Stirling v Earl of Lauderdale* (1733) Mor 2930.
22 *Royal Bank of Scotland plc v Watt* 1991 SC 48, 1991 SLT 138, IH.
23 See for instance *Royal Bank of Scotland plc v Watt* 1991 SC 48, 1991 SLT 138.
24 Stair put it thus: 'but industrial and artificial profits, in so far as they arise from the haver's industry, and not from the thing, fall not under restitution, if once separate therefrom' (I.7.10).
25 See G C Borland, 'Change of Position in Scots Law' 1996 SLT (News) 139.
26 (1901) 9 SLT 93.

'In my opinion, the defenders in order to establish such a defence would require to show (1) that they had reasonable grounds for believing the money was theirs; and (2) that having that reasonable belief, they acted upon it so as to alter their position in such manner as to make repetition unjust.'[27]

It has been rightly noted[28] that Lord Kyllachy's proposition in fact imposes three requirements for the defence: (1) a reasonable belief on the defender's part that he was entitled to the benefit; (2) a causal link between the belief and the change of position; and (3) that it would be unjust to order restoration of the benefit. The defence has been successfully pled in a number of cases,[29] but refused where, for instance, the defender has been held to have been at fault in parting with the benefit received.[30]

(b) *Personal bar*. Where a pursuer has by words or conduct led the defender to believe that a certain state of affairs exists, the pursuer is not permitted to maintain that a different state of affairs is the case in order to found a claim of repetition.[31]

(c) *Money paid under compromise settlement*. Where a sum has been paid pursuant to a compromise settlement between parties entered into in order to settle an uncertain state of affairs between the parties, and thus to extinguish any further debt due by the payer, the sum paid cannot subsequently be recovered if it is discovered that it was not due.[32]

(d) *Payments relating to an immoral or illegal transaction*. In such cases, if the parties are *in pari delicto*, the loss lies where it falls, that is to say, a payment made cannot be recovered by the payer. The topic of enrichment remedies in relation to immoral or illegal transactions is considered further below.[33]

(e) *Where the obligation to make repetition has prescribed*. The obligation to make repetition prescribes five years from the date when the obligation became enforceable,[34] which will be the date when the undue payment was received by the enriched party.[35]

(f) *Where a valid debt has been paid by a party other than the debtor*. It was asserted by Bankton[36] that, where a creditor A had received payment of a debt from B, where B paid A believing that in so doing he was discharging a debt which he owed to C, but where B later discovered that he was not in debt to C, B could not claim back the sum in repetition from A, if C had indeed been A's

---

27 (1901) 9 SLT at 95.
28 See Borland, op cit, fn 25.
29 See for instance *Duke of Argyll v Lord Halcraig's Representatives* (1732) Mor 2929; *Kerr v Rutherford* (1684) Mor 2928.
30 *Royal Bank of Scotland plc v Watt* 1991 SC 48, 1991 SLT 138, IH.
31 *Dixon v Monkland Canal Co* (1831) 5 W & S 445, IH.
32 See for instance Stair I.7.9, I.17.2; *Manclark v Thomson's Trusteess* 1958 SC 147, IH, at 162, 167, 168.
33 See **4.72–4.74**.
34 Prescription and Limitation (Scotland) Act 1973, s 6, Sch 1, para 1(b).
35 On the assumption that the action of repetition would lie from the moment that the defender became enriched by receipt of the sum.
36 Inst. I.8.32

debtor, but *B* had to seek redress from *C* (a defence referred to by Stair as *suum receipt*[37]). This view has been approved of by the Scottish Law Commission.[38]

Pleading a case of restitution

Elements of the action

4.17 For the action of restitution to lie, *A* must have transferred a thing to *B*. Whilst the transfer will normally be a transfer of ownership, there seems no theoretical objection to the transfer of another real right being the subject of an action of restitution.[39] Thus a real right of security or of lease, for instance, might be the subject of a restitution claim.[40] The thing may be moveable or heritable property, although there is less authority on its application to heritage.[41] There is no authority on the issue of whether recovery of incorporeal property may be sought, but there would seem to be no theoretical objection to this.[42] As with repetition, the pursuer will be required to make the necessary averments relevant to the particular *condictio* within which his case falls.[43]

Measure of recovery

4.18 The pursuer is entitled to the return of the specific thing transferred to the defender.[44] The pursuer is also entitled to those things which are the natural accessions and fruits of the property transferred.[45] Thus, young born to animals would be recoverable. As with repetition, gains which are solely the result of the defender's industry and ingenuity are irrecoverable by the pursuer.[46]

Two specialities in relation to the measure of recovery ought to be noted at this point:

---

37 I.7.9
38 SLC Discussion Paper No 95, vol 2, paras 2.174–2.181. For a recent comparative discussion of the issues surrounding payment of another's debt, see H L MacQueen, 'Payment of Another's Debt', in R Zimmermann and D Johnston (eds), *Unjustified Enrichment: Key Issues in Comparative Perspective* (Cambridge University Press, 2002).
39 See K Reid, 'Unjustified Enrichment and Property Law' 1994 JR 167 at 174.
40 Thus if party *A* granted a real right of lease to party *B* in the expectation of *B*'s marriage, reduction of the lease could be sought via the *condictio causa data causa non secuta* if *B* did not marry.
41 See cases cited by Whitty in *The Taxonomy of Unjustified Enrichment* at para 1.36, among them *Grieve v Morrison* 1993 SLT 852, OH, a case concerning the *condictio causa data causa non secuta* in which Lord Morison remarked (obiter): 'No doubt the condictio can apply to a gift made by transfer of title to heritable property ... so as to require the donee to reconvey the heritage to the donor if the consideration for which the gift has been made fails' (at 855B–C). K Reid, 'Unjustified Enrichment and Property Law' 1994 JR 167, states that 'there seems no reason to doubt that the *condictiones* apply to heritable property as well as to moveable property' (at 174).
42 K Reid, 'Unjustified Enrichment and Property Law' 1994 JR 167 at 174, n 22, states that 'there is no reason to doubt that [the *condictiones*] apply also to incorporeal property. So when a debt is assigned by mistake it can be recovered under the *condictio indebiti*'.
43 As to which, see **4.13** above.
44 Bell, *Principles*, s 537.
45 Stair I.7.10
46 Stair I.7.10.

4.19 (a) *Thing no longer in existence.* If the specific thing transferred no longer exists because it has been consumed by the defender, then the pursuer may be entitled to substitutionary restitution, that is, to a sum of money in place of the thing. Consumption in bona fides probably defeats such a claim, so that it is only the mala fides consumer who will be subject to liability.[47] There is no conclusive authority on the exact value to which a pursuer may be entitled where liability for consumption lies. Arguably the appropriate amount ought either to be the value of the thing when transferred to the defender or the value of the thing when consumed.[48]

4.20 (b) *Thing alienated by the defender.* Where the defender has alienated the thing to a third party in bona fides, he is liable to account to the pursuer only for the amount of any profit (that is, in the measure *quantum lucratus*) made on the transfer.[49] In such a case, the claim is not in fact categorised as one of restitution. The entitlement to restitution ends when possession is parted with by the defender. The claim for profit made by the defender is categorised as a *recompense* claim, stemming from interference by the defender in the pursuer's property rights. Consider the following cases:[50]

Example 1: A transfers goods to *B* under a void contract. The price of the goods is £500, which *B* pays. *B*, being unaware of the void nature of the contract, sells the property on to *C* for £750. *A* is entitled to recover from *B* in recompense in the amount of £250, being the amount of profit which *B* has made on the transfer to *C*.

Example 2: A, an executor under a will, dispones heritable property (valued at £30,000) for no value to *B* under a supposed but non-existent obligation to do so. *B*, being in good faith, sells the heritable property to *C* for £20,000. *A* is entitled to recover £20,000 from *B*, being the amount of profit which *B* has made on the transfer to *C*.

4.21 If the thing has been disposed of in mala fides, the defender must restore the monetary value of the thing to the pursuer, such claim being categorised as one of restitution:[51]

Example 3: A wrongly delivers goods worth £300 to *B*. *B* knows that he is not entitled to the goods, but sells them on to *C* for £150. *A* is entitled to recover the full value of £300 from *B*.

The foregoing says nothing of any direct claim which the pursuer may have against the third party. A pursuer may seek to avoid the title to goods held by a third party, although this will often not be possible if the third party has acquired them in bona fides for value.[52]

4.22 While the pursuer has a prima facie right to demand the return of specific property if still in the hands of the defender, it may be that the pursuer is entitled, as an alternative, to ask for its monetary value. The pursuer's right to demand this where specific restitution would be available and is offered by the defender is

---

47 Bell, *Principles*, s 537, states that it is only where the thing received has been destroyed through the receiver's fault, or where it was received in mala fide, that substitutionary redress will be due.
48 See further the discussion in K Reid, 'Unjustified Enrichment and Property Law' 1994 JR 167 at 179–180.
49 See further on this issue **6.08**.
50 See *Stair Memorial Encyclopaedia*, vol 15, para 57.
51 Stair I.7.2. See *Stair Memorial Encyclopaedia*, vol 15, para 56.
52 See further K Reid, 'Unjustified Enrichment and Property Law' 1994 JR 167 at 180–181.

unclear. A defender's right to offer substitutionary restitution rather than the thing itself is also unclear.

Defences

4.23 The defences of change of position, prescription, and transfer made for an immoral or illegal purpose, are all applicable to restitution.[53] It is also thought that a plea of personal bar could be maintained in an action of restitution.

Pleading a case of recompense

Elements of the action

4.24 Stair described the remedy of recompense as lying 'for that whereby we are enriched by another's means, without purpose of donation'.[54] This definition was essentially repeated by the later institutional writer, Bell,[55] but has been subject to criticism for being too simplistic. Lord President Dunedin felt compelled to comment:

> 'I do not think it is possible—it certainly would not be easy—but I do not think it is possible to frame a definition of recompense which shall by itself in terms at once include all classes of cases which fall within the doctrine and at the same time successfully exclude those which do not. A very much greater framer of definitions than any of us can hope to be—Mr George Joseph Bell— tried it, and I am afraid that he failed, because there is no question that the definition of "recompense" in Bell's Principles will not do'.[56]

4.25 Nonetheless, in a legal system which prides itself on its principled approach it should be possible to identify the essential elements which require to be present to justify the remedy of recompense. The following are generally recognised as necessary elements of a claim:

(a) a loss suffered by the pursuer;[57]
(b) a gain made by the defender;[58]
(c) a causal connection between the loss and the gain, in other words that the gain was made 'at the pursuer's expense';[59]
(d) that the pursuer neither intended to make a donation to the defender, nor

---

53 See **4.16** for discussion of these defences.
54 I.8.6.
55 Bell, *Principles*, s 538.
56 *Edinburgh and District Tramways Co Ltd v Courtenay* 1909 SC 99 at 105, per Lord President Dunedin.
57 See for instance the comment to that effect of Lord President Dunedin in *Edinburgh and District Tramways Co Ltd v Courtenay* 1909 SC at 105. See **4.29** below on the question of whether an interference with one's rights falls to be classified as a loss.
58 See for instance the comment to that effect of Lord President Emslie in *Lawrence Building Co Ltd v Lanark County Council* 1978 SC 30 at 41, 1979 SLT 2, IH.
59 The necessary connection has not been discussed greatly by the courts, but one may note in this regard the discussion by Kames, *Principles of Equity* (3rd edn, 1778), at pp 137–141.

undertook his actings in *suo*, that is, with the intention of benefiting himself alone; and

(e) that there is no other remedy available to the pursuer (the so-called requirement of 'subsidiarity').[60]

Error has not been insisted upon as a requirement for recompense. As shall be seen later,[61] the foregoing requirements bear a remarkable resemblance to the requirements generally accepted in civilian systems for the constitution of an action for the redress of unjustified enrichment.

4.26 It should be noted that Scots law has not traditionally followed the growing English tendency to develop a list of 'unjust factors' which will determine when retention of a benefit is unjustified. In relation to recompense, the Scottish courts have, on the whole,[62] remained content to rely upon the nebulous requirement that the pursuer must not have intended to make a donation of the benefit, and to treat the various factual circumstances which have given rise to the action of recompense as simply instances of the action without seeking to crystallise them in any way.

4.27 There are a diverse number of factual circumstances which have given rise to a recompense claim. Some arise from a voluntary transfer from the pursuer to the defender (loss caused by transfer); some from interference by the defender in a right of the pursuer's (loss caused by interference).[63] Examples of cases where recompense claims have been permitted by the courts include: the provision of services where no valid contract exists in relation to such provision;[64] improvements to heritable property in the bona fide but erroneous belief that it belonged to the improver;[65] payment of another's debt;[66] and profit on the resale of a thing which would have been subject to the obligation of restitution had it remained in the hands of the defender.[67] As may be appreciated, these circumstances are much more diverse than those which may give rise to a repetition or restitution claim. This is a reflection of the fact that the nature of recompense is, unlike repetition and restitution, not tied to the type of benefit received by the defender.

The elements of a recompense claim require further elucidation and are now considered in turn.

(a) Loss suffered by pursuer

4.28 For the purposes of recompense, loss (like gain) is a fluid concept. It may be constituted in a number of ways, including by the pursuer having expended time and effort in the defender's interests—for instance, through the provision of

---

60 Discussed further below at **4.52–4.55**.
61 See **4.47**.
62 Although, as noted below at **4.32**, there are signs of a judicial shift in attitude in this respect.
63 Further on interference with rights, see **6.03–6.09**.
64 Either because a contract was never concluded, was frustrated, or was void. These situations are discussed further below at **4.61–4.71** (formation), **4.80–4.82** (void contracts) and **4.121–4.124** (frustration).
65 *Newton v Newton* 1925 SC 715, 1925 SLT 476, IH.
66 See further **4.28**.
67 See further **4.20** and **6.08**.

services to the defender—or through the pursuer's assets being diminished—for instance, through paying another person's debt.[68]

4.29 It is thought that loss can also be caused by the interference with a right of the pursuer at the hands of the defender. For instance, the pursuer may discover that the defender has occupied a house owned by the pursuer without permission. It might be argued that in such a case of interference with rights, there is no actual loss to the pursuer, merely a gain to the defender.[69] On the other hand, it is suggested that it is preferable to treat such a claim as falling within a widely drawn concept of loss: the interference by the defender with the pursuer's rights can be said to have caused the pursuer to lose the quiet enjoyment of those rights, something which may be described as a loss. Such a view is consistent with the Scottish courts having granted recompense in such cases of interference whilst insisting upon loss as an element of the recompense claim.[70] Scots law, to date, has not clearly separated cases of recompense stemming from interference from those stemming from a transfer, although it has been cogently argued that it ought to do so.[71]

(b) Gain made by defender

4.30 Stair defined gain by the defender widely: 'We are enriched either by accession of gain or prevention of loss'.[72] Included therefore within the notion of gain are the following:

(i)   the performance of services for the defender;
(ii) increase to the defender's patrimony through the receipt of money or other property;
(iii) reduction in the defender's liabilities - for instance through having a debt reduced;
(iv) protection of the defender's property from harm or destruction;[73]
(v)   profits made from the possession or use of the pursuer's property.

The measure of enrichment is discussed below.[74]

(c) Causal connection between the loss and the gain

4.31 Lord President Inglis put it thus: 'in every case there must be, in order to ground the claim, the loss to one party resulting in a benefit to the other'.[75] The

---

68 See for instance *Edinburgh Life Assurance Co v Balderston* (1909) 2 SLT 323, OH. See further H L MacQueen, 'Payment of another's debt', in R Zimmermann and Johnston D, *Unjustified enrichment: key issues in comparative perspective* (2002).

69 In German law, a claim for interference with the rights of an owner would lie under the *Eingriffskondiktion*, or action for interference, although in the German action the requirement of loss is not strictly insisted upon: see R Zimmermann, 'Unjustified Enrichment: The Modern Civilian Approach' (1995) 15 Oxford Journal of Legal Studies 403.

70 Further on enrichment for interference with rights, see **6.03–6.09**.

71 See the arguments advanced by Dr Andrew Steven in 'Recompense for Interference in Scots Law' 1996 JR 51–65.

72 I.8.8.

73 In *SMT Sales and Services Co Ltd v Motor and General Finance Co Ltd* 1954 SLT (Sh Ct) 107, where the defender's vehicle had been garaged by the pursuers, this was held to amount to an enrichment.

74 See **4.37–4.39**.

75 Lord President Inglis in *Stewart v Steuart* (1878) 6 R 145, IH, at 149.

Scottish courts have given no clear guidance as to how precisely the causal connection between the two is to be assessed. There has, however, been clear rejection of certain types of claim on the basis, inter alia, that the alleged enrichment is too indirect.[76] One such type of case is the so-called 'garage repair' scenario:[77]

Example: A garage owner carries out repairs upon a vehicle at the instructions of a third party who is not the owner, for instance an insurance company. If the insurance company does not pay, either because it is unwilling or unable to do so, the garage may look to the owner of the vehicle for recovery of its account. Can the garage require the owner to pay on the basis that, if the owner does not pay, he will be unjustifiably enriched?

The Scottish courts have not permitted an enrichment claim to lie against the owner in such a case.[78] This position can be justified in a number of ways, among them the following:[79] (i) the garage already has a valid claim in contract against the third party: to permit an alternative enrichment claim would subvert the subsidiary nature of enrichment; (ii) there is no direct causal connection between the owner's gain and the garage's loss: the loss has been caused by the insurance company's refusal to pay, not any behaviour of the owner; and (iii) where the third party is insolvent, any claim by the garage against the owner would subvert the policy of the statutory rules concerning ranking in insolvency.

(d) No intention of donation, and actings undertaken in suo

4.32 As mentioned above, Scots law has not traditionally followed the English approach of developing a list of unjust factors, that is to say, a list of specific factual circumstances within which the pursuer must bring his case in order to demonstrate that retention of the gain by the defender would be unjustified. By contrast, reliance has been placed upon the twin concepts that (i) the pursuer must not have intended to make a donation of the benefit to the defender, and (ii) the pursuer must not have undertaken the actings in question for his own benefit, that is, they must not have been undertaken *in suo*. There are, however, nascent signs[80] of a judicial drift from the traditional criterion of lack of donation towards a criterion of lack of justification, a shift which could encourage development of a categorisation based upon unjust factors. This shift is linked to the movement towards a unified concept of unjustified enrichment away from the old tripartite classification of the law.

---

76 Further on indirect enrichment see Niall Whitty, 'Indirect Enrichment in Scots Law' 1994 JR 200.
77 For a comparative analysis of this type of case see Danie Visser and Saul Miller, 'Between Principle and Policy: Indirect Enrichment in Subcontractor and 'Garage-Repair' Cases' [2000] 117 SALJ 594.
78 See *Kirklands Garage (Kinross) Ltd v Clark* 1967 SLT (Sh Ct) 60.
79 See, further, Whitty, op cit, fn 76.
80 For instance, Lord Cullen's comments in *Dollar Land (Cumbernauld) Ltd v CIN Properties Ltd*, 1996 SC 331, that 'A person may be said to have received unjustified enrichment at another's expense when he has obtained a benefit from his actings or expenditure, *without there being a legal ground which would justify him in retaining that benefit*' (at 348–349, emphasis added). Even more clearly, in the same case, Lord Hope commented in the House of Lords (1998 SC (HL) 90, 1998 SLT 992) that 'In general terms it may be said that the remedy [of recompense] is available *where the enrichment lacks a legal ground* to justify the retention of the benefit.'(at 1998 SC 98H–I, emphasis added).

4.33 Behaviour which is undertaken intentionally to promote or protect the pursuer's own position cannot found the basis of an enrichment claim. Where such expenditure has occurred then it is to be inferred that, if the defender gained any incidental benefit from the expenditure, the pursuer intended to donate this benefit to the defender. Thus, where parties are negotiating a contract, it is to be presumed (in the absence of any contrary agreement) that, if one party undertakes expenditure designed to assist it in securing the contract's conclusion, this expenditure is to be considered *in suo* and irrecoverable from the other party.

4.34 An example of irrecoverable expenditure is seen in *Edinburgh and District Tramways Co Ltd v Courtenay*:[81]

> The pursuers had rented advertising space on their tramcars to the defender. The defender was obliged under the contract to provide boards for attachment to the tramcars onto which the advertisements would be placed. The pursuers subsequently decided to bring into service new tramcars onto which boards were already affixed, thus obviating the need for the defender to provide its own boards. The pursuers sought to recover the cost of providing the boards from the defender. The Inner House held that the cost of providing the boards was not recoverable from the defender in recompense.

The decision may be explained on the basis that the pursuer had intended to undertake the expenditure on new tramcars for its own benefit (*in suo*), or simply by saying (as Lord President Dunedin did)[82] that the pursuers had not in essence suffered any loss.

4.35 It can be argued that the requirement that the pursuer's actings were not undertaken *in suo* is merely a facet of the requirement that the pursuer must not have intended to donate the benefit: on this view, actings which are for the pursuer's own benefit, but which incidentally benefit the defender, may impliedly be said to have been made with a donative intent.[83]

(e) There must be no other remedy available to the pursuer

4.36 This requirement is discussed more fully below (in relation to the interaction of unjustified enrichment and contract), but it may be noted at this point that the availability of any other legal remedy to the pursuer, whether at common law or by statute, will defeat a claim for recompense, unless an exceptional case is made out for the availability of such. Lord Fraser put the position thus:

> 'I do not know that it is absolutely essential to the success of an action for recompense that the pursuer should not have, and should never have had, any possibility of raising an action under the ordinary law, but in my opinion it would at least require special and strong circumstances to justify an action for recompense where there was, or had been, an alternative remedy open to the pursuer.'[84]

---

81 1909 SC 99, IH.
82 See Lord President Dunedin, 1909 SC at 105.
83 This is the position adopted by W D H Sellar, *Stair Memorial Encyclopaedia*, vol 15, para 63.
84 *Varney (Scotland) Ltd v Burgh of Lanark* 1974 SC 245 at 259, 1976 SLT 46, per Lord Fraser.

Measure of recovery

4.37   The pursuer is in general entitled to recover to the extent of the defender's enrichment, a measure referred to by the term *'quantum lucratus'*. This is in distinction to the measure of recovery under implied contract, *quantum meruit*, the market value of the benefit received, although in many cases the two measures may produce the same valuation. Where enrichment has occurred through the defender saving an expense, the amount of the saving made will be the measure of the enrichment. It has been asserted that the extent of the pursuer's loss limits recovery under recompense,[85] although there is no solid line of authority to support this view.

4.38   Whilst in general the defender's enrichment is the measure of recovery, this is not so in all cases. Thus, where a defender has bona fide used the pursuer's property in the creation of a new species of property, the measure of the claim by the pursuer in recompense will be for the value of the property lost, and not the enrichment of the defender; whereas, if the defender was in bad faith, the pursuer's recovery is for the 'utmost value'[86] of the goods, permitting the pursuer to argue circumstances which would justify a higher claim.

4.39   The time when the enrichment falls to be measured has not clearly been settled by the courts. There are a number of options: the time when the pursuer suffered the loss, the time when the defender first made the gain, or the time that the action is raised. Whitty has taken the view that 'in most cases it is the time of the action (or demand?) for recompense'.[87] On the other hand, Lord President Hope's statement in *NV Devos Gebroeder v Sunderland Sportswear*[88] that 'the obligation to make recompense in this case first became enforceable when the defenders became enriched or *lucrati*'[89] suggests that it is the time of receipt of the enrichment by the defender. Under either approach, a court will require to take account of any available defences.

Defences

4.40   As with repetition and restitution, bona fide consumption or alienation of the enrichment (or part thereof) will operate as a valid defence to a claim of recompense. It might further be suggested that the requirements (discussed above) that the pursuer's actings must not have been *in suo*, that there be no other remedy available to the pursuer (the requirement of subsidiarity), and that the benefit acquired by the defender be not merely incidentally acquired, ought best to be discussed under the heads of defences to an action of recompense, rather than, as they have been treated in this text, as part of the substantive requirements of an action of recompense. The question is a

---

85   This view was adopted by Whitty in 'The Taxonomy of Unjustified Enrichment in Scots Law', Appendix B, at p 80.

86   Per Bankton, *Institute*, I.ix.43.

87   Whitty, op cit, fn 85, at p 81.

88   1987 SLT 331, 1989 SLT 382, OH; 1990 SC 291, 1990 SLT 473, IH.

89   1990 SC at 297.

moot one, and there has been insubstantive discussion by the courts to provide a clear answer.

4.41 It has been argued that the requirement that the loss was not made *in suo* does not, in any event, add anything to the other established components of recompense, an argument which has merit.[90] In relation to the issue of subsidiarity, whilst it may be sensible for a pursuer to state in its written pleadings that there is no other remedy available to it, it would be difficult to prove such, and it seems more appropriate that the defender should raise this issue in its defences if it believes this to be the case.

The 3 Rs as themselves distinct obligations?

4.42 In the modern law, unjustified enrichment is seen as a distinct, unified obligational head. At the time of Stair, however, this concept had not yet been acknowledged as drawing together the various actions into a single category. Stair recognised restitution (subsuming within it repetition) and recompense as distinct obediential obligations,[91] to be counted alongside other discrete obligations such as that of reparation (the obligation to compensate for loss wrongfully caused). With the subsequent development of the concept of unjustified enrichment, the individual actions are no longer perceived as distinct obligational headings, although it would still be perfectly correct to describe them as individual obligations in the second alternative meaning of the term obligation described at **1.02** above.

Criticisms of current scheme of the law

4.43 The current tripartite division of the law along the lines of the 3 Rs has been widely criticised. Amongst the legitimate criticisms of the current taxonomy may be numbered the following:

(1)   The division between the actions is not made according to a consistent criterion. The distinction between repetition and restitution lies in the nature of the benefit received, but recompense is not so characterised. Rather it has the appearance of a residual action, gathering together a diverse collection of cases linked through the measure of recovery *quantum lucratus*. Any properly ordered taxonomy of the law requires consistency in the method of subdivision.

(2)   In relation to all three actions, there has been no clear analysis of the nature of the requirement of the causal connection between the loss to the pursuer and the gain by the defender.

---

90   See further reference at fn 83.
91   See further on this point W D H Sellar, '*Shilliday v Smith*: Unjust Enrichment through the Looking Glass?' (2001) 5 ELR 80 at 82.

(3)   There is no uniform measure of recovery in operation. If the concept of unjustified enrichment underlies all three actions, then a uniform measure of recovery, based upon the amount of the defender's enrichment, should apply in all cases.

(4)   There is no clear understanding as to the correct time for assessing the extent of enrichment under each action.

(5)   The inclusion of specific factual situations within specific actions seems to lack any clear rationale. Why, for instance, should profit made on resale of a thing be treated as recompense rather than an aspect of restitution? Or why should recovery of a sum of money from a defender lacking full capacity be classified as a recompense claim?[92]

These criticisms are serious and compelling. The case for reform has been made from all sides. As shall now be seen, there is however no agreed route by which to proceed.

Proposed schemes to reformulate the law

4.44   A number of suggestions have been made for law reform. They are worth restating here briefly:

(1)   *Reform along English lines.* Peter Birks has suggested that Scots law adopt an English model, proposed by him as a division of the law of unjustified enrichment into enrichment by subtraction and enrichment by wrong.[93] Additionally, he proposes that enrichment by subtraction be triggered by reference to various recognised unjust factors, a method which has gained strong support in English law. Bill Stewart has developed a taxonomy which builds upon the English approach.[94]

(2)   *Reform along the lines of the German Wilburg/von Caemmerer taxonomy.* Niall Whitty, a former law commissioner, has proposed that Scots law be remodelled along the lines adopted by German law (largely as the result of the academic contributions from Wilburg and von Caemmerer).[95] This scheme divides enrichment into four main heads: (a) enrichment by performance of the pursuer (performance encompassing payment, transfer or performance of services); (b) enrichment by the pursuer's unauthorised improvement of the defender's property in the bona fide but mistaken belief it belonged to the pursuer; (c) enrichment by the pursuer's discharge of the defender's debt; and (d) enrichment by the defender's unauthorised interference with the pursuer's property.

(3)   *Codification:* Eric Clive, a former law commissioner, out of a belief that the existing law has become so muddled that starting from scratch provides the

---

92   As to which, see the sources cited by Whitty, op cit, fn 85, at p 43, n 217.
93   For the Birks view, see 'Six Questions in Search of a Subject—Unjust Enrichment in a Crisis of Identity' 1985 JR 227 and 'Restitution: A View of the Scots Law' (1985) 38 CLP 57.
94   See W J Stewart, *The Law of Restitution in Scotland.*
95   For the Whitty view, see 'Rationality, nationality and the taxonomy of unjustified enrichment' in D Johnson and R Zimmermann (eds), *Unjustified Enrichment: Key Issues in Comparative Perspective* (CUP, 2002), pp 658–729.

best way to proceed, has produced a very succinct draft Code to reformulate the law.[96] It is based upon a basic anti-enrichment principle enshrined within section 1 of the Code: 'A person who has been enriched at the expense of another without justification is bound to redress the enrichment.' The sections of the Code thereafter proceed by fleshing out the component parts of this basic principle.

(4) *Development of recompense as a general enrichment action.* Hector MacQueen and David Sellar have proposed that recompense has developed to become the general enrichment action in Scots law.[97] Its equitable foundations in the civilian brocard *nemo debet locupletari aliena jactura* uniquely placed it as the ideal vehicle for the general restoration of unjustifiably retained enrichments. MacQueen and Sellar view recompense as the ideal foundation upon which to continue the development of a general action.

(5) *Judicial development of an innominate general enrichment action.* As explained below, a strong possibility for future development is the abandonment by the courts of the constraints and uncertainties imposed by the existing threefold classification of the law, and the development of an innominate action for the redress of unjustified enrichment. The elements and limitations of such an action would require further development by the courts. Whether any sub-categories of such a general enrichment action would be desirable would also be a question to be addressed by the courts.

4.45 Which of the above suggestions for reform most commends itself? Proposals to adopt an English approach have generally not found favour amongst Scottish commentators, not least because the English law of restitution is arranged around the remedy of restitution, rather than the ground of action of unjustified enrichment. Such a fundamental difference makes Scots lawyers looking for inspiration for reform wary of drawing support from England. The German approach, whilst providing a workable and logical model, has nothing specially to commend it and is unlikely to attract sufficient political support.

4.46 The last three models for reform from the above list are the front runners for possible adoption. The Scottish legal community has remained somewhat sceptical of codification, although the recent higher profile achieved by projects such as the Principles of European Contract Law may be beginning to soften some of the critics of codification. Legislative impetus would be necessary for such a project to succeed, however, and it must be said that codification of enrichment law is unlikely to be a domestic legislative priority. That is not to say that the impetus could not come from the European Union, but the prospects of such are slim in the short term.

4.47 The development of recompense as a general action has merit. Recompense has similar marks to those commonly recognised as forming the foundation of

---

96 The Code is framed for possible adoption at a European level, while permitting national law to specify local remedies and procedure. The Code is reproduced as an appendix to the Scottish Law Commission's Discussion Paper No 99 on *Judicial Abolition of the Error of Law Rule* (1996), and also appears within chapter 25 of *Towards a European Civil Code* (eds Hartkamp et al).

97 See H L MacQueen and W D H Sellar, 'Unjust Enrichment in Scots Law', in *Unjust Enrichment: The Comparative Legal History of the Law of Restitution* (ed E J H Schrage).

enrichment law in civilian systems, namely[98] (a) enrichment, (b) impoverishment, (c) a causal connection between the two, (d) absence of justification or cause,[99] and (e) subsidiarity. While there are those who have been sceptical as to its functioning as a general action in the past, there is no doubt that the similarities with the requirements of the modern civilian action would render recompense suitable for development as a general action even if it historically had not fulfilled such a role.

4.48 The final candidate for reform, development of an innominate general action, provides a common law equivalent of the codification route. Adoption of this route would permit the courts to take leave of previous jurisprudence and forge a new unified action based firmly upon the principle that no one should be permitted to be unjustifiably enriched at the expense of another. The Scottish courts might well be reticent to divorce themselves from the prior law, feeling that to do so would be too sharp a break from the past and would smack of judicial law making, but such a position might be reached in stages:

Stage 1: the courts maintain the current actions (the 3 Rs), but emphasise that the foundation of each is a principle against unjustified enrichment.

Stage 2: the courts encourage a shift of the focus in written pleadings away from specification of a pursuer's case by reference to a specific native action or to the *condictiones*, and towards a general statement that the pursuer's case is based upon the anti-enrichment principle. This stage would culminate in an authoritative statement that the courts had now recognised a general action.

Stage 3: there would then follow a period of development in which the courts would require to develop the component parts of the general action. It is suggested that prior to this stage being reached, relevant bodies, such as the Scottish Law Commission, might undertake a thorough consultation and discussion process designed to provide the courts with guidance in this respect.

4.49 An examination of the cases indicates that the courts have already reached stage 1 and are proceeding to stage 2. Recent pronouncements of Lord Presidents Hope and Rodger have emphasised the general principle underlying all three native actions. In *Morgan Guaranty* Lord Hope stated:

'[T]he important point is that these actions are all means to the same end, which is to redress an unjustified enrichment upon the broad equitable principle *nemo debet locupletari aliena jactura.*'[100]

In a similar vein, in *Shilliday v Smith* Lord Rodger said:

'repetition, restitution, reduction and recompense are simply examples of remedies which the courts grant to reverse an unjust enrichment'.[101]

98 The criteria listed were suggested by Barry Nicholas in 'Unjust Enrichment in the Civil Law and Louisiana Law' (1962) 36 Tulane LR 605. See also Schrage, 'Unjustified Enrichment: Recent Dutch developments from a comparative and historical perspective', 1999 NILR 57.
99 The parallel for recompense being Stair's requirement that there be no purpose of donation.
100 1995 SLT 299 at 309L.
101 1998 SC 725 at 728B.

Lord Hope, commenting later from the House of Lords on this statement of Lord President Rodger, thought that it might perhaps be

> 'unrealistic to expect those who practise in the courts to depart from such terminology. In the context of the written pleadings which are used in our practice the pursuer is expected to state the nature of the remedy which he seeks, as well as the legal basis for it. For my part I see no harm in the continued use of these expressions to describe the various remedies, so long as it is understood that they are being used merely to describe the nature of the remedy which the court is being asked to provide in order to redress the enrichment.'[102]

This might suggest a certain reticence to judicial embarkation upon stage 2 of the process outlined above. Nonetheless, Lord President Rodger had commented in *Dollar Land* that

> 'a distinct feature of the argument for both parties was that counsel did not spend much time identifying into which class of enrichment action the present case falls'[103]

which suggests that practitioners may have reached this stage at the level of oral pleadings at least. Since the decision in *Dollar Land* this trend appears to have continued, as is witnessed by Lord Penrose's summary of the submission of counsel in *Bank of Scotland v Junior*[104] on the enrichment aspect of the case:

> 'One had to have regard to the fundamental requirements of a remedy for unjustified enrichment. Those were that one person was enriched at the expense of another in circumstances in which it was unjust and unintended that the person advantaged should retain the benefit obtained at the expense of the person who was disadvantaged by the other's enrichment. If those requirements were established, the form of the remedy was a secondary matter.'[105]

Such comments suggest that stage 2 is indeed underway, but as yet at an early point. There are optimistic signs that the Scottish courts will feel up to the task at hand, the development of a general action for the redress of unjustified enrichment which is untrammelled by much of the historical baggage of the law. Those pleading cases are in a prime role to assist development through focusing their pleadings on the principle of unjustified enrichment rather than on one of the traditional actions recognised by the law.

Future of a general action

4.50 How might the courts develop a general action for the redress of unjustified enrichment? What issues will they have to address in order properly to do so? The following suggestions are offered:

---

102 *Dollar Land (Cumbernauld) Ltd v CIN Properties Ltd* 1998 SC (HL) at 98.
103 1996 SC at 353A–B.
104 1999 SCLR 284, IH.
105 1999 SCLR at 292G–293A.

(1)   A general action should exist for the redress of an enrichment retained without justification. Loss to the pursuer should be a requirement, although this might be demonstrated by an interference with the pursuer's rights.

(2)   There should be no separate action for the return of an undue payment, as is the case in some civilian systems. A claim for an undue payment should be treated as a species of the general enrichment action, there being no compelling reason to treat it separately.

(3)   The enrichment claim should lie for the extent to which the defender has been enriched during the period for which the defender was not entitled to retain the enrichment. The pursuer's loss should not, in general, act as a ceiling for any claim.[106] However, the extent of any enrichment which accrues as the result of the defender's bona fide industry or ingenuity should remain with the defender.

(4)   The enrichment claim should be measured (as with damages claims) at the time of the action. However, the defender should be liable for any mala fide or culpable consumption or alienation.

(5)   A causal connection should be shown between the loss and the enrichment. Causality might be demonstrated in a number of ways, which should include: (i) a transfer of money or property from pursuer to defender;[107] (ii) the performance of services by the pursuer for the defender; (iii) interference by the defender with the pursuer's patrimony (including rights possessed by the pursuer); (iv) fulfilment by the pursuer of an obligation due by the defender, eg a monetary debt.[108]

(6)   The retention of the enrichment should be without justification, that is, without a valid underlying purpose. There might be a great number of specific circumstances which could be so characterised, but there is no need to crystallise these into a list of unjust factors. Examples of a valid underlying purpose should include a valid contract and donation.

(7)   Where a specific piece of property has been transferred, the pursuer should be entitled to its return if it remains in the hand of the defender. The defender may offer substitutionary monetary redress, but the pursuer is not bound to accept this.

(8)   The enrichment claim should be prima facie a claim of right. It should be for the defender to raise any equitable considerations which might defeat the claim.

4.51   There are a number of matters of detail which have been omitted from the above suggestions, and which would require to be addressed by the courts.[109] As suggested earlier, the Scottish Law Commission and other interested parties

---

106   This may be a controversial view. Some may feel that the pursuer's loss ought to act as a ceiling. However, this would penalise the pursuer, for during the time in which the asset has been in the hands of the defender, or he has otherwise benefited from the gain, the pursuer has been deprived of his right to make a similar gain.

107   This might include bona fide but mistaken improvements to the defender's property.

108   The courts will require to develop an understanding of those situations where the connection is deemed to be too indirect.

109   Eric Clive's Draft Code goes into much greater detail in relation to the component requirements of a general enrichment action.

might helpfully provide impetus for judicial completion of stage 2 (in the staged list noted above)[110] and embarkation upon stage 3 by consulting on a general action.

PART II: UNJUSTIFIED ENRICHMENT AND CONTRACT

SUBSIDIARITY: ENRICHMENT POSTPONED TO CONTRACT

4.52 In relation to the action of recompense, the requirement that there be no other remedy available to the pursuer was discussed at **4.36** above. This requirement can be stated more broadly in relation to the wider interaction of unjustified enrichment and the obligation of contract: enrichment remedies will not be available to a pursuer where there is a valid contract in existence by which a transfer of the enrichment to the defender can be justified. Whilst this requirement is not always insisted upon in other systems, in Scots and indeed English law[111] the presence of a valid contractual remedy is in general[112] held to be fatal to an enrichment claim. This exclusionary effect of contract vis-à-vis enrichment is referred to as the principle of subsidiarity of unjustified enrichment.

4.53 This principle has been affirmed at various points by the Scottish courts, and most recently by the House of Lords in *Dollar Land (Cumbernauld) Ltd v CIN Properties Ltd.*[113]

> The pursuers were subtenants of a shopping centre under a complex leasing arrangement. The defenders were the tenants. The defenders terminated the sublease on account of the pursuers' failure to pay rent. The termination allowed the defenders to collect rental payments directly from the sub-subtenants who occupied the units at the shopping centre. The pursuers raised an action of recompense claiming that, by retaining the rental payments from the sub-subtenants, the defenders were unjustifiably enriched at the pursuers' expense. The defenders argued that, as by virtue of the termination they were contractually entitled to use and enjoy the shopping centre free of all claims by the pursuers, they were justifiably entitled to retain the payments from sub-subtenants. On appeal, the House of Lords dismissed the pursuers' claim, holding that the terms of the contractual arrangement justified the defenders' retention of the rental payments.

---

110 See **4.48**.
111 In this respect, one may note the remarks of Lord Goff of Chieveley in *Pan Ocean Shipping Ltd v Creditcorp Ltd* [1994] 1 All ER 470, HL, who, commenting on the facts of the case, stated (at 473j–474a): 'there is a contractual regime which legislates for the recovery of overpaid hire. It follows, that as a general rule, the law of restitution has no part to play in the matter; the existence of the agreed regime renders the imposition by the law of a remedy in restitution both unnecessary and inappropriate'.
112 As was seen in relation to recompense, the judicial view has been expressed that there may be exceptions to this general principle (see Lord Fraser's remarks in *Varney*, noted above at **4.36**). It is difficult, however, to envisage what such exceptional circumstances might amount to. It may be that what Lord Fraser had in mind was the operation of enrichment remedies in certain circumstances of breach of contract, where certain contractual remedies might also remain. This is discussed below at **4.83** ff.
113 1998 SC (HL) 90, 1998 SLT 992, HL.

In his speech, Lord Jauncey of Tullichettle, commenting upon the enrichment in the hands of the defenders, said: 'I simply do not see how results for which parties or their predecessors had specifically and willingly contracted could be said to be unjust.'[114] In a similar vein, Lord Hope of Craighead commented: 'The benefit which has enriched CIN is one which was provided for them expressly in the contract of sublease.'[115] In this view of the subsidiarity of enrichment law and its postponement to contractual remedies, English law concurs.[116]

4.54 It must be asserted, however, that the general postponement of enrichment remedies to contract is not to be seen in any respect as supporting a dichotomy between 'legal' and 'equitable' remedies. Whether or not this is the case under English law, Scots law knows of no such dichotomy, equitable considerations underlying all of our law, albeit with particular emphasis in an area such as enrichment. In this respect, notions of a legal-equitable divide hinted at by Lord Justice Clerk Wheatley in *Varney (Scotland) Ltd v Burgh of Lanark*[117] cannot be approved of.

4.55 As discussed in the following paragraphs, the general postponement of enrichment remedies to contractual ones does not preclude the operation of the former in certain cases where the parties are, or have been, in a contractual relationship. In particular, the cases of breach of contract, frustration and void contracts are discussed below.

REMEDYING A BREACH OF CONTRACT: COMPENSATION FOR LOSS, NOT DISGORGEMENT OF GAIN

4.56 In chapter 3 the function of contractual damages to compensate for loss was explored. It is no part of the law that damages for breach of contract are to be assessed by gains made by a contract breaker unrelated to the loss suffered by the pursuer. This principle was clearly laid down in *Teacher v Calder*:[118]

> The pursuer lent the defender £15,000 to be invested in the defender's timber business. The pursuer sued the defender in damages for breach of contract, alleging that the defender, in breach of their agreement, had withdrawn the pursuer's capital from the timber business and instead invested it in a distillery. It was held, inter alia, that the pursuer was not entitled to recover any profits made by the defender in so breaching the contract.

The rule that damages are to be assessed by reference to the pursuer's loss is not circumvented by permitting to the pursuer any other remedy whose purpose is to disgorge gains made by the defender. Thus, an 'account of profits', a remedy distinct from damages, is not, save exceptionally,[119] permitted to the pursuer. The two principal examples of exceptional circumstances are those where the

---

114 1998 SC at 93F–G.
115 1998 SC at 100C.
116 See the comments of Lord Goff, noted at fn 111.
117 1974 SC 245, 1976 SLT 46.
118 (1898) 25 R 661, IH; on appeal (1899) 1 F (HL) 39, 1899, 7 SLT 153; (1899) 36 SLR 949; [1899] AC 451, HL. See, in English law, *Surrey County Council v Bredero Homes Ltd* [1993] 1 WLR 1361, CA.
119 See **4.58–4.60**.

contracting parties are in a fiduciary relationship, or where the contract imposes an obligation of confidence on one or both parties.

4.57 The English courts have exceptionally allowed recovery in damages for breach of contract in a measure not mirroring the loss of the claimant in cases where a negative covenant relating to the use of land has been breached. This occurred in *Wrotham Park Estate Co Ltd v Parkside Homes Ltd*,[120] where an award of damages was made against a builder who had built on land adjoining the plaintiff's in breach of an agreement not to do so. The loss to the plaintiff was nominal. However, the plaintiff was permitted to recover in an amount equating to what the court estimated the plaintiff might reasonably have demanded for a relaxation of the restrictive covenant, even though the plaintiff might never in fact have agreed to such relaxation. This approach was recently affirmed in *Amec Development Ltd v Jury's Hotel Management (UK) Ltd*,[121] but it has been held inapplicable where the covenant broken does not relate to land.[122]

Disgorgement of profits

4.58 An account of profits by a contract breaker was ordered by the House of Lords in the English appeal *Attorney-General v Blake*.[123]

> The defendant, George Blake, was a convicted spy who had escaped from prison and fled to Russia where he had settled. Blake had written an autobiography, which disclosed confidential information obtained by him during his service as a member of the British Secret Intelligence Service. The Crown sought an injunction preventing Blake from receiving any financial benefit from his publishing arrangement and in addition seeking disgorgement of the benefits received by Blake as a result of his breach of contract with the Crown. On appeal to the House of Lords, the request for an injunction was refused. However, an order requiring Blake to account for the profits made by him as a result of the breach of contract was granted by the court.

4.59 One way to regard the nature of the decision is as an application of the tightly defined exception to the normal rule on assessment of contractual damages based upon a breach of an obligation of confidence owed by the defendant. So characterised, it is of one of those few exceptions to the general principle against disgorging benefits from contract breakers dependent upon aspects of the contractual relationship which bring the parties into an extremely close relationship. The difficulty with such a characterisation of the case is that the test for application of the exception adopted by Lord Nicholls of Birkenhead, who delivered the leading speech, is framed much more widely, restricted only by considerations of justice and equity. His Lordship stated:

> 'There seems to be no reason, in principle, why the court must in all circumstances rule out an account of profits as a remedy for breach of contract. ... When, exceptionally, a just response to a breach of contract so requires, the court should be able to grant the discretionary remedy of

---

120 [1974] 1 WLR 798, Ch.
121 [2001] 1 EGLR 81, Ch.
122 *World Wide Fund for Nature v World Wrestling Federation Entertainment Inc* [2001] FSR 32, Ch.
123 [2001] 1 AC 268. It has been reported that Mr Blake is to challenge the decision of the House of Lords before the European Court of Human Rights.

requiring a defendant to account to the plaintiff for the benefits he has received from his breach of contract ... the plaintiff's interest in performance may make it just and equitable that the defendant should retain no benefit from his breach of contract.'[124]

Lord Nicholls went on to suggest that exceptional cases were those where the existing contractual remedies 'are inadequate'.[125] But how does one define inadequacy? Could inadequacy not be said to occur wherever a pursuer's loss is less than the gains made by a contract breaker? Lord Nicholls did, however, make the further suggestion that a 'useful general guide, although not exhaustive, is whether the plaintiff had a legitimate interest in preventing the defendant's profit-making activity and, hence, in depriving him of his profit.'[126] This may act as some break on the generality previously expressed by his Lordship.

4.60 The *Blake* approach has subsequently been held inapplicable in a commercial arbitration where the breach of contract concerned failure to provide a commodity readily available on the open market.[127] However, it was followed in *Esso Petroleum Co Ltd v Niad Ltd*,[128] which concerned the breach by the defendant garage owner of a price-limitation contract entered into with the claimant petrol supplier. The defendant had increased his petrol prices beyond the price agreed, thus increasing his profits. Ordinary compensatory damages were deemed inadequate in this case, as Esso were unable to attribute any particular losses to the defendant's breach. However, on the basis that the very purpose of the agreement was to cap the price of petrol, disgorgement of profits was awarded against the garage owner. In such a case, where a disgorgement of profits is permitted, it may well be very difficult for the pursuer to assess the profits made by the party in breach, especially where the relationship between the parties is an ongoing one in which profits made may not relate clearly to any one transaction.

PRE-CONTRACTUAL ACTINGS

4.61 One area in which it may be argued that enrichment remedies have a role to play is in the realm of pre-contractual actings. The following situations may be distinguished:

(1) cases where the parties have been directly negotiating a contract, but no contract has arisen (eg because negotiations have broken down) and no works directly forming the basis of the contract have been undertaken, but some preliminary expenditure has been incurred by one or both parties;

(2) cases where the parties have been directly negotiating a contract, no contract has arisen, but some, or all, of the work which is to form the substance of contractual performance has occurred;

---

124 [2001] AC at 284G–285A.
125 [2001] AC at 285G.
126 [2001] AC at 285H.
127 In *AB Corporation v CD Company* [2002] 1 Lloyd's Rep 805, concerning a breach of a charterparty agreement, a claim by the party suffering the breach for disgorgement of profits from the party in breach was held inappropriate.
128 Ch, 2001 WL 1476190 (unreported).

(3)   cases where the parties have not been directly negotiating a contract, but a tender (for example) has been submitted, and expenditure has been incurred, but no contract has followed; and

(4)   cases where the parties have reached an informal agreement, but the final contract was not in the correct form and services have been rendered under the informal agreement.

Is it appropriate that enrichment has any role to play in any of the above cases?

Case (1)

4.62   The general principle applicable to pre-contractual negotiations is that where expenditure is incurred by A in the expectation of winning a contract, but no contract is concluded, such expenditure is to be treated, in the absence of any contrary agreement,[129] as undertaken at A's own risk, without the possibility of recovery from B.

An illustration of the principle is seen in the decision of the English High Court in *Regalian Properties plc v London Dockland Development Corporation*:[130]

> The plaintiffs entered negotiations for the development as residential accommodation of an area of the London Docklands owned by the defendants. An agreement was entered into 'subject to contract' and to various other matters. Whilst these matters remained outstanding, the plaintiffs incurred considerable expenditure in professional fees and other costs in preparing for the proposed contract. Due to failure to agree on outstanding matters, and other factors, no contract was ever concluded. The plaintiffs raised an action in restitution for recovery of £3 million, being the amount of their wasted expenditure. The High Court held that as the agreement was 'subject to contract' this necessarily implied that the parties were free to walk away from the proposed contract without incurring any liability. Moreover, the costs sought had been expended by the plaintiffs in the hope of the contract being won, and had conferred no benefit upon the defendants.

4.63   This seems correct both on the facts and in principle. One cause for concern, however, might be that part of the expense incurred by the plaintiffs was in providing further designs which had been requested by the defendants. It could be argued that, where a negotiating party explicitly requests that certain work be carried out during the negotiating process, the costs of this should be recoverable by the burdened party. However, responding to such an argument, the judge in *Regalian Properties*, Rattee J, commented:

> 'I do not accept that it incurred this expenditure or any part of it at the request of LDDC, save in the sense that some of it was incurred in an attempt to satisfy LDDC's requirements as to design which was a precondition of Regalian obtaining the building lease it wanted. This expenditure was

---

129   Where protracted negotiations are to occur in relation to a substantial contract in terms of which a party may be required to undertake expensive pre-contractual preparations which will not necessarily confer any benefit upon the other, there is much to be said for the parties reaching a formal agreement on who is to bear the costs of such expenditure should negotiations fail to produce a contract. Of course, such a preliminary contract may not be practicable in the circumstances.

130   [1995] 1 WLR 212, [1995] 1 All ER 1005, Ch.

incurred by Regalian in an attempt to put itself in the position of obtaining and complying with the terms of the proposed building lease from LDDC.'[131]

The situation might have been different had the work conferred some positive and tangible benefit upon the defendants, but that was not so. A party seeking to win a contract must therefore be aware that expenditure which it carries out, even if in response to specific requests from the other party as to its requirements, is likely to find such expenditure irrecoverable.[132]

4.64 There may be some cases where, as noted in chapter 3, negotiations have been carried out in bad faith—for instance, with no genuine intention of entering into a contract—and in such cases liability may lie for losses caused in delict.[133] In addition, in a restricted category of case where B has led A to conclude that a contract exists between them, but, due to some defect, no contract exists, a remedy for wasted expenditure may lie on the authority of the line of cases following *Walker v Milne*.[134] This is discussed more fully in chapter 5.[135]

Case (2)

4.65 In case (2), where some benefit has been transferred by one party to the other, whether it is all or merely part of the anticipated contract works, it is equitable that a remedy should lie in recompense. A classic example of this scenario is the case of *British Steel Corporation v Cleveland Bridge Engineering Co Ltd*:[136]

> The plaintiffs and defendants entered into negotiations for the manufacture by the plaintiffs of a quantity of steel nodes, to be used by the defendants in a construction project. While negotiations as to the terms of the contract were ongoing, the defendants issued a letter of intent to the plaintiffs asking them to begin production of the steel nodes. The parties were unable to reach agreement on a number of issues, including the contract price, and when negotiations broke down the plaintiffs sued for payment on a *quantum meruit* basis. The defendants counterclaimed for damages for breach of contract, alleging inter alia late delivery of the nodes. In the High Court it was held that there was no contract between the parties, the counterclaim of the defendants being dismissed. The defendants were ordered to pay a reasonable sum for the steel nodes on a *quantum meruit* basis.

The measure of recovery in this case was *quantum meruit* (the value of the work done), which is the English restitutionary measure of recovery. Had the same result been reached in Scotland, which it is submitted it would have, then recovery *quantum lucratus* would have been awarded against the defenders in an action of recompense.

4.66 An enrichment approach to cases such as *Cleveland Bridge*, while providing a much needed remedy, is not wholly satisfactory. While the expectations of the

---

131 [1995] 1 All ER at 1009d–e.
132 No doubt such expenditure will, in cases where the contract is successfully concluded, be factored into the projected profits to be expected from the contract.
133 See **3.23**.
134 (1823) 2 S 379, IH.
135 See **5.11–5.18**.
136 [1984] 1 All ER 504; 1983 Build LR 94, QB.

party claiming for the work done may have been largely met, the expectations of the party commissioning the work are much less satisfactorily met. In *Cleveland Bridge* the defendants' expectations as to quality, timing and order of delivery of the goods finds no adequate expression, there being no contract between the parties by which these expectations can be measured. The case highlights the dangers of allowing negotiations to drag on in a protracted fashion whilst accepting a non-contractual performance.

4.67 An alternative approach which may be adopted in some cases, those where negotiations have been all but completed, is for a court to imply a missing term in order to hold a contract to exist between the parties. Such an approach was adopted by the Inner House in *Avintair Ltd v Ryder Airline Services Ltd*.[137]

> The pursuers, aviation consultants, sought declarator that a contract existed between them and the defenders, an aircraft engineering company, in terms of which the defenders were obliged to pay the pursuers for work undertaken in introducing the defenders to a third party, an airline company, from whom the defenders had obtained work. The defenders argued that, as no commission had been agreed for such services, no contract therefore existed, and further that, as the pursuers had not averred a case of recompense, no claim for the work undertaken could be maintained. The Inner House held that a term was to be implied into the contract that the defenders would pay the ordinary or market rate for the services provided (payment *quantum meruit*).

The Inner House distinguished cases where 'nothing has been done by either party to implement the alleged contract' from cases where 'a party to the alleged contract has already provided the goods or services for which he seeks payment'.[138] Whilst in the former case it would be difficult to enforce the alleged contract because 'in the ordinary case the price is one of the essential matters upon which agreement is required', in the latter case 'the usual rule is that there is an obligation to pay for them [ie the goods or services] unless they have been provided gratuitously'.[139] Even with this restriction upon the ratio, the decision is controversial. There is much to be said for the view that in any onerous contract determination of the price is so fundamental a matter that judicial contract making is inappropriate, unless legislation so permits.[140] The alternative solution lies in enrichment.

4.68 A court will not adopt an *Avintair* approach when, as in *Cleveland Bridge*, the parties are still at odds on a *number* of contract terms. Additionally, in England at least, the caveat to a complete contract that it is 'subject to contract' will be fatal to a determination that a contract has been concluded between the parties.

4.69 It should be noted that even where *B* may have gained as a result of *A*'s pre-contractual actings, an enrichment claim by *A* may be barred if the gain is deemed to be merely incidental to *A*'s primary purpose in winning the contract. This point is exemplified by the decision in *Site Preparations Ltd v Secretary of State for Scotland*.[141]

---

137 1994 SC 270, 1994 SLT 613, 1994 SCLR 401, IH.
138 1994 SLT at 615K–L.
139 1994 SLT at 615L.
140 As is the case in contracts for the sale of goods, where the Sale of Goods Act 1979, s 8(2), as amended, stipulates that, in the absence of agreement, a buyer is to pay a 'reasonable price' for goods.
141 1975 SLT (Notes) 41, OH.

The pursuers made an unsolicited approach to the defender in relation to a development proposed by the pursuers at Peterhead Harbour. In connection with the proposal, the pursuers prepared various plans and other materials which they submitted to the defender. The pursuers were aware that their proposal was only one of a number being considered by the defender, and that it was possible that the defender might reject all proposals and proceed with a development of its own devising. In the event, the defender rejected the pursuers' proposals and informed the pursuers that it was to develop the harbour itself. The pursuers raised an action of recompense against the defender, claiming that the defender had been *lucratus* to the extent of £30,000 through use of the plans submitted to it. The Lord Ordinary dismissed the action as irrelevant, holding that the expenditure had been carried out for the purpose of winning the contract, and that a recompense claim was excluded where work was undertaken primarily for the benefit of the impoverished party.

Case (3)

4.70 In cases where the parties have not been in direct contractual negotiations, there is even less reason to treat pre-contractual expenditure as recoverable by the party upon whom it falls. A party who, for instance, is tendering for a contract must bear its costs should its tender be unsuccessful.

Case (4)

4.71 In cases where a lack of formality may invalidate a contract, but performance has occurred, one of two approaches may be adopted. Either, the statutory personal bar provided by the Requirements of Writing (Scotland) Act 1995, s 1(3) may prevent a party or parties from denying the validity of the contract, or, where this is inapplicable, unjustified enrichment may provide redress for the impoverished party (either through recompense, or through a demand for repetition or restitution).

ENRICHMENT AND ILLEGAL CONTRACTS

4.72 The effect of illegality upon a contract is a complex matter, and reference is made to the specialised literature in this field.[142] Only some brief comments will be made here. In contracts tainted by illegality, where both parties are equally culpable (*in pari delicto*), courts will not entertain any action upon the contract: *ex turpi causa non oritur actio*.[143] This includes any unjustified enrichment action for the return of money or property that may have been passed by one party to the other. The recipient of such a benefit is permitted to retain it, even if expected counter-performance has not been made: *in turpi causa melior est conditio possidentis (defendentis)*.[144]

---

142 See McBryde, para 13-29 f.; L Macgregor, 'Unjustified Enrichment and Illegal Contracts' 2000 ELR 19 and *'Pacta Illicita'* in K Reid and R Zimmerman (eds), *A History of Private Law in Scotland* (2000), vol II, ch 5.

143 From a disgraceful cause, no action arises.

144 In a disgraceful cause the better position is that of the possessor (or defender). Stair, I.7.8: 'But in things received *ex turpi causa*, if both parties be *in culpa*, *potior est conditio possidentis*: so there is no restitution'.

4.73 Restitutionary remedies may be permitted by the courts where:

(1) the parties are not *in pari delicto*. If the pursuer is deemed to be less blameworthy, then restitutionary remedies may be permitted to him;

(2) the illegality is statutory in origin and the statute was designed to protect a particular class of person; in such cases, members of that class may be permitted a restitutionary remedy; and

(3) although the contract is affected by illegality, there is no moral turpitude associated with it. Such a case is *Cuthbertson v Lowes*,[145] which concerned a sale of goods by reference to a measurement prohibited by the relevant weights and measures legislation. The pursuer, who sought recompense for the amount of the goods delivered, was permitted a claim, Lord President Inglis commenting:

> 'There is no turpitude in a man selling his potatoes by the Scotch acre and not by the imperial acre. ... I know of no authority, in the absence of *turpis causa*, to prevent the pursuer from recovering the market value of the potatoes.'[146]

4.74 The above brief summary might suggest that there is a reasonably settled approach of the law in this area. In fact, however, there is great uncertainty in determining when exactly a contract is tainted by illegality. A contract the express purpose of which is to do an illegal act is clearly so tainted; on the other hand, not every act the performance of which may be illegal will necessarily render a contract under which it is performed illegal. As the commentaries on this subject indicate, the law is in need of restatement and reform.[147]

VOIDABLE CONTRACTS: THE NATURE OF *RESTITUTIO IN INTEGRUM*

4.75 Before a voidable contract may be avoided[148] *restitutio in integrum* must be possible. *Restitutio in integrum* has been used in Scots law in two senses: first, to describe a requirement to be fulfilled by a pursuer before avoidance of a voidable contract may be permitted; and second, to describe a remedy sought by the pursuer in consequence of the avoidance of such a contract, namely restoration of the pursuer to his pre-contractual position.

4.76 As to the first aspect of the concept, it has sometimes been asserted that restoration of both parties must be possible before avoidance of the contract may occur. However, in *Western Bank of Scotland v Addie*[149] Lord Cranworth stated that *restitutio in integrum* was available where 'the party seeking it is able to put those against whom it is asked in the same situation in which they stood when the contract was entered into'.[150] This statement was subsequently approved of by

---

145 (1870) 8 M 1073, IH.
146 (1870) 8 M at 1075.
147 The English Law Commission has made suggestions for reform: Law Commission Consultation Paper No 154, The Effect of Illegality On Contracts and Trusts, April 1999.
148 Avoidance of a voidable contract may be affected by raising an action of reduction, or by intimation of avoidance (sometimes referred to as 'rescission') to the other contracting party.
149 (1867) 5 M (HL) 80, HL.
150 (1867) 5 M (HL) at 89.
151 1939 SC (HL) 52, HL.

Lord Thankerton in the House of Lords in *Spence v Crawford*[151] when he said 'it is to be noted that the condition of the relief is the restoration of the defender to his pre-contract position, and that no stress is placed on whether the pursuer is so restored'.[152] The better view therefore is that restoration must be offered by the pursuer to the defender before avoidance of the contract may be sought, but that it is not strictly necessary that the pursuer be restored to his pre-contractual position. Clearly, in many cases the pursuer will also be seeking the return of money or property passed to the defender (that is, *restitutio* in the second sense of the term), but if this is not possible because, for instance, the defender has consumed the property, then the pursuer may seek substitutionary redress in damages.

Restoration of the defender to his pre-contractual position will not always be possible,[153] although it has been asserted that the requirement should not be taken as extending to the *minutiae* of the pre-contractual position.[154]

4.77 As to the second aspect of the concept, the case law clearly indicates that *restitutio in integrum* has been described as a remedy which may be sought by the pursuer. In *Western Bank of Scotland v Addie*, Lord Chancellor Chelmsford said of the pursuer's pleadings that he 'demands a reduction and restitution *in integrum*', a clear characterisation of *restitutio in integrum* as a remedy sought. Where the term is used to denote restoration sought by a pursuer to his pre-contractual position, it is not entirely clear, however, what claims are encompassed. No doubt the claim for the return of the exact thing transferred by the pursuer is encompassed, a sum of money or a specific *res*. But does substitutionary redress fall within *restitutio in integrum* as a remedy, for instance, a sum of money representing a thing consumed by or no longer in possession of the defender? Would a claim for recompense for services rendered fall within *restitutio in integrum* in the sense of a remedy? If substitutionary redress or recompense is not properly viewed as an aspect of *restitutio in integrum*, then they must be seen as free-standing remedies in unjustified enrichment. Whilst the answer to this question is not certain, it seems safer to treat *restitutio in integrum* as a remedy as only extending to restitution *in forma specifica* and any other 'restitutionary' remedies, in the wider sense, as falling within the realm of unjustified enrichment.

RESTITUTIO IN INTEGRUM AS A CONTRACTUAL REMEDY

4.78 *Restitutio in integrum* so described above has traditionally been viewed as an aspect of contract. It has been argued by one leading South African academic that it would be preferable to view *restitutio in integrum* in its remedial sense as part of the law of enrichment rather than contract, because it is aimed at 'the removal of an advantage unjustifiably retained by one party'.[155] In support of such a view, it is argued that to view *restitutio in integrum* in its remedial sense as

---

152 1939 SC (HL) at 69.
153 Thus, where construction works have been undertaken, restoration will (in practical terms) usually be impossible: *Boyd & Forrest v Glasgow & South Western Railway Co* 1915 SC (HL) 20.
154 *Spence v Crawford* 1939 SC (HL) 52; McBryde, para 14-64.
155 D Visser, 'Rethinking Unjustified Enrichment: A Perspective of the Competition between Contractual and Enrichment Remedies' 1992 Acta Juridica 203 at 224.

an enrichment remedy would be to open up the possibility of the defender pleading enrichment defences, such as change of position, and would also permit substitutionary redress to be claimed by the pursuer.

4.79 Such an approach would raise some problems, however, including the following:

(1) To treat a pursuer's claim for restoration as part of enrichment law would be to adopt a categorisation based upon *effect* rather than *cause of action*. But the remedy of restitution is not necessarily tied to enrichment. After all, a proprietary claim can give rise to restitution. But one would not, for instance, treat a contractual damages claim in which compensation for wasted expenditure was sought as lying within the law of delict simply on the basis that what was sought was protection of the restoration interest. Similarly, one cannot ignore the contractual background to a claim for restoration following avoidance of a contract.

(2) If *restitutio in integrum* were viewed as an enrichment remedy, it would be measured by the gain made by the defender. One would not be effecting mere restoration of the pursuer to his pre-contractual position, and the pursuer might be able to claim more than the value of what he had transferred.[156] On the other hand the pursuer might receive less than the value of what he had transferred, thus leaving him worse off than prior to the contract. Thus, the pursuer's claim would be an uncertain one, and injustice might be occasioned to him. An enrichment remedy might be subject to a claim for change of position, whereas it is the pursuer's position which should be favoured in cases of voidable contracts.

It is suggested that it is preferable to treat the pursuer's restorative remedy as an aspect of contract law. Nonetheless, there is much to be said for extending the pursuer's claim to encompass substitutionary redress, and the common law should be developed to effect this.

VOID CONTRACTS

4.80 Where a contract is void, and thus a complete nullity, a party which has performed (whether in whole or in part) under the supposed contract but has not received the expected counter-performance may raise a claim in unjustified enrichment in respect of such performance. Where the performance amounted to the transfer of money or property, the appropriate claim is repetition or restitution; in other cases, the claim is one of recompense. An important recent example of a claim for unjustified enrichment following a void contract is *Morgan Guaranty Trust Co of New York v Lothian Regional Council*,[157] concerning ultra vires (and thus void) contracts entered into by a local authority.

4.81 There is no question that the remedy available in such cases is properly classified as stemming from unjustified enrichment. As there never is a valid

156 Unless the pursuer's loss was to act as a ceiling to the claim.
157 1995 SC 151, IH.

contract, it is not arguable that the remedy falls to be classified as contractual in nature.

4.82 A difficult theoretical issue surrounds the void contract where both parties have performed thinking that a valid contract existed. Take the example of a void sale of goods contract, where *A* has paid for goods which have been supplied by *B*. Can *A* demand repetition of the price paid for the goods under the void contract? The difficulty is that *B* is not unjustifiably enriched because *B* has given value for the enrichment received by transferring the goods to *A*.[158] If *A* rejects the goods, then it can claim that *B* has been unjustifiably enriched, but not if *A* keeps the goods. Where *A* has been the recipient of services provided by *B*, then rejection will not be possible in practical terms, and in such a situation it seems that an enrichment claim will not be possible. *A* must simply accept that, whether or not the contract is void, it has benefited irrevocably from the services provided by *B* and has no claim against *B*.

This difficult issue also affects a contract the performance of which has been frustrated after formation of the contract.

BREACH OF CONTRACT—ONE PARTY IN BREACH—INNOCENT PARTY'S REMEDIES

4.83 Where a breach of contract occurs in a bilateral contract, both parties may be guilty of breach, or only one may. First considered is the position where only one party is in breach, and whether any enrichment remedies are available to the party suffering the breach, the so-called 'innocent party'.

4.84 The principle of subsidiarity of enrichment remedies dictates that, in general terms, a party seeking redress for breach of contract should have recourse to his contractual remedies.

4.85 Cases of material and immaterial breach may be distinguished. Where the breach of contract is not material, the contract may not be rescinded. In this case, the innocent party is restricted to contractual remedies. It may claim damages for breach; it may seek to enforce an obligation *ad factum praestandum* by an action of specific implement; it may seek interdict. But, because the contract cannot be avoided, there is no room for the operation of enrichment remedies in these circumstances.

4.86 In cases of material breach, the innocent party may, of course, choose to affirm the contract and not to release the breaching party by rescinding. In such cases the innocent party is confined to its contractual remedies. Where the innocent party chooses to rescind the contract for material breach, the following cases may be distinguished:

(1) cases where performance has not yet been tendered by the innocent party, but preliminary expenditure may have been incurred by it;

---

158 For development of this point, see K Reid, 'Unjustified Enrichment and Property Law', 1994 JR at 167.

(2)　cases where the innocent party has transferred money or other property to the breaching party; and

(3)　cases where the innocent party has tendered services under the contract.

Where innocent party has undertaken preliminary expenditure in expectation of performance of contract

4.87　As no benefit has been transferred to the breaching party, no enrichment claim will lie. The pursuer is restricted to a claim for damages.

Where money or property has been transferred by innocent party

4.88　Can a party rescinding a contract for material breach seek repetition of an advance payment or restitution of property passed to the contract breaker? If so, is such a remedy to be treated as arising in unjustified enrichment, or is there a species of contractual restitutionary claim? It might be thought, as Lord Brand put it, that it is 'no more than common sense that a vendor who has been fully paid but is unable to fulfil his obligation under the contract should be liable to make restitution of the price'.[159] There is much to be said for this common sense view.

4.89　Clearly, where a contract is rescinded for breach (rather than where it is void) restitution cannot be sought of money or property in respect of which a counter-performance has been received by the pursuer. Thus, an advance payment or part-payment for performance which has been received gives no right to restitution. Additionally, it has been held that a deposit whose character is not advance part-payment but is a pledge of performance cannot be reclaimed. This was the situation in *Zemhunt (Holdings) Ltd v Control Securities plc*.[160]

> The pursuers had successfully bid at auction for the purchase of heritable property. One of the conditions of sale was the payment of a deposit amounting to £165,000, which the pursuers duly paid. The remainder of the price was to be paid by a specified date, after which the defenders were given the right to terminate the sale agreement. The pursuers failed to pay the remainder as required, and the defenders exercised their right to terminate the sale. The pursuers raised an action of repetition for the repayment to them of the deposit. The Inner House held that the proper characterisation of the deposit in the circumstances of the case was a pledge of performance, which had not followed, and not as an advance part-payment. In consequence, the pursuers could not reclaim the deposit.

4.90　The decision in *Zemhunt* is relatively uncontroversial and can be accommodated within the traditionally understood view that a reciprocated advance

---

159　This, of course, must be taken as subject to any insolvency or bankruptcy of the creditor, in which event the party reclaiming an advance payment would have to rank as a creditor in the insolvency or bankruptcy. As to whether a mistaken payment made to a party prior to (or indeed after) bankruptcy or insolvency should give rise to any preference, see Hogg and Backx, 'Restitution in bankruptcy: a Scots law view of *Ontvanger v Hamm*' (2000) 8 ERPL 509.

160　1992 SLT 151, IH.

performance may not be reclaimed. It is not so easy to accommodate the decision of the Inner House in *Connelly v Simpson*[161] with the traditional view.

> The pursuer agreed with the defender to purchase 33 shares in a company controlled by the defender. The pursuer understood that this would secure for him a one-third ownership and control of the company. The pursuer paid £16,000 for the shares, but requested that their transfer to him be postponed until after his divorce had settled. Subsequent to this sale, the defender authorised an increase in the share capital of the company, which authorisation was back-dated to a date prior to the pursuer's purchase, and at the same time allotted to himself 4,500 shares. The following year, the company went into voluntary liquidation. The shares were never transferred to the pursuer. The pursuer raised an action in which he sought declarator that the contract was void, in consequence of the defender's fraud, or else that the defender was in material breach of contract. In either case the pursuer sought the sum of £16,000 as damages. The pursuer's pleadings were subsequently amended to indicate that the return of the £16,000 was sought by way of an action of repetition, based on the principle of *condictio causa data causa non secuta*. On appeal, the Inner House held that an action of repetition was not permissible in such circumstances. All that the pursuer would have been entitled to in these circumstances was damages, to be assessed at the date of the breach of contract, which would have amounted to £400. In any event, as the pursuer had no longer sought damages for breach, he was entitled to nothing.

4.91 From the pursuer's pleadings as originally drafted, it appears that he was seeking to rescind the contract at the date when the action was raised, although there is no evidence that he had attempted to rescind before this date. However, as the case proceeded, the reference to rescission was lost from the pleadings. It is questionable therefore whether one can read the decision of the majority as proceeding on the basis of rescission having taken place, so one may only surmise that this may have been the basis upon which they proceeded.[162]

4.92 The majority of the bench in the Inner House was of the view that the defender was in breach of contract. Lord McCluskey took the view that 'the defender was guilty of breach of contract ... by failing to deliver the shares, or by having so acted as to render performance impossible'.[163] Lord McCluskey's point was that, by increasing the share capital of the company, Simpson was no longer able to offer to transfer shares totalling one-third of the nominal capital of the company. Whether or not, on the facts recited, Simpson had undertaken such a thing as a matter of contract, or whether his behaviour ought more properly to have been characterised as a fraudulent misrepresentation, the breach approach was that adopted by the majority of the Inner House.

4.93 The finding of material breach is not the problematic aspect of the case. What is troubling is the Inner House's conclusion that the pursuer was not to be permitted a repetition claim as an alternative to a damages claim. Lord McCluskey appears to come close to the view that wherever a damages action

---

161 1993 SC 391, 1994 SLT 1096, IH.
162 On one view, intimation in the original summons of rescission should have been enough to operate as rescission of the contract, whether or not the pleadings continued to show this. This view would proceed from the argument that rescission once intimated is effective and subsequent withdrawal is irrelevant.
163 1993 SC at 407H, 1994 SLT at 1106F.

for breach of contract is available to a pursuer, a claim for restitution of an advance payment will always be barred:

> 'Leaving aside the other remedies which might arise following a breach of contract, the only remedy available to a person for breach of contract, if he seeks a monetary remedy, is to claim damages which will compensate him for his loss. ... I see no room, in a breach of contract case, and especially one where a long time has elapsed without performance ever having been demanded, for a remedy in the form of restitution of the price as such.'[164]

If this is correct, then it is an important restriction upon a pursuer's rights in a situation of breach of contract. It puts the innocent pursuer in a breach of contract case in a worse position than the pursuer in a case of frustration or voidability. The preferential treatment of the defender seems unfair when it is the defender who has been at fault.

4.94 Lord Sutherland, while agreeing with the result reached by Lord McCluskey, reached this result by another route. Lord Sutherland, referring favourably to the decisions in *Cantiere* and *Zemhunt*, took the view that Connelly was not entitled to the return of his money because it was not truly to be seen as an advance payment:

> 'The payment made by the pursuer could not be described merely as an advance towards the price which would only be due and payable when he was in receipt of a completed transfer. The payment was in fact in consideration of the pursuer acquiring a personal right against the defender to demand a transfer of the shares and that consideration he received.'[165]

Lord Sutherland took the view that Connelly got what he paid for, because he was buying the right to require the transfer of the shares to him, and he could immediately have chosen to raise an action of specific implement had he requested the transfer of the shares and these not been delivered to him. The case was not therefore one of an advance payment for a future performance, but a payment for a performance presently due.

4.95 In distinguishing advance payments from other payments, Lord Sutherland referred to the important decision of Lord President Inglis in *Watson v Shankland*,[166] in which an advance payment against freight had been recovered by the pursuer. Lord President Inglis had said in that case:

> 'There is no rule of the civil law, as adopted in all municipal modern codes and systems, better understood than this—that if money is advanced by one party to a mutual contract, on the condition and stipulation that something shall be afterwards paid or performed by the other party, and the latter fails in performing his part of the contract, the former is entitled to repayment of his advance on the ground of failure of consideration. In the Roman system the demand for repayment took the form of a *condictio causa data causa non secuta*, or a *condictio sine causa*, or a *condictio indebiti*, according to the

---

164 1993 SC at 407D–408A, 1994 SLT at 1106C–G.
165 1993 SC at 414G–H, 1994 SLT at 1110G.
166 (1871) 10 M 142, IH, affd in 1873 11 M (HL) 51, HL.

particular circumstances. In our practice these remedies are represented by the action of restitution and the action of repetition.'[167]

On the face of it, this dictum strongly favoured the pursuer. However, both Lord Sutherland and Lord McCluskey were at pains to stress that the comments of Lord President Inglis had to be understood in the context of the facts of *Watson*. Because *Watson* concerned a case of an advance payment made in respect of an amount which might never become due (because, unless performance occurred, no freight would become due), it was a different situation from that where an individual paid for shares because the debt was presently due and where that individual might then seek transfer of the shares whenever he wished.

4.96 One may query whether this distinction ought to be significant, and whether cases where payment is tendered because it is now due should not also give rise to a right to restitution where counter-performance does not occur. Even if there is scant authority on this point,[168] it is submitted that the pursuer who tenders a performance which is due and does not receive the counter-performance expected ought equally to be entitled to receive restitution of his performance. It is surely the case that the equities of the circumstances do not substantially differ, if at all, from advance payments for a future performance.

4.97 The concern has been expressed by some that allowing a restitutionary claim to a party who has suffered a breach of contract in respect of his tendered performance, might allow some parties to escape a bad bargain. Consider these circumstances:

> A enters into a contract with B under which A agrees to purchase a ship from B for £500,000. A fails properly to inspect the ship. The ship is in a poor state of repair and is worth only £300,000. A pays the contract price. B subsequently fails to deliver the ship, in breach of the contract. A has by this time realised that the ship is worth only £300,000. A rescinds the contract. If A is entitled to the return of the £500,000 it may be said to have avoided the consequences of its carelessness in not properly inspecting the ship. On the other hand, if B is required to pay only £300,000 in damages, it will be entitled to keep £200,000 having failed to deliver the ship.

While in situations such as this, allowing A a repetition claim may enable it to avoid a bad bargain, it is suggested that this consequence is less undesirable than allowing B to profit from its breach of contract. The policy of the law should favour the innocent party in a situation of breach, even if this may allow some innocent parties to escape from foolish contracts.

Nature of claim for restitution following breach of contract

4.98 If, as suggested, restitution of performance tendered ought to be permitted to a party who has suffered a breach of contract, where such party has not

---

167 (1871) 10 M 142 at 152.
168 Gloag stated 'In cases of breach of contract the party aggrieved has an action for damages, but in addition to this, and whether damages have been suffered or not, he is clearly entitled to recover any part of the price or other consideration which he may have been paid.' (*Contract*, at pp 59–60). It is clear from the context that Gloag saw this as an instance of repetition.

received the counter-performance in respect of which its own performance was tendered, is this restitutionary remedy to be seen as flowing from unjustified enrichment or from contract?

4.99 Dieckmann and Evans-Jones have suggested that the restitution to be awarded to a pursuer who has tendered performance but who rescinds for breach is to be regarded properly as a contractual claim:

> 'The source of the obligation to restore ... arises from fully valid contracts and it is therefore by reference to the law of contract that the solution for these cases, in our opinion, is best found. Under this approach restitution is merely one of a range of responses, including damages and specific implement, provided by the law of contract.'[169]

This makes the important point that merely because a response is restitutionary in measure it does not follow that the source of the obligation to restore should be seen as lying in unjustified enrichment. This is a valid point, for indeed proprietary restitution—the claim by an owner to have that restored to him which belongs to him—clearly lies in property law and not in unjustified enrichment.

4.100 The alternative view is that restitution in such a case is to be classified as stemming from unjustified enrichment by reference to the object of the claim:

> 'If one says that a remedy which is aimed at achieving the objectives created by the parties' consensus or reliance (whether it does so in a real sense or by way of delivering the economic equivalent) is contractual, while one which merely aims at restoring the position as it was before the contract was entered into (by effecting the return of unjustly retained benefits) is enrichment based, one has, I believe, a working distinction by which one may classify some actions as belonging to the one or the other sphere.'[170]

On this approach, the claim of Connelly, had it been allowed, would be classified as an enrichment remedy, as it looked towards reversing an unjustly retained benefit in the hands of Simpson. The difficulty with this second view is that it smacks of the approach of English law of lumping all remedies which are restitutionary in effect into one large subject box of the law. It would treat the restitutionary claim of an owner to the return of a *res* as enrichment in nature, when under Scots law it is seen quite properly as a proprietary remedy. It might, absurdly, treat a damages claim for breach of contract under which protection of the *restoration* interest was sought as being delictual in nature.

4.101 It is suggested that the claim of a party who has suffered a material breach of contract for the restoration of a tendered performance ought to be viewed as a *contractual* remedy. This is perfectly consistent with the view, expressed in chapter 1, that while a contractual claim protects primarily the pursuer's performance interest, it is quite acceptable in certain cases for the pursuer's restoration or disgorgement interests to be protected. A claim for restitution in the circum-

---

169 J A Dieckmann and R Evans-Jones, 'The Dark Side of *Connelly v Simpson*' 1995 JR 90 at 100.
170 D Visser, 'Rethinking Unjustified Enrichment: A Perspective of the Competition between Contractual and Enrichment Remedies' 1992 *Acta Juridica* 203 at 209–210.

stances discussed would be just such an instance of contractual protection of the disgorgement interest.

4.102 Does it make a difference which of these two routes is viewed as the appropriate one? At least two important differences lie in respect of defences which may be available, and in the question of the prescription of any claim. In relation to the first issue, 'change of position' as it is commonly called is now established as a defence in an enrichment based claim, but would not be clearly so if the restitutionary claim of the innocent party is deemed contractual. It is a difficult question as to whether change of position ought to be extended to a restitutionary claim if it is deemed contractual in nature. On one view, it may seem odd to treat the position of the defender as different merely because of the way the claim is treated by the law, but the point is that an enrichment claim is an equitable one, whereas a contractual claim lies as of right. This may mitigate against extension of any change of position defence to a contractual restitutionary claim. As to prescription, *NV Devos Gebroeder v Sunderland Sportswear Ltd*[171] has settled that contract and enrichment claims are considered to be of a different nature, such that the raising of either one of them is not considered to be a 'relevant claim' under the head of the other for the purposes of the Prescription and Limitation (Scotland) Act 1973. The issue, then, is not merely an academic one.

Non-monetary restitutionary claims

4.103 The discussion thus far has centred mainly on claims for the return of money. What of claims for the return of property? Several interesting questions may be posed in relation to such claims:

(1) Is a pursuer entitled to seek the restoration of property transferred under a contract rescinded for breach where the expected payment for such property has not been forthcoming? Or is the pursuer restricted to a damages claim?
(2) If the pursuer is entitled to restitution of property, can a substitutionary claim be maintained if the property has been consumed or transferred to a third party?
(3) If the pursuer is entitled to restitution of property, may he elect instead to seek damages or substitutionary redress if he does not wish to pursue a claim for restoration of the specific property? In other words, if a defender is willing to effect specific restitution, can this be refused?

4.104 *Connelly* suggests that the answer to the first question should be in the negative. However, as it has been suggested above that a monetary restitutionary claim should be allowed, there is no reason not to allow a claim for the return of property. Clearly if it is heritable property which has been transferred, then reduction of the disposition will also have to be sought.

4.105 In relation to the second question, there seems nothing objectionable in principle in permitting a substitutionary restitution claim for property which has

---

171 1990 SC 291, 1990 SLT 473, IH.

been consumed or transferred to a third party. If the claim for restitution were enrichment based, then a transfer of the goods to a third party would render the defender liable in *recompense* only to the extent to which he had profited from such onward transfer,[172] which raises the question whether such a restriction ought to apply to any substitutionary claim if it is treated as contractual in nature. Again, because the contract claim would lie as of right, rather than in equity, the imposition of such a restriction might seem inappropriate.

4.106 As to the final question, damages are always available for breach of contract, so a pursuer could not be restricted to a restitutionary claim. As to whether a pursuer could seek the monetary equivalent of any property transferred rather than pursue a claim for restoration of the property itself, while the answer is unclear, it is difficult to imagine a court, faced with a defender who was willing to restore the property, requiring him instead to pay substitutionary redress in money. Such an approach might place some defenders in a difficult financial position.

Where innocent party has tendered services under the contract

4.107 Where the innocent party has performed services (which may include, as part of the overall services contracted for, the transfer of property) under the contract, then it is necessary for such party to seek enforcement of a claim for breach through contract, the appropriate claim being an action for payment. The innocent party may of course choose to rescind the contract for material breach and sue for damages.

BREACH OF CONTRACT—ONE PARTY IN BREACH—GUILTY PARTY'S REMEDIES

4.108 Is a contracting party which is in breach of contract (the 'guilty party') permitted any remedy in unjustified enrichment where the non-breaching party (the 'innocent party') rescinds the contract for material breach? This is a crucial question, for the contracting party which is in material breach of contract is precluded from judicial enforcement of the other party's obligations in relation to any period after the breach.[173] Thus, a contracting party which is in breach of contract may be prevented from suing for the price due under the contract by the innocent party. If no remedy in unjustified enrichment were to be available to the guilty party, this might be productive of inequity, for the innocent party would be permitted to retain performance (albeit defective) without the requirement to make any payment for it.

---

172 See further **6.08**.
173 The leading example is *Graham v United Turkey Red Co Ltd* 1922 SC 533, IH, where an agent was barred from suing for payment of its commission in respect of the period after the agent was in breach of contract.

4.109   The law in this area is far from clear and in much need of restatement,[174] but the following is a broad summary of the current state of the law:

(1)   *Action for payment by the guilty party—trivial breach.* The guilty party who is in only trivial breach is permitted to sue for payment under the contract, subject to a deduction for the defective performance.[175]

(2)   *Action for payment by the guilty party—material breach.* Where the breach is material, the guilty party is precluded from suing for payment, but is permitted a remedy in recompense.[176] This rule may be applicable to lump sum contracts alone, and not measure and value contracts.[177]

(3)   *Action for restitution of goods.* If the innocent party has rejected defective goods supplied by the guilty party, then the guilty party is entitled to the return of the goods: this is implicit in the right of the purchaser of defective goods to reject them.[178]

(4)   *Action for repetition of price paid.* Where the guilty party has paid the contract price, or part of it, but is nonetheless in breach, he is entitled to the return of such payment, unless he has received the expected counter-performance, or the sum paid is forfeited as a deposit.[179]

In all cases, the innocent party has an action for damages for any losses caused by the defective performance.

Something more requires to be said of the first two categories of case listed above:

Trivial breach—right to the price, subject to a deduction

4.110   The leading authority is *Ramsay & Son v Brand*,[180] although doubt has been expressed as to whether it accurately represents the present law.[181]

> A builder was employed to undertake masonry work on a cottage under a lump sum contract. The works had been executed defectively, with the result that the builder was found to be in breach of contract (although the breach was not deemed material). The builder sued for the contract price. As the breach was merely trivial, the Inner House permitted the builder the contract price less the cost of curing the defective works.

---

174   See the discussion in McBryde at paras 20-132–20-147.
175   See **4.110** below.
176   See **4.113** below.
177   See the discussion below at **4.113**. The better view in respect of measure and value contracts may be that the guilty party is permitted to claim the agreed contract price for those parts of the contract works which have been undertaken in conformity with the contract.
178   Sale of Goods Act 1979, s 15B(1). Although the buyer in such a case is not bound to return rejected goods (see s 36), a buyer who refused to allow the seller to reclaim them would be open to an action for restitution of the goods.
179   See the obiter comments of Lord Morison in *Zemhunt (Holdings) Ltd v Control Securities plc* 1992 SC 58, 1992 SLT 151 at 155H–I, IH.
180   1898 25 R 1212, IH. The report at (1898) 35 SLR 927, IH, is more extensive and generally thought to be of greater assistance.
181   See McBryde, para 20-133.

The Lord President (Robertson) noted that had the builder been in material breach he would have been barred from raising an action for the price, but would have been permitted an action in recompense for the extent to which the employer was *lucratus* by the works.

4.111 The approach in *Ramsay* is an equitable, common sense one, but may be problematic in some situations:

(1) What if the cost of cure is excessive (as it would have been in the later case of *Steel v Young*[182])? If cure of the defects would necessitate wholly undoing the work which has already been done, it would seem inequitable to leave a contracting party with no recompense whatsoever, especially if the innocent party has no intention of carrying out remedial works.

(2) What if an action of recompense is worth more than the agreed contract price, because the value of the works, even in their defective state, is now worth more than originally envisaged? This may occur in some situations where the market price of services is fluctuating. Although there is no case authority on the proper solution to this problem, commentators are generally agreed that the contract price must act as a ceiling to recovery in any recompense case.[183] If that were not so, a cynical contractor could deliberately breach the contract in the hope of increasing his remuneration.

4.112 In cases where defective performance cannot be cured, it may be simpler to deny any recovery to the contract breaker for that portion of the works which is defective. This was the approach adopted in one sheriff court case, *Culter Mill Restaurant v Hogg*.[184]

> The defender and some friends had dined at the pursuer's restaurant. The meal had been satisfactory, until liqueurs were served at the end of the evening. These were wholly unsatisfactory, and the defender refused to pay for any part of the meal. The restaurant sued for the contract price. The sheriff principal, holding the restaurant to be only in trivial breach, allowed its claim for the price, subject to a deduction of 'the cost of the offending liqueurs.'

Clearly, in such a case, where goods provided have been consumed, no question of cost of cure can arise. Furthermore, this not being a lump sum contract (as was the case in *Ramsay*), it was easier to identify a specific sum relating to the defective item which could be deducted for the price claimed. In lump sum contracts, where a specific item has been consumed (and remedial works are thus impossible), equity suggests that a court must do its best to affix a proportion of the price to the defectively consumed item, and such proportion should be deducted from the sum due.

---

182   1907 SC 360, IH.

183   See the sources noted at MacQueen, 'Unjustified Enrichment and Breach of Contract' 1994 JR 137 at 163, n 96.

184   1996 SCLR 182, Sh Ct.

Material breach—action of recompense

4.113 Consideration under this head must be given to *Steel v Young*:[185]

A builder was employed under a measure and value contract.[186] The builder used different materials in construction than those specified in the contract and was thereby held to be in material breach of contract. The Inner House held that, being in material breach, he was precluded from suing for the price. However, with reference to the dictum of the Lord President in *Ramsay*, the court added that the builder would have been entitled to raise an action of recompense.

This approach to measure and value contracts was subject to later criticism in the Inner House,[187] the criticism being that if parts of the works have been performed conform to contract, there is no reason to deny the contractor the agreed value of those parts. There is much sense in such a criticism, and one can see similarities with the approach of the sheriff in *Culter Mill Restaurant*, [188] although in that case the breach was not deemed material. Lump sum contracts are clearly in a different category, where the work is seen as an entirety for which one sum is to be claimable or not.[189] If later criticism of *Steel* is well founded, then in contracts under which the work is to be divided, measured and valued, a party (even one which is in material breach as regards some of the work) may be entitled to an action for the price in respect of the work properly performed.

4.114 Contracts for the sale of goods are in a special category by virtue of the provisions of the Sale of Goods Act 1979. A buyer of goods is entitled to reject part of the goods, if some are conform to contract but some are not.[190] In such case, the buyer is required to pay the contract price for those goods which are retained. Thus the seller in breach is not precluded from maintaining an action for the price for those goods which are conform to contract. This clearly has no application in the case of a sale of a single good which is defective.

BREACH OF CONTRACT—BOTH PARTIES IN BREACH

4.115 Where both parties are in breach, then, if the breach is material, they are both precluded from suing for performance (subject to what was said above in relation to measure and value contracts[191]). Although it has been maintained by some members of the judiciary that a party in breach of contract is

---

185 1907 SC 360.
186 In terms of which the actual work done was to be measured and paid for according to rates set out in the contract.
187 See Lord Skerrington's comments in *Forrest v Scottish County Investment Co Ltd* 1915 SC 115, IH, affirmed at 1916 SC (HL) 28, HL.
188 See discussion at **4.112**.
189 See the comments of Lord Parmoor in *Steel v Young* 1916 (HL) 28, HL, at 35.
190 Sale of Goods Act 1979, s 35A(1).
191 See **4.113**.

precluded from suing for damages,[192] the more persuasive authority is against such a view.[193]

4.116 Given the foregoing, the following examples may be considered:

Example 1: A building contract, under which the works are to be performed in three stages, is entered into between an employer and a contractor. Each stage is to be performed according to a measure and value basis. Stage 1 is performed according to contract, and the architect certifies the works as completed; the stage 2 works are, however, defective to a material extent. The employer withholds payment in respect of the stage 1 works, hoping that this will encourage the builder to remedy the defects in stage 2. The builder is unwilling to accept the employer's refusal to pay for the stage 1 works and ceases work under the contract. The employer states its opinion that the builder has repudiated the contract, and that the employer therefore considers the contract to be at an end.

Example 2: A contract under which a catering company is to provide a buffet lunch and staff to serve it at a reception to be hosted by another company (the client). A lump sum is agreed for provision of the services. When the catering company arrives to set up for the reception, it finds that, due to failure by the client properly to arrange access (as agreed in the contract), it is unable to enter the building to set up in good time for the function, which is consequently delayed. The catering company has provided insufficient staff to properly serve the function, and has not provided champagne for the guests, as agreed in the contract. The client refuses to pay for the reception.

4.117 In both examples, the question is: what remedies are available to the parties?

Example 1: In the first example, the builder is in material breach of contract. According to *Steel v Young* the builder is precluded from suing for the price; however, the better view may be that, as the structure of the contract permits a division to be made between the amounts due under the various stages, the builder is entitled to sue for the price due under stage 1. The employer is not entitled at common law to retain the amount due under stage 1, as this is not a reciprocal obligation in respect of stage 2.[194] By refusing to release the stage 1 payment, the employer is thus also in material breach. As such, the employer cannot insist upon completion of the works. The builder may be able to raise an action of recompense in respect of the stage 2 works (as suggested in *Ramsay*). Both parties will have a damages claim in respect of any loss caused by the other's breach.

Example 2: In the second example, the client is in breach by not arranging timeous access to the building. This may or may not be deemed a material breach. The catering company is likely to be held in material breach by failing to provide sufficient staff and by failing to provide the champagne. As such it will be unable to sue for the price due under the lump sum contract. The catering company will have an action in recompense in respect of the services provided for the extent to which the client has been *lucratus* by provision of the services (there may well be difficulties in assessing the figure in this case). Both parties will have a damages claim. However, the catering company may not have suffered any loss; if the client has suffered loss, it may be hard to quantify in financial terms.

---

192 See the dictum of Lord McLaren in *Thornloe v McDonald* (1892) 29 SLR 409, IH, at 411; also *Hayes v Robinson* 1984 SLT 300, OH.

193 *Graham & Co v United Turkey Red Co Ltd* 1922 SC 533. See the discussion in McBryde at paras 20-48–20-52.

194 *Bank of East Asia Ltd v Scottish Enterprise* 1997 SLT 1213, HL.

PRE-CONTRACTUAL FRUSTRATION

4.118 If parties' intentions to conclude a contract are frustrated by events outwith their control, is there any room for the operation of unjustified enrichment liability between the parties? The issues here are, to some extent, similar to those situations where negotiations break down through an irreconcilable difference between the parties.[195]

4.119 The general rule in such a situation is that, unless there is an enforceable undertaking to the contrary, each party negotiating a contract accepts the risk that the contract may fail to be concluded due to frustrating circumstances beyond the control of the parties. Any wasted expenditure falls upon the party which has suffered the loss.

4.120 If property has been transferred in expectation of a contract which is frustrated prior to its conclusion, then an action will lie for the restitution of the property; similarly, an action will lie for the repetition of any sum of money transferred. In both cases the situation gives rise to the *condictio causa data causa non secuta*. If services have been performed or begun to be performed under an expected but frustrated contract, an action of recompense will lie.

POST-CONTRACTUAL FRUSTRATION

4.121 Where, following the valid conclusion of a contract, the future performance of the contract is frustrated due to external events beyond the control of the parties, an equitable adjustment may be permitted if performance, or part-performance, by one party of its obligations has given rise to an unjustified enrichment in the hands of the other party. The seminal authority is *Cantiere San Rocco SA v Clyde Shipbuilding and Engineering Co Ltd*.[196]

> In May 1914, a contract was concluded for the supply of marine engines by the defender to the pursuer (an Austrian company). The contract price was £11,550, to be payable by instalments. The first instalment of £2,310 was paid shortly after conclusion of the contract. During the course of the summer, the defender undertook various preliminary works in preparation for performance of the contract. However, in August 1914 war was declared between the United Kingdom and Austria. This had the effect of frustrating further performance of the obligations under the contract. Following the cessation of hostilities, the pursuer brought an action of repetition before the Scottish courts, seeking the return of the deposit. At first instance, the pursuer's claim succeeded, although this was overturned on appeal to the Inner House. Upon further appeal to the House of Lords, the original verdict was restored, and repetition of the advance part payment was ordered.

At all levels of the case, there was much discussion of both Roman and Scots law, and in particular of the *condictio causa data causa non secuta* as the appropriate analogy for the award of repetition in the action. The House of Lords' use of

---

195 See the discussion at **4.61** ff.
196 1923 SC (HL) 105, HL.

Roman sources has been criticised,[197] and the alternative view proposed that a solution to the problem ought to have been found in contract rather than unjustified enrichment.[198] The significance of the decision has been assessed somewhat differently by another commentator: 'Arguably, the most important point about the decision was the determination that there should be a remedy: whether that remedy is considered as arising from contract or from unjust enrichment is less important.'[199]

4.122 One might argue whether the remedy of the party who has part (or wholly) performed under a frustrated contract but has not received its expected counter-performance ought to lie in contract or unjustified enrichment, just as a similar discussion can be had in relation to enrichment following breach of contract.[200] However, unlike breach of contract, where the authorities are still somewhat mixed, the authority of the decision of the House of Lords in *Cantiere* is now well settled, and there seems little likelihood of it being overturned by the courts. As the claim is classified as one of repetition, then the recognised defences to such a claim would be available.[201]

4.123 One interesting aspect of the decision which does require further exploration, however, is the terse reference in the interlocutor of the Lord Ordinary (Hunter) in the case, restored by the House of Lords, that the claim of the buyer was 'subject to such counter-claim as may be afterwards established '.[202]

There is no reported evidence of any subsequent counterclaim by the Scottish seller, but the interlocutory reference is an important one. Whilst an action in unjustified enrichment might well satisfy the claim of the buyer, if that were to be the only permitted action then the seller who had begun preparations for performance under the frustrated contract might find itself out of pocket as a result of wasted expenditure. We know that the seller in *Cantiere* had begun to make just such preparations for carrying out the contract works. The opinion of the Lord Ordinary notes that

'it appears that the defenders carried out a certain amount of preparatory work required by the contract'[203]

although the report continues that 'The preparatory work referred to by the Lord Ordinary included the interchange and approval of the plans and measurements provided for ... but no part of the engines had been constructed by the outbreak of war'.[204] As no value could have been conferred upon the pursuer by this preparatory work, then a counterclaim by the defender based upon unjustified enrichment would not have been possible. What therefore might have been the

197 R Evans-Jones, 'Unjust Enrichment, Contract and the Third Reception of Roman Law in Scotland' (1993) 109 LQR 663.
198 Note the comments of R Evans-Jones, op cit, at 679: 'Frustration and rescission operate to terminate future performance of a contract, not to annul it. Since it still exists, it is preferable if the relations of the parties are seen to be regulated by the contract.'
199 W D H Sellar, 'Unjust Enrichment', in the *Stair Memorial Encyclopaedia*, vol 15, para 43.
200 See the discussion above at **4.98–4.102**.
201 As to which, see **4.16**.
202 See the interlocutor of the Lord Ordinary, as reported in 1922 SC 723 at 725.
203 1922 SC at 724.
204 1922 SC at 724.

basis for such a counterclaim, for the wasted expenditure of the defender? Several possibilities present themselves, the most likely being *negotiorum gestio* or implied contract. Another solution might lie in the development of a wider doctrine of unjustified impoverishment[205] although this is unlikely. On the facts of *Cantiere*, the quantum of any possible claim of the seller was likely to have been minimal, which may explain the absence of any further reference to such in the reports.

4.124 As with void contracts,[206] a difficult issue arises in cases of frustrated contract where both parties have received the expected performance. Is there any room for the application of unjustified enrichment in such a case? If, for instance, *A* had paid a proportion of the contract price, and had received from *B* a proportion of the expected performance, an unjustified enrichment claim by either might well be untenable. Each might simply have to accept the situation as it stood.

---

205 As to which, see the discussion in chapter 5.
206 See the earlier discussion at **4.82**.

Chapter 5

Unjustified Impoverishment

GENERAL RECOGNITION OF UNJUSTIFIED IMPOVERISHMENT?

5.01 Scots law does not recognise a general obligation of what might be called 'unjustified impoverishment' or 'unjustified sacrifice'. That is to say, it is not universally the case that where party *A* has been impoverished through its efforts in connection with an anticipated contract with party *B* which fails to materialise, or through efforts undertaken to safeguard *B*'s interests, *A* will be able to reclaim any expenditure undertaken by it from *B*. It is unlikely that the law will develop such a general obligation, as it would be difficult successfully to delimit its application, and it would be open to abuse. Were such a general obligation to exist, unsuccessful tenderers might, for instance, seek to claim costs of their failed tenders, a situation which would be clearly undesirable.

5.02 Nonetheless, while there is no general obligation of unjustified impoverishment or unjustified sacrifice, Scots law has recognised two circumstances where costs incurred by one party on behalf of another may be reclaimed, even though no benefit has accrued to the latter party (which might otherwise have grounded a claim for unjustified enrichment). The relevant doctrines—of *negotiorum gestio*, and of a limited right to claim wasted pre-contractual expenditure— apply to specific circumstances where the law considers it improper that expenditure undertaken by one party should be borne by it, and where therefore the party who has been impoverished is permitted to reclaim its expenditure from the other party.

NEGOTIORUM GESTIO[1]

5.03 The obligation of *negotiorum gestio* is recognised as an independent obligation in Scots law, distinct from contract, promise, delict, or unjustified enrichment. Whilst not recognised by English law, it exists in civilian and other mixed legal systems (such as South Africa). Its existence in Scots law is an aspect of its civilian legal heritage, the obligation being found originally in the Roman law.[2] The term

---

1 For the only thorough treatment in Scots law, see N Whitty 'Negotiorum Gestio', in Stair Memorial Encyclopaedia, vol 15.
2 See D 49.1.24.

negotiorum gestio means literally the management of (another's) affairs. In the standard work in South African law, the obligation was succinctly described as 'the voluntary management by one person (the *negotiorum gestor*) of the affairs of another (the *dominus negotii*) without the consent or even knowledge of the other'[3] which also serves as an accurate description of the nature of the obligation in Scots law.

5.04   Whereas there was a tendency in the past in some quarters to treat the obligation as an aspect of the law of unjustified enrichment, it is not properly so treated, there being no requirement that the *negotiorum gestor* has enriched the *dominus negotii*. Even where the *gestor's* actions have enriched the *dominus*, this is not, as shall be seen,[4] the measure of the *gestor's* recovery. Furthermore, *negotiorum gestio*, while sharing some similarities with maritime salvage, is distinguishable therefrom.[5]

5.05   *Negotiorum gestio* arises where the following requirements are met:

(1)   *A* (the *gestor*) has undertaken the administration of the affairs of *B* (the *dominus*);
(2)   the administration is without a mandate or other authorisation from *B*;
(3)   *B* is unaware of the administration or is unable to consent to it through absence or incapacity;
(4)   *A* has acted for the welfare of *B*; and
(5)   the administration was useful when it occurred, even if it did not ultimately benefit *B*.

Where these requirements are met then the *dominus* must reimburse the *gestor* for expenses reasonably incurred by him, and relieve him of any obligations undertaken on behalf of the *dominus*.

5.06   A couple of examples of the operation of *negotiorum gestio* will serve to make its application clearer:

Example 1: A farmer notices that his absent neighbour's field has caught fire. The farmer makes efforts to put out the fire. The farmer is entitled to claim from his neighbour any expenses incurred in putting out the fire.

Example 2: A householder notices that, during a cold weather snap, his neighbour's pipes have burst and that his property will be flooded when the temperature thaws unless immediate action is taken. His neighbour is in intensive care in hospital, and is thus incapable of consenting to the necessary repairs. The householder employs a plumber to fix the burst pipes, settling the plumber's account. The householder is entitled to claim the cost of settling the account from the neighbour.

In all the above examples, the requirements of the *actio negotiorum gestorum* are met, and the *gestor* may claim the sum expended from the *dominus*.

---

3   D H van Zyl, *Negotiorum Gestio in South African Law*, 1985, at p 3.
4   See **5.09** below.
5   See Whitty, op cit, fn 1, at para 93.

Negotiorum gestio a bilateral obligation

5.07 *Negotiorum gestio* is a bilateral obligation. Both the *gestor* and *dominus* are bound to the obligation. In addition, each party comes under duties to the other. The *gestor* is obliged to complete any administration begun by him,[6] must exercise due care when performing the administration,[7] must transmit to the *dominus* all money and other property received on behalf of the *dominus*,[8] and must account to the *dominus* for any profit made from the management.[9] The *dominus* is obliged to pay to the *gestor* the costs of the administration reasonably undertaken by the *gestor*,[10] and to relieve the *gestor* from any obligations undertaken on behalf of the *dominus*.[11]

Enrichment of *dominus* a ceiling to some claims

5.08 Whilst the administration must have been useful at the time it was carried out, in general the *gestor's* claim is not related to any enrichment of the *dominus*. However, there are a limited number of cases where the *gestor* is entitled only to the amount of his expenses *or* to the enrichment of the *dominus*, whichever is the lesser amount. There are four such cases:

(1)   where the management is undertaken for the *gestor's* own benefit;
(2)   where the management is against the express wishes of the *dominus*;
(3)   where the *gestor* believes in good faith that the management relates to his own affairs; and
(4)   where the *dominus* is not fully *capax* on account of want of age.

These cases are discussed fully by Whitty,[12] who notes that the factor linking each of them is that they are impure *gestio*, lacking one of the essential requirements of the *actio negotiorum gestio*.

Enrichment claim or *negotiorum gestio*?

5.09 In *negotiorum gestio* proper, the enrichment of the *dominus* is irrelevant as regards the claim of the *gestor*. The *gestor's* claim is in respect of the expenses of his administration. It matters neither that the *dominus* was not ultimately enriched by the *gestor's* actions, nor that the *dominus* may have been enriched beyond the costs of the *gestor's* administration: the quantum of the *gestor's* claim is the amount of

---

6   D.3.5.5.14; 3.5.20.2.; Stair, I.8.5.
7   *A S Kolbin & Sons v William Kinnear & Co* 1931 SC (HL) 128, 1931 SLT 464.
8   Stair I.8.4; Bankton, *Institute*, I.9.25; Erskine, *Institute*, III.3.52; Bell, *Principles*, s 541.
9   Stair I.8.4. See also cases of count and reckoning to enforce this obligation cited by Whitty, op cit, fn 1, at para 132, n 3.
10 Bell, *Principles*, s 541.
11 Erskine, *Institute*, III.3.52.
12 See Whitty, op cit, fn 1, paras 137–141.

the costs of the administration. It is generally agreed that an additional claim by the *gestor* in respect of his labour or services is not permitted.[13]

5.10 Where the nature of the *gestor's* behaviour was truly that of uninvited intervention on behalf of the *dominus*, the *gestor* is not permitted to raise a claim in unjustified enrichment in order to increase the amount sought. The proper nature of the claim is determined by the characterisation of the behaviour of the claimant: if the requirements of *negotiorum gestio* are met, then this precludes a claim in unjustified enrichment.

PRE-CONTRACTUAL LIABILITY—LIABILITY FOR WASTED EXPENDITURE IN FAILED CONTRACTS

5.11 The question of whether liability for wasted pre-contractual expenditure may ever be claimed was raised in chapter 3.[14] It was there noted that circumstances where delict can provide recovery are limited. However, reference was made to a line of cases, beginning with the case of *Walker v Milne*,[15] which are authority for the availability to a pursuer, in limited circumstances, of a claim for the reimbursement of expenditure in connection with an anticipated contract which fails to materialise.

5.12 The extent of the remedy for reimbursement of expenditure based upon this line of authority was explained by Lord Cullen in his judgment in *Dawson International plc v Coats Paton plc*.[16] His Lordship summed up the cases deriving from *Walker v Milne* thus:

'Having reviewed the cases in this field to which I was referred I am not satisfied that they provide authority for reimbursement of expenditure by one party occasioned by the representations of another beyond the case where the former acted in reliance on the implied assurance by the latter that there was a binding contract between them when in fact there was no more than an agreement which fell short of a binding contract.'[17]

5.13 In summarising the remedy in this way, Lord Cullen identified the following as essential elements of a claim for the reimbursement of expenditure:

(1) party B has given an implied assurance[18] to party A that a valid contract has been entered into between the parties;
(2) due to a defect in the contract (whether of form or of some other type) no valid contract exists between the parties; and
(3) A has incurred wasted expenditure in reliance upon the assurance given by B.

---

13 Bankton *Institute*, I.9.27; Erskine, *Institute*, III.3.52.
14 See **3.24**.
15 (1823) 2 S 379, IH.
16 1988 SLT 854, OH.
17 1988 SLT 854 at 866A. Lord Cullen's view on this line of cases was approved on appeal: 1989 SLT 655, IH.
18 The giving of an express insurance could be seen as a misrepresentation.

5.14 The need for recourse to this remedy for wasted expenditure will be obviated if *A* is able to rely upon the statutory form of personal bar provided by the Requirements of Writing (Scotland) Act 1995, s 1. Where this statutory remedy is available, a contracting party is able to prevent the other party from denying the validity of the contract on the basis of a failure to comply with the statutory requirements as to form for certain contracts. It is an interesting question whether, if this statutory form of personal bar is available, a pursuer might choose in the alternative to exercise the remedy for wasted expenditure outlined above. Comments made by Lord Cameron of Lochbroom in *Bank of Scotland v 3i plc* suggest that the remedy of reimbursement will not be available where the facts of the case support an alternative remedy.[19]

5.15 The remedy for reimbursement of expenditure has been successfully used in a number of circumstances, among them the following:

A landowner successfully sued the subscribers to a monument which was to be erected on the landowner's property. As the agreement to erect the monument related to heritable property, it required to be in properly subscribed writing. On the faith of an agreement not yet in the correct form, the landowner altered his plans for development of the land to incorporate the monument, and allowed various preliminary preparations to be carried out on the land in preparation for the erection of the monument. When the subscribers subsequently indicated that they intended to erect the monument elsewhere, the landowner sued them for breach of contract. The Inner House held that there was no properly concluded contract. However, they held the landowner 'entitled to indemnification for any actual loss and damage he may have sustained, and for the expenses incurred in consequence of the alteration of the site of the monument.'[20]

A son erected a house on land belonging to his father, following a verbal promise by the father to convey the land to him. The father subsequently refused to convey the land to his son, and instead conveyed it to his daughter. The father's promise, being verbal, was unenforceable for want of formal writing. The son sued his father, and was awarded the amount of his wasted expenditure in erecting the house.[21]

A woman arranged to care for certain children for a number of years. In order to effect the arrangement, she entered into the lease of a property, and incurred certain expenditure. Subsequently, following a dispute, the children were removed from the woman's care. The Inner House held that the arrangement was not a legally enforceable contract, but merely a 'family arrangement'. However, they permitted the woman to recover her losses in reliance upon the agreement.[22]

In all such successful cases, the claim was not in respect of any enrichment that may have accrued to the defender, but in respect of the expenditure incurred in reliance upon the belief in the existence of a valid contract.

---

19 See further **5.16** below.
20 *Walker v Milne* (1823) 2 S 379, IH, at 380.
21 *Bell v Bell* (1841) 3 D 1201, IH.
22 *Dobie v Lauder's Trs* (1873) 11 M 749, IH.

Restriction on the remedy: an implied assurance

5.16 The restrictive interpretation on these earlier cases given by Lord Cullen in *Dawson International*, particularly the stress that there must have been an implied assurance as to the existence of a valid contract, will exclude the vast majority of cases of failed contracts from the remedy of reimbursement of expenditure, as indeed happened in the subsequent case of *Bank of Scotland v 3i plc*.[23] On the facts of that case, there was held to be no evidence of such an implied assurance, the pursuer's claim for reimbursement being in consequence rejected.

Restriction on the remedy: its subsidiary nature

5.17 In the *Bank of Scotland* case, Lord Cameron of Lochbroom made a further point about the nature of the remedy of reimbursement of expenditure:

'The remedy given by the court is an equitable one and is only available in limited circumstances.'[24]

In so stating, he was repeating similar remarks made by Lord Cullen in *Dawson International*.[25] In Lord Cameron's view, as the factual basis of the claim for reimbursement of expenditure was precisely the same as that upon which a claim by the pursuer for misrepresentation in delict was proceeding, equity did not favour the availability of the remedy of reimbursement of expenditure.

5.18 Such an approach imports the characteristic of subsidiarity into the remedy of reimbursement of expenditure, much as with the available remedies in unjustified enrichment. This requirement that the pursuer must use another avenue if it is available to him represents a further limit upon the availability of the remedy.

CONCLUSION ON UNJUSTIFIED IMPOVERISHMENT

5.19 The obligation of *negotiorum gestio* and the limited remedy of reimbursement of expenditure in relation to a failed contract may be seen as recognition that there are some circumstances where the law considers that it would be unjust for a party to bear the costs of expenditure undertaken by it. At present, the only circumstances which have been recognised as creating such an injustice are where the expenditure has been undertaken in the administration of the affairs of another (*negotiorum gestio*) or where it has been undertaken in reliance on an implied assurance as to the existence of a contract between the parties (the remedy of reimbursement). The remedy in both such cases protects the pursuer's restoration or *status quo ante* interest.

---

23 1990 SC 215, OH.
24 1990 SC 215 at 225.
25 1988 SLT 854 at 865K–L, 1988 SCLR 371, OH.

5.20   It might be argued that there ought to be other circumstances recognised at law where a party ought not to be required to bear the costs of a sacrifice of time, money or other efforts, but ought to be able to recover such costs from another party. It is unlikely, however, that any such circumstances will attract protection through development of the common law, unless it is through development and application of a common law doctrine of good faith.

Chapter 6

Delict and Unjustified Enrichment

'RESTITUTION FOR WRONGS' IN GENERAL

6.01 It was suggested in chapter 4 that the development of a general action of unjustified enrichment in Scots law ought to encompass claims where the defender has interfered with the pursuer's patrimony, including certain of the pursuer's rights. Such a claim for enrichment derived from interference with rights is considered below[1]. Any such claim is properly treated within the law of unjustified enrichment.

6.02 It is, however, a separate question whether a pursuer in a delictual action is ever entitled to recover damages in a measure representing not his loss, but a gain made by the defender, or whether any other remedies are available to him which would allow recovery to an extent not mirrored by any quantifiable loss of his. This question is also considered below[2]. If any such claims do arise in delict, then they ought properly not to be considered as part of the law of unjustified enrichment, but as stemming directly from the commission of the wrong and thus to be treated as part of the law of delict.

UNJUSTIFIED ENRICHMENT—INTERFERENCE WITH RIGHTS[3]

6.03 Scots law does not provide that the interference with every right possessed by an individual gives rise to a claim on his part for any enrichment made by the interferer from that interference. What Scots law has provided for is that a recompense claim will be available in a limited number of situations where a particular right of the pursuer's has been interfered with by the defender.

6.04 It is important to recognise that, while in some of the cases outlined below one may be able to point to the commission of a recognised wrong (ie delict) by the defender, this is not a necessary pre-requisite for the availability of recompense. It is not for the commission of a delict (if any) that the remedy is

---

1 At **6.03–6.08**.
2 At **6.10–6.16**.
3 This topic was touched upon at **4.29**. See further on this topic: J Blackie, 'Enrichment, Wrongs and Invasion of Rights in Scots Law' 1997 Acta Juridica 23; A Steven, 'Recompense for Interference in Scots Law' 1996 JR 51. The issue is considered from a modern civilian standpoint in R Zimmermann, 'Unjustified Enrichment: The Modern Civilian Approach' (1995) 15 Oxford Journal of Legal Studies 403.

available, but rather for the unauthorised gain made by the defender through interference with the pursuer's right. This topic is considered specifically in this chapter because interference, while not necessarily delictual, may be regarded as 'wrongful' behaviour in a wide sense of that term.

Unauthorised use of property by defender

6.05 The paradigm situation of interference with rights is where A has made use of B's property without B's permission giving rise to an enrichment on the part of A. There is authority for the application of this rule in cases both of heritable as well as moveable property.[4] The oft cited example of this as regards heritable property is *Earl of Fife v Wilson*:[5]

> The defender was in possession of shootings on the pursuer's estate under a supposed lease granted by the pursuer's predecessor in title. The pursuer challenged the defender's lease, which was declared invalid. Thereafter the pursuer sought recovery from the defender for enjoyment of the shootings. The Lord Ordinary held that the defender should pay £40 per annum for each year of possession as a 'just and reasonable consideration'.

6.06 In cases under this category, it may be disputed whether A has suffered any loss. It may be argued, for instance, that where A would not have permitted another party to occupy and use the property, or would not have occupied it himself, A has suffered no loss; on the other hand, it can be argued either that mere deprivation of use is a loss in itself, or that the loss of the opportunity to permit another to occupy it (whether or not this opportunity would have been exercised) constitutes the loss. It was suggested in chapter 4 that such circumstances should be considered as falling within a widely drawn concept of loss. This has the merit of ensuring that there is no category of enrichment claim lacking the requirement of loss to the pursuer.[6]

6.07 In cases where A has permitted B to occupy and use his property without intention of donation, this would be an ordinary case of enrichment by transfer, and not of enrichment by interference.[7]

Other cases of interference with rights

6.08 There are other cases where, if B has made a gain without the knowledge and consent of A, then the concept of an invasion of or interference with A's rights can explain the basis for ordering recompense. These are:[8]

---

4   See A Steven, op cit at 53–54.
5   (1867) 3 M 323.
6   Blackie appears to suggest that there may not have been a loss in all such cases: see op cit, fn 3, at p 285. Zimmermann (op cit, fn 3), discussing civilian claims for interference with rights, states (at p 418) that the law would still provide a remedy even in 'many situations where the plaintiff has not suffered any loss'.
7   Such as *Glen v Roy* (1882) 10 R 239.
8   See further Steven, op cit, fn 3 at pp 52–63. Steven also suggests a category of B's misappropriation of A's funds, although notes that this category is not clearly established in Scots law.

(1) Profit made by B on a bona fide resale of A's property. For instance, where B sells a car wrongly delivered to him to C at a profit, he is liable in recompense for such profit. Examples of this head were discussed in chapter 4.[9] Where B is in bad faith, he is liable in restitution for the full value of the property.[10]

(2) The consumption or destruction of A's property by B. Where, for instance, B has received A's goods wrongly delivered to him, and has consumed or destroyed them, B is required to make restitution of the value to A. The classic example is the case of the salted ox, *Findlay v Monro*:[11]

> The pursuer sent a present of a live ox to a friend in Edinburgh. However, the ox was delivered in error to the defender who, considering it either the gift of a friend who had forgotten to write or of some unknown benefactor, promptly killed and salted it. The pursuer sued the defender for the value of the ox. The Court of Session found the defender liable in restitution for the value of the ox.[12]

> If B was in good faith, then it appears that he would be liable in recompense to A for any profit made (as in the previous category of the profit made on a bona fide resale of A's property).[13]

(3) A gain made by B in the acquisition of original title in property achieved by means of A's property—for instance, where B has used A's cement powder in order to make concrete, he will be liable in recompense to A. In such a case, if B was in good faith, he will be liable for the value of the cement powder; if he was in bad faith, his liability may be extended to 'the greatest value, according to the estimation of the former owner'.[14]

6.09 It is worth noting that in all such cases there is a clearly identified loss suffered by A. It is also worth noting again that if any of the above factual circumstances have obtained through a voluntary transfer of property by A to B, then it is this voluntary transfer, rather than an invasion of rights, which explains the basis on which the enrichment remedy rests.

ENRICHMENT MEASURE IN DELICT

6.10 Where a defender has committed a delict, the pursuer may not have suffered any loss, but the defender may have benefited from his wrongdoing. Even where the pursuer has suffered some loss, the defender's position may have been benefited to an extent greater than the pursuer's loss. In either case the pursuer may wish to have gains made by the defender transferred to him. Does the law ever permit a pursuer to claim in damages an amount representing the defender's gain, or permit to him any other remedies which will transfer gains made by the defender to the pursuer?

---

9 See **4.21**.
10 See Stair I.7.2. Also Steven, op cit, fn 3 at p 58.
11 (1698) Mor 1767.
12 There is some uncertainty as to whether the case is best seen as one of recompense, or a vindicatory claim resting upon the right of ownership.
13 See Steven, op cit, fn 3, at 59–60.
14 Stair II.1.39.

6.11 In relation to damages, the general rule, as with contractual damages, is that the purpose of an award of damages is to compensate the pursuer for loss suffered. As Stair put it, the obligation of the wrongdoer is of 'repairing his [that is, the injured party's] damage, putting him in as good condition as he was in before the injury'.[15] Thus, punitive damages play no part in the law of delict, with one exception.[16]

6.12 The issue of whether an injured party in a delictual action may ever claim a greater sum in damages than loss sustained by him has not been fully researched in Scots law.[17] The topic, when discussed, is sometimes referred to as 'restitution for wrongs'. This term is misleading, for it obfuscates whether what is being granted is the remedy of damages for a delict, albeit in a measure which protects the pursuer's disgorgement or restitutionary interest, or whether what is being granted is a remedy in unjustified enrichment which, as explained above, may on occasion be the case where the circumstances giving rise to the delict also constitute an invasion of rights for which a remedy in unjustified enrichment is granted. Where it is genuinely an award of damages which is at issue, in a measure protecting the pursuer's disgorgement or restitutionary interest,[18] then the term 'disgorgement damages for wrongs' is to be preferred.

6.13 In relation to disgorgement damages for wrongs, the position adopted by Scots law is that there are no clearly recognised circumstances where a pursuer is entitled to recover more than his losses (if any) in damages. It has on occasion been suggested that there are exceptional circumstances where such a claim is permitted. Two such categories for which an exception has been argued are discussed directly hereafter. The better view, however, is that the enrichment measure plays no part in either case.

DAMAGES IN AN ENRICHMENT MEASURE

Violent profits from the occupation of property

6.14 It has been argued that the recovery of 'violent profits'[19] for the un-authorised occupation of property is an enrichment measure of damages for wrongful behaviour.[20] The authorities do not, however, support a link to an enrichment measure.

6.15 In relation to urban heritable property, the arbitrary figure of double the rental value that the property could have been let for during the offending period is awarded as violent profits (which, in the case of tenants who have stayed on

---

15 Stair I.9.2.
16 Namely violent profits for unauthorised possession of property, as to which see **6.14–6.15** below.
17 The only treatment of any note being J Blackie's article 'Enrichment and Wrongs in Scots Law' 1992 Acta Juridica 23.
18 As to which, see **1.34**.
19 The notion of violent possession indicates that it was without the consent of the owner of the property: see Stair IV.29.2.
20 See Blackie, 'Enrichment and Wrongs in Scots Law', at pp 31–35.

beyond the term of an agreed lease, will be twice the contractually agreed rent).[21] In other cases, as Stair noted,[22] the precise measure to be awarded is unclear. One commentator on lease has suggested that it is 'based on the greatest profit that the landlord could have made, either by possessing the property itself or by letting it to others, together with compensation for any damage caused to it by the illegal possessor'.[23] If this is correct, and it is suggested that it is, then it is a measure which is without reference to any profit made by the wrongdoer, and cannot thus be seen as protection of the owner's disgorgement or restitutionary interest. It is better to see violent profits as a penal measure designed to deter unlawful occupation.

Fraud

6.16 It has also been said that the law relating to fraud may 'give rise to a claim for enrichment that is not mirrored by a loss'.[24] There is, however, almost no authority for such a view,[25] and it is more usually asserted that 'The pursuer is entitled to reparation for all *losses* which arose directly or naturally from the defender's fraudulent conduct'[26] (emphasis added).

DOES THE LAW REQUIRE TO BE REFORMED?

6.17 From the foregoing, it will be evident that there is no established category of case in Scots law where an enrichment measure of damages is awarded in respect of the commission of a delict. This begs the question whether Scots law *ought* to recognise that certain types of wrongful behaviour should furnish the pursuer with a right to seek damages in an amount greater than his loss (if any), to the extent of any gain made by the defender.

6.18 If such an award were to be permitted, then the exceptional cases when it could be claimed would require to be delineated very tightly. One possible criterion might be to restrict enrichment damages claims to cases where the defender had in bad faith exploited a wrong committed against the pursuer with the intention of profiting thereby. Recovery in such a case might be supported by the maxim *nemo ex suo delicto meliorem suam conditionem facere potest*, which is to say, no one is permitted to improve his position by his delict, or no one may take advantage of his delict. Clearly, this maxim has not, to date, been thought inevitably to lead to a general, or even restricted, right to an enrichment measure of damages in a delictual action. It has, however, been used to justify the award of an account of profits in a breach of confidence case before the House of Lords.[27]

---

21 For an example, see *Jute Industries Ltd v Wilson & Graham Ltd* 1955 SLT (Sh Ct) 46, 71 Sh Ct Rep 158.
22 IV.29.3.
23 Angus McAllister, *Scottish Law of Leases* (2nd edn) at pp 219–220. Blackie has expressed a preference for a similar measure (Blackie, 'Enrichment and Wrongs in Scots Law', at p 32).
24 Blackie, 'Enrichment and Wrongs in Scots Law', at p 35.
25 Blackie, op cit, suggests a sole sheriff court authority.
26 J Thomson, 'Fraud', in *Stair Memorial Encyclopaedia*, vol 11, para 731.
27 Discussed below at **6.20**.

6.19 It is suggested that there is good reason not to alter the current position of the law in relation to the calculation of delictual damages to include gains made by the defender. Unless one were to suggest that such measure ought to be available in every case, a course of action which would radically alter the accepted understanding of the purpose of an award of damages, one would require to find a clear principle by which to describe those exceptional types of case in which the measure would be available. A suggestion was made in the previous paragraph that such principle might lie in the notion of deliberate exploitation of wrong-doing with the intention of making a profit. Such a principle would be difficult to apply in practice, however, requiring as it would an examination of the subjective state of mind of the wrongdoer. It might also be seen as introducing an element of punishment into the modern law of delict, something which may well seem out of place in a system with a developed criminal law. Nonetheless, these are not insurmountable objections to reform of the law, and it may be that policy arguments will eventually favour a move to a restricted availability of the enrichment measure as damages for commission of a delict.

OTHER TYPES OF CLAIM FOR MORE THAN LOSS SUFFERED

Account of profits for breach of confidence

6.20 It has been suggested that where the defender has committed the delict of breach of confidence the pursuer may seek to recover any profits made by the defender from such breach of confidence through an action of an account of profits.[28] Unfortunately, the one Scottish case of any substance in relation to the proper amount to be awarded to a party who has suffered a breach of confidence, is vague as to the nature and measure of any such award.[29] The English view is clearer, however. In *Attorney-General v Guardian Newspapers (No 2)*,[30] an account of profits was ordered by the House of Lords. Lord Keith of Kinkel, who distinguished the remedy from that of an award of damages, described the remedy as 'to be attributed to the principle that no one should be permitted to gain from his own wrongdoing'.[31] This principle is clearly not seen as being of general application, as the availability of the remedy of an account of profits has not been extended to other torts (or delicts).

---

28 See H L MacQueen, 'Breach of Confidence', in *Stair Memorial Encyclopaedia*, vol. 18, para 1490.
29 *Levin v Caledonian Produce (Holdings) Ltd* 1975 SLT (Notes) 69, OH. A proof before answer was ordered in respect both of a damages and a recompense claim.
30 [1990] 1 AC 109, HL.
31 [1990] 1 AC 109 at 262E.

Bibliography

Atiyah, P S, 'Contracts, Promises and the Law of Obligations', in *Essays on Contracts* (Clarendon Press, 1986)

Barker, K, 'Unreliable Assumptions in the Modern Law of Negligence' (1993) 109 LQR 461

Beatson, J and Friedmann, D (eds) *Good Faith and Fault in Contract Law* (Clarendon Press, 1995)

Beatson, J and Schrage, E (eds) *Cases, Materials and Texts on Unjustified Enrichment* (Hart Publishing, 2003)

Birks, P, 'Restitution: A View of the Scots Law' (1985) 38 CLP 57

Birks, P, 'Six Questions in Search of a Subject—Unjust Enrichment in a Crisis of Identity', 1985 JR 227

Blackie, J, 'Enrichment and Wrongs in Scots Law', 1992 Acta Juridica 23

Blackie, J, 'Enrichment, Wrongs and Invasion of Rights in Scots Law', 1997 Acta Juridica 23

Borland, G C, 'Change of Position in Scots Law', 1996 SLT (News) 139

Bridge, M, 'Good faith in commercial contracts', in *Good Faith in Contract: Concept and Context*, R Brownsword et al (eds) (Dartmouth, 1998)

Burrows, A, *Understanding the Law of Obligations* (Hart Publishing, 1998)

Dieckmann, J A and Evans-Jones, R, 'The Dark Side of Connelly v Simpson', 1995 JR 90

Evans-Jones, R, 'Some Reflections on the Condictio Indebiti in a Mixed Legal System' (1994) 111 SALJ 759

Evans-Jones, R, 'Unjust Enrichment, Contract and the Third Reception of Roman Law in Scotland' (1993) 109 LQR 663

Forte, A D M (ed), *Good Faith in Contract and Property Law* (Hart Publishing, 1999)

Friedmann, D, 'The Performance Interest in Contract Damages' (1995) 111 LQR 628

Fuller and Purdue, 'The reliance interest in contract damages' (1936) 46 Yale LJ 52 (part 1) and 373 (part 2)

Hartkamp, A, et al (eds) *Towards a European Civil Code* (Kluwer, 2nd edn 1998)

Hogg, M, 'Concurrent Liability in the Scots Law of Contract and Delict', 1998 JR 1

Hogg, M, 'Lost chances in contract and delict', 1997 SLT (News) 71

Hogg, M, 'Lowlands to Low Country: Perspectives on the Scottish and Dutch law of Unjustified Enrichment', Ius Commune Research School, 2001

Hogg, M, 'Paul v Ogilvy: A Lost Opportunity for Lost Chance Recovery' (2003) 7 ELR 86

Hogg, M and Backx, J, 'Restitution in bankruptcy: a Scots law view of Ontvanger v Hamm' (2000) 8 ERPL 509

Hogg, M and Lubbe, G, 'Formation of Contract' in *Mixed Legal Systems in Comparative Perspective: Property and Obligations in Scotland and South Africa*, K Reid and R Zimmermann (eds) (OUP, forthcoming 2004)

Kames, Lord (Henry Homes) *Principles of Equity* (Bell & Creech, 1778 (3rd edn))

Kessler, Friedrich and Fine, Edith, 'Culpa in Contrahendo, Bargaining in Good Faith and Freedom of Contract: A Comparative Study' (1964) 77 Harvard LR 401

Kötz, H and Flessner, A, *European Contract Law*, vol 1 (Clarendon Press, 1998)

McAllister, A, *Scottish Law of Leases* (Butterworths, 3rd edn 2002)

McBryde, W W, 'Promises in Scots Law' (1993) 42 International and Comparative Law Quarterly 48

Macgregor, L, 'The expectation, reliance and restitution interests in contract damages', 1996 JR 227

Macgregor, L, 'The House of Lords "Applies" O'Brien North of the Border' (1998) 2 ELR 90

MacQueen, H L, 'Concrete Solutions to Liability: Changing Perspectives in Contract and Delict' (1998) 64 Arbitration 285

MacQueen, H L, 'Offers, Promises and Options', 1985 SLT (News) 187

MacQueen, H L, 'Payment of Another's Debt', in *Unjustified Enrichment: Key Issues in Comparative Perspective*, R Zimmermann and D Johnston (eds) (CUP, 2002)

MacQueen, H L (ed) *Scots Law into the 21st Century: Essays in honour of W A Wilson* (W Green, 1996)

MacQueen, H L, 'Unjustified Enrichment and Breach of Contract', 1994 JR 137

MacQueen, H L and Brodie, D, 'Private Rights and the Private Domain', in *Human Rights and Scots Law*, A Boyle et al (eds) (Hart Publishing, 2002)

MacQueen, H L, and Sellar, W D H, 'Unjust Enrichment in Scots Law', in *Unjust Enrichment: The Comparative Legal History of the Law of Restitution*, E J H Schrage (ed) (Duncker & Humblot, 1995)

Mason, A, 'Contract, good faith and equitable standards in fair dealing' (2000) 116 LQR 66

Nicholas, B, 'Unjust Enrichment in the Civil Law and Louisiana Law' (1962) 36 Tulane LR 605

Normand, W G, 'Consideration in the Law of Scotland' (1939) 55 LQR 358

Phillips, A, 'Lost Chances in Delict: All or Nothing?' (1995) 5 JR 401

Reece, H, 'Losses of Chance in the Law', 1996 MLR 188

Reed, Hon Lord, *A Practical Guide to Human Rights in Scotland* (W Green, 2001)

Reid, K, 'Obligations and property: Exploring the Border', 1997 Acta Juridica 225

Reid, K and Zimmermann, R (eds) *A History of Private Law in Scotland*, 2 vols (OUP, 2000)

Rickett, C E F, 'The Financiers Duty of Care to a Surety' (1998) LQR 17

Schrage, E J H, 'Unjustified Enrichment: Recent Dutch developments from a comparative and historical perspective', 1999 NILR 57

Scottish Law Commission Discussion Paper No 99, Judicial Abolition of the Error of Law Rule (1996)

Scottish Law Commission Memorandum No 39, Constitution and Proof of Voluntary Obligations (1977)

Scottish Law Commission Report No 144, Formation of Contract: Scottish Law and the United Nations Convention on Contracts for the International Sale of Goods (1993)

Sellar, W D H, 'Shilliday v Smith: Unjust Enrichment through the Looking Glass?' (2001) 5 ELR 80

Smith, T B, 'The Common Law Cuckoo', in *Studies Critical and Comparative* (W Green, 1962)

Smith, T B, *A Short Commentary on the Law of Scotland* (W Green, 1962)

Stapleton, J 'Duty of Care—Peripheral Parties and Alternative Opportunities for Deterrence' (1995) 111 LQR 301

Stapleton, J, 'Good faith in private law' (1999) 52 Current Legal Problems 1

Stapleton, J, 'The Normal Expectancies Measure in Tort Damages' (1997) 113 LQR 257

Steven, A, 'Recompense for Interference in Scots Law', 1996 JR 51-65

Stewart, H, 'Medical Lost Chances' (2000) SLPQ 147

Stewart, W J, 'The theory of the Scots law of contract', 1996 JR 403

Stewart, W J, *The Law of Restitution in Scotland* (W Green, 1992)

Treitel, G, *The Law of Contract* (Sweet & Maxwell, 11th edn, 2003)

Unberath, H, *Transferred Loss: Claiming Third Party Loss in Contract Law* (Hart Publishing, 2003)

van Zyl, D H, *Negotiorum Gestio in South African Law* (Butterworths, 1985)

Visser, D and Miller, S, 'Between Principle and Policy: Indirect Enrichment in Subcontractor and 'Garage-Repair' Cases' [2000] 117 SALJ 594

Visser, D, 'Rethinking Unjustified Enrichment: A Perspective of the Competition between Contractual and Enrichment Remedies', 1992 Acta Juridica 203

von Bar, C, van Gerven, C, et al, *Cases, Materials and Text on National, Supranational and International Tort Law* (Hart Publishing, 1998)

von Bar, D, *The Common European Law of Torts*, 2 vols (Clarendon Press, 1998 (vol 1) and 2000 (vol 2))

Whittaker, S, 'The application of the "broad principle of Hedley Byrne" as between parties to a contract' (1997) 17 LS 169

Whitty, N, 'Indirect Enrichment in Scots Law' 1994 JR 200

Whitty, N, 'Rationality, nationality and the taxonomy of unjustified enrichment' in *Unjustified Enrichment: Key Issues in Comparative Perspective* (CUP, 2002), pp 658–729

Wilson, W A, *The Scottish Law of Debt* (W Green, 2nd edn 1998)

Zimmermann, R and Whittaker, S (eds) *Good Faith in European Contract Law* (CUP, 2000)

Zimmermann, R, 'Unjustified Enrichment: The Modern Civilian Approach' (1995) 15 Oxford Journal of Legal Studies 403

Index